Riding to Jerusalem

RIDING TO JERUSALEM

Evelyne Coquet

*Translated from the French
by Kitty Black*

THE TRAVEL BOOK CLUB
LONDON

First published by Editions Robert Laffont – Opera Mundi, Paris,
Original text and illustrations © Opera Mundi 1975
English translation © Kitty Black 1978
All other material © John Murray (Publishers) Ltd 1978

The Travel Book Club
125 Charing Cross Road
London WC2H OEB.

This edition by arrangement
with John Murray.

Printed and bound in Great Britain by
REDWOOD BURN LIMITED
Trowbridge & Esher

Contents

1 Deus le Volt 1

2 One Foot in the Stirrup 6

3 Choosing the Elect 12

4 Excitement at Square One 18

5 The Day Continues 24

6 Chateau and Champagne 33

7 Marching through Lorraine and Alsace 36

8 Fantasia in the Black Forest 44

9 A Curious Noah's Ark 49

10 Shopping in Ulm 56

11 D for Disaster 63

12 We Meet the Bundeswehr 68

13 Capoue on the Inn 74

14 Guardian Angels 79

15 Gschwendhof: 'Luxury, Peace and Delight' 85

16 The Priest and the Pilgrim 91

17 Our Graceful Travelling Companions 95

18 En Route for the Land of the Magyars 100

19 Goulash and Pork Fat 108

20 Donald's Illness 115

21 Panic-Stricken 127

22	To Hell with the Militia	*136*
23	Surprise, Surprise	*147*
24	An Unusual Christmas	*152*
25	Terror on the Motorway	*156*
26	Well Guarded through Bulgaria	*166*
27	Turkish March	*181*
28	The Paradise of Unliberated Women	*185*
29	Man's Best Friend	*192*
30	The Bosporus and Beyond	*196*
31	Apotheosis at Eskisehir	*203*
32	Olivier Throws in the Towel	*208*
33	*Dolce Far Niente*	*214*
34	The Camels are Coming	*219*
35	Over the Taurus Alone	*224*
36	The Little Horse is Sick	*230*
37	Two Nights in Gaol	*239*
38	The Runaways	*245*
39	Home Thoughts from Abroad	*251*
40	An Unfriendly Village	*256*
41	Grass and Lettuce	*267*
42	A Very Persistent Aeroplane	*276*
43	On the Banks of the Jordan	*287*
44	A Farm in the Desert	*298*
45	The End of the Road	*307*
	Index	*323*

Illustrations

between pages *182* and *183*

1   Off at last! Ready to leave from outside Notre-Dame

2   Studying the itinerary with our guide in the Vosges

3   Pluto catching up after a diversion

4   A rest and a snack with our friends from the Alsace riding-school

5   Good-bye to France, leaving our friends at the West German frontier

6   Evelyne plays her harmonica while leading Mickey in the Black Forest

7   A rather unusual bridge; Pluto bravely goes first

8   A rest and a snack on the banks of the Danube, Austria

9   It can be quite hazardous riding through long grass

10   Serenity in Austria

11   You can lead a horse to water . . .

12   An unexpected hitch in Hungary

13   Our Hungarian escort with his big black horse

14   Pluto has a drink of snow in Hungary

15   Going to the fair on the road to Šid, Yugoslavia

16   Crossing the Balkans, not too much snow here

17   A cautious welcome to Turkey

18   Turkish hospitality

19 Pluto sports his protective spikes

20 Turkish schoolchildren pose for a class photograph

21 We stop for a drink at an Anatolian village well

22 The usual reception from the Anatolian menfolk

23 A meeting with camels in the Taurus Mountains

24 Dining in style, Turkish fashion

25 Pluto views the Taurus Mountains

26 Trimming a cow's hoof in Adana, Turkey

27 The Turkish vet about to give Donald his injection

28 Donald is sick, so we have to walk

29 Ready to cross into Syria

30 The orange-seller at Dam Sharko

31 Adnan's house, Jeble, Syria

32 Leaving Payas Castle

33 Riding through the gateway of Baniyas Castle

34 The lettuce-buyer

35 Grinding coffee at Jebel ed Druz

36 Dressed *à la mode* in Ramtha, Jordan

37 Carrying problems solved in Jordan

38 Trading for cucumbers

39 Barbed wire divides Lebanon and Israel

40 Pluto passes an abandoned tank by the roadside

41 We cross Allenby Bridge into Israel on 17 April 1974

42 The Jericho to Jerusalem road

43 Mickey and Donald are reluctant to greet a camel

44 We have arrived: Jerusalem at last!

45 We give a press conference in Jerusalem

46 Homeward-bound, ready to load the horses onto the *Iris*

Sketch-map of author's route   *between pp. 6–7*

CHAPTER ONE

Deus le Volt

I haven't the slightest doubt: Godfrey de Bouillon was the cause of it all. Of course, others had a hand too, but in no way comparable to the role played by the great Crusader. You may wonder how that proud cavalier, who became the first King of Jerusalem, influenced in this modern age the destiny of two young French girls from Nevers. Well, here goes.

I was ten and in a dream most of the time, when I first heard the story of the Crusades: all those nobles, priests and ruffians, who set out to restore the Holy Sepulchre to Christianity, leaving work, family, country, palaces and farmsteads, flocks and fields—all material possessions, in fact—I was completely bowled over. Corinne, my younger sister, was barely three, so the deliverance of the Holy Land didn't mean much in her young life. I'm not sure that her attitude's any different even now.

At twelve my life changed, rather in the manner of a fairy-story. My aunt had married a very rich man with a private house in Paris, hunting lodge in Sologne, villa at Deauville, *mas* at St Tropez. She took a fancy to me, as did my uncle. As their only daughter was exactly my age, it was fixed that I would spend my holidays with my cousin, a strange double life, watching every penny at home, having a really easy, luxurious time with them.

One wet summer's day at Deauville, they took us to an indoor riding-school and sat me on a horse. The instructor couldn't believe it was truly the first time: he insisted I must take it up. Some weeks later, I was tossed up onto one of my uncle's hunters, and the very next day he took me to a meet. I found in him the perfect mentor and we became firm friends. We would go off on long rides, with him holding forth about nature and the countryside, while we tracked a hare or hind. But even fairy-stories come to an end. Midnight struck: my uncle died, and my aunt sold the horses. The pumpkin carried me home to Nevers.

I had to put away all thoughts of such a rich man's hobby as riding, but the virus had taken hold and the symptoms kept reappearing. No pop stars for me, but horses' heads scrawled all over my schoolbooks and my dreams were filled with fiery black steeds, too wild for anyone but me to ride. And I was mad about the Crusades—shades of things to come. But I was seventeen before I could scrape up enough to join a riding-club and learned to jump, to groom and feed a horse, with all the fervour of someone who had had to wait for years. I worked through every stage until I became what is known as a *cavalière accomplie*. Meanwhile I had gone to work in Paris, stifling all week and pawing impatiently for the week-ends and my riding.

Years passed. Horse trekking became popular and I had a pretty low opinion of it until I heard of a colourful type called Henri Roques who had followed the pilgrim route from Paris to Compostela on horseback. Why couldn't I do the same—or better?

One day a friend made me an offer:

'I've got a horse in Greece. I'll pay your air fair to Athens and you can ride him back to France during your holidays. Can it be done?'

No, it couldn't be done, because Greece was a long way away and my holidays were much too short. And then, I don't know why, pictures of columns of knights, with crosses worn over their coats of mail, flashed into my mind, and I heard myself saying: 'What I'd really like to do is ride to Jerusalem.'

My friend shook his head: 'What woman wills, God wills.'

'"*Deus le volt!*" The motto of the first Crusaders, when Pope Urban II made his appeal at the Council of Clermont in 1905.'

My sister Corinne interrupted by saying: 'I'm coming with you!' It wasn't a suggestion—it was a decision.

I looked at her, and realised that my baby sister had grown up. So I said, 'Why not?'

I ran my fingers over the maps. We could go this way, or that. So many roads lead to Jerusalem. I didn't know then that some even go through Alès and New York.

Talking of Jerusalem, I landed in New York a few weeks later. The American way of life, the hurry-scurry of Manhattan, a job on a women's magazine, weren't enough to cure me of my obsessions. I found time to go to the Theological Library and devour everything I could find on the Crusades. I became an expert on the tribulations of the Tancreds, the Bohemonds, Gautiers-sans-Avoir, on William II of Nevers (!), on the rivalries of the Byzantines, Fatimids, Armenians, Seljuks, their intrigues and battles, and on everything from the routes taken by the soldiers of the Cross down to their victualling problems. Thanks largely to Steven Runciman, I knew that the crossing of the Dalmatian coast and the Yugoslavian mountains had cost Raymond of Toulouse half his troops, that the Duke of Normandy and the Comte de Blois had also paid dearly for the crossing of the Alps: that Godfrey de Bouillon did best of all, having followed the Danube for the greater part of his journey: his crusade was the only one that had been carried out entirely on horseback. I learned that it takes a full day to cover thirty kilometres; that Istanbul can be reached in three and a half months; that between Belgrade and Niš there is a dense forest; and between Eskisehir and Konya the Anatolian plain is an arid desert better avoided in time of drought—and much more.

However ancient the chronicles, I believed that in the main they were still valid. One thing seemed obvious: the man to follow was Godfrey de Bouillon.

Having decided on our route, I called on the consular attachés of the countries we intended to cross. When I explained that I wanted to ride through, accompanied by my sister and a dog, these officials dissolved into fits of helpless laughter. Yet my project was clear, my questions precise. I talked of vaccinations, large-scale maps, stabling and feed for the horses, possible quarantine. They obviously didn't take me seriously. Several even asked how I intended to ride across the Atlantic. But some were kind, and promised to write to their ministries at home.

That's how I acquired dozens of travel folders, and lists of recommended hotels. Some of the more optimistic said: 'Get to the frontier, and then play it by ear.'

Back in France, I started again from scratch, with Corinne helping. I tried to find serious backers and useful introductions. The *Guilde du Raid*, experienced in off-beat undertakings (Paris–Kabul by motorcycle, for example), put me in touch with the Ministry of Youth and Sports and the Tourist Office, both of which took me under their wing, and armed me with a semi-official stamp.

But first I had to pass a sort of preliminary exam with two companions: Concorda, my horse, an ex-trotting champion, and my faithful Pataud, a mongrel I wouldn't part with for the world. On 15 August 1972, I stuffed my sleeping-bag with a few trifles for myself, a dandy brush and a hoof-pick for the horse, strapped the lot on my saddle-bow, and all three of us struck out for the south. Three weeks later I arrived, convinced that if I had been able to cover 600 odd kilometres with no problems, why couldn't I manage a distance ten times greater? Jerusalem was definitely on.

The months passed. By the beginning of the following summer I could draw up a balance sheet. The Germans were agreeable if the Austrians were agreeable. There were no serious objections from the Hungarians, the Yugoslavs, Bulgarians or Lebanese: they merely asked for vaccinations and certificates of health. The Bulgarians were particularly co-operative: not only were they the first to reply, but General Stoytchev, their delegate to the International Olympic Committee, President of the Bulgarian Equestrian Club and a great friend of France, proposed to have us escorted by four cavalrymen, who would see to everything.

From the Austrians came nothing for a long time. And then we discovered that an epidemic of foot-and-mouth disease had only just been stamped out and they were not at all anxious for our animals to spread the virus again. It was annoying, because the Germans wouldn't allow us to cross the Rhine unless they were sure we could enter Austria. So we might never be able to leave our own country.

From the Turks, nothing definite, but it so happened that the Turkish Minister for Tourism came to Paris and agreed to see me. He explained that what he feared for us was not the famous Anatolian brigands but the cold!

'You will be crossing the plateau in the depth of winter. Do you know that at Konya, last March, the thermometer fell to minus forty degrees! How will you be able to ride in such conditions?'

I assured the Minister that we would be properly equipped, but he wasn't convinced. I insisted. He promised to do something.

From the Syrians, absolutely nothing. The Jordanians and Israelis said we'd be welcome. Probably they both doubted we'd ever get that far.

So much to organise: money to finance our expedition, buying two horses capable of carrying us with bag and baggage, over hill and dale, through hell and high water, for 6,000 kilometres. Yes, I know. As the Boeing flies, it's only 4,000 kilometres from Paris to Jerusalem, but on horseback, the shortest route isn't necessarily a straight line.

CHAPTER TWO

One Foot in the Stirrup

In a magnificent panelled room, filled with books, an apparently shy young girl confronts an impressive, white-haired gentleman. His moustache is silvered, his eyes searching, his smile welcoming. The young girl is me. The man is Paul Winkler, a big wheel in newspapers and publishing. My purpose is to convince him that by providing me with the necessary, he will be making a wise investment. What am I asking for? Fifty thousand francs, to set my foot in the stirrup. How did I get to see Paul Winkler? By seducing the director of a publicity agency—with my enthusiasm, let me hasten to add.

I talked about my wonderful week-ends, galloping over our green fields. From the Nièvre to Jerusalem is only a step, and I imagined aloud what a fantastic, mad gallop that would be through forests and fields, over deserts and dunes.

So that's how I found myself in the office of the director of *Le Journal de Mickey*, a Walt Disney publication, read by hundreds of thousands of French children every week, not to mention their parents.

'If you could send them regular accounts of your adventures, they'd find it fascinating. It might even be possible to include some kind of publicity for Mickey Mouse . . .'

I wondered if I ought to dress up for this vitally important appointment. And then decided I wouldn't. I chose my most casual outfit: well-faded jeans, and a tee-shirt printed with a Women's Lib slogan, 'I'm the boss'.

Did this declaration bring a gleam of irony into M. Winkler's

UMANIA

BULGARIA

Danube

BLACK SEA

*nac
*ela Palanka
*Pirot
*Balkan Mts
*Sofia *Vakarel
*Pazardzhik
*Belovo *Plovdiv
Kapitan Androvo *Edirne
Istanbul
Silivri
Izmit

GREECE

TURKEY

*Eskisehir
Mahmudiyé *Emirdağ
Bolvadin *Arğithani
Ilgin *Kadinhani
Konya

A N A T O L I A

Ereğli *Porsuk
*Pozanti
Camalan *Karaisali
Adana *Ceyhan
*Payas
*Alexandretta
*Yonikoy

Taurus Mountains

Antioch *Kislac
Yayladaği
El Ladhiqiya *Dam-Sharko
Jeble *Orontes SYRIA
Baniyas
Tartus *Hamidiya

CYPRUS

LEBANON

Beirut
Sidon
Tyre
Acre
Haifa
Caesarea
Tel Aviv
Jerusalem
ISRAEL

*Damascus

JEBEL
ED DRUZ
Dera *Ramtha
*Irbid
Jordan *Shunat
Jericho

DEAD SEA

JORDAN

CRETE

AN SEA

eye? He is a man who sees straight to the heart of things, and knows a great deal about horses. I came under an instant barrage of questions.

'What experience have you had of long-distance riding? Would you know how to describe your adventures? Do you know how to handle a camera?'

Reassured on these points, he continued:

'If you're attacked, can you defend yourself? Can you use a gun? Have you had your appendix out? Any number of expeditions have failed because an appendix got infected at the wrong moment. . . . Have you had all the right vaccinations?'

And then he started on visas for the riders, the horses, the dog. And the difficulties we might meet in countries permanently at war.

I painted a slightly rosy picture of the situation. I produced an argument which I considered sensible: there was no point in asking for visas for the countries of the Near East: once we arrived, they probably wouldn't be valid anyway. I added that I was relying on the help of the local French Embassies: if they hadn't replied to my letters it was because they probably thought they were being taken for a ride, but once we got there . . .

'How do you expect to enter Israel from an Arab country?'

'There is one sector open: the Allenby bridge over the Jordan, opposite Jericho.'

'What about horses?'

'I must buy two, and I haven't any money. I need you to finance me.'

'What kind of horses?'

'Several countries won't allow stallions or mares, so I thought I would take two six- or eight-year-old geldings.'

'Do you know where to find them?'

'Yes, there are plenty of horses in France.'

There I was bluffing. I couldn't very well tell him that I had had to reject all the horses I had tried. When I sent his horses back, one owner was very angry: 'You won't find any better at this time of year.'

I had told him: 'I'm not asking for thoroughbreds. I just want a healthy horse, with strong legs, who can walk without stumbling.'

And he had said: 'You're asking for the moon.'

Paul Winkler went on:

'Why this time of year? You'll find it very cold in the Balkans and in Turkey . . .'

'The horses will do better in cold weather. Besides, germs are much less likely to be around at ten or twelve degrees below zero. We'll be safe from epidemics.'

The real truth was that I wanted to start at once. I was too much afraid that if the journey was postponed, it would never happen at all. There would always be another good reason for starting at the next blue moon.

'What do your parents think?'

'They are a little worried.'

'Very understandable. By the way, your sister is still a minor. I can't do anything without formal permission from your parents.'

'Of course. I'll have it for you next week.'

I was bluffing, desperately—Paul Winkler had put his finger on my weakest spot. I knew I'd have to pull off a miracle. In dealing with other men, I could still use my childish charms, play the innocent, that kind of thing. But with my father, there wasn't a hope in hell.

'What have I done that God should inflict such daughters on me?' he had grumbled. 'Why should you want to go and be killed by bombs in the Middle East?'

At times I was shaken myself. I wondered if I had the right to expose my little sister to such hazards: tourists stoned by Serbian beggars; campers violated by Turkish mountaineers; hitch-hikers disappearing without trace in the Arabian deserts . . . not to mention that the Syria–Lebanon–Jordan–Israel borders were peppered with minefields. But as far as I was concerned, none of that mattered. I'd seen so many pile-ups every week-end on the Paris–Nevers road that nothing could be worse. What was there to choose between being chopped into tiny pieces by the cutlass of a randy Anatolian or being squashed flat by an articulated lorry?

I even toyed with the idea of going alone, and immediately discarded it, because it's more fun to be two; a trouble shared is a trouble halved, and I just couldn't leave Corinne behind. For heaven's sake, we'd have our good times too.

Corinne was in Paris the day I saw Paul Winkler, and within

minutes of leaving him, quite sure I had won him round, I had put her in the picture, typed up a few lines and piled her into my car.

When we arrived, Papa and Maman were already at table, but before we could open our mouths, we realised we were in for trouble. Better to jump in at the deep end, I thought, and opened fire:

'We need your agreement to accept 50,000 francs. You only have to sign this authorisation for Corinne,' and I held out the sheet to Papa. I saw him frown and turn pale.

'I'll sign nothing,' he declared, without even glancing at the paper. But he took it with a shaking hand and read:

I have been informed that my daughter Corinne, aged nineteen, plans to accompany her sister Evelyne on a ride from Paris to Jerusalem. I acknowledge that this idea stems entirely from their personal initiative. Consequently I shall have no claim to make against *Le Journal de Mickey* if it finances and sponsors this journey. I appreciate the very real dangers of the enterprise. I do not wish to help my daughters, and I have done all I can to dissuade them. However, since one of them is of age and the other soon will be, I give my consent regarding my daughter Corinne.

No verbal reaction. His face was paler and his hand trembled even more. I brought out my trump.

'You agreed last year to let Corinne go to Paris, on condition that she passed her exam, and she's done it. Now she needs practical experience, as they do in the States. She'll learn far more in eight months than she would in four years. Imagine, she hasn't even been taught how to use a traveller's cheque. It's appalling.'

'It was your mother's idea. I never believed in your crusading story.'

'Yes, but now everything's organised. It's serious. Papa, you don't have to worry. I'm not completely mad and I don't want to die. Everyone is intrigued by our idea. Look at this letter from the Bulgarian Minister: he's having us escorted by four cavalrymen. The Turks will probably do the same. Look at these papers, we're under the patronage of the Ministry for Youth and Sports.

If we didn't have some chance of success, *Le Journal de Mickey* wouldn't have agreed to give us five million.'

No reaction. I attacked from another angle:

'Papa,' I said, my voice trembling with emotion, 'it's a chance which will never come again. You can't make us miss it.'

Corinne provided a counterpoint. I held out a pen. My father wouldn't take it.

'You won't get very far,' he warned us. 'By the time you reach Bar-le-Duc your bottoms will be so sore you'll come home.'

'Then you agree there's no real danger . . .'

He seized the pen, held it poised for a moment, gritting his teeth. Please God, don't let the phone ring. Papa signs. No one heaves a sigh of relief but everyone relaxes. Papa has given in.

Maman's eyes were moist. I said:

'Thank you, Maman. I don't know what you did to Papa this week, but it's worked. Don't worry too much. We'll be careful.'

'If you ride to Jerusalem with that dog that walks sideways, you'll end up in Siberia. Poor Pataud! You're planning to make him run for thousands of kilometres. Have you asked him what he thinks? He'll crawl home on his belly, poor chap . . . he'll never stay the course, that's for sure. By the time you get to Vienna he'll be worn down to a dachshund. You'd better send him home from there, or he'll be gobbled up by wolves.'

'Maman, his passport is ready. He is described as "a large fox-terrier". He's had all the necessary injections, and he'll be happy as long as he's with us. You can't expect to keep him at home.'

From then on, my watchword was 'Forward'. I wanted to be on Godfrey's heels before the month was out, and there were still so many things to do. First objective: the Austrians. Without their authorisation, no question of entering Germany. I said to Corinne:

'Let's run over to Vienna. Everything is always much easier on the spot. I've got an introduction to the Austrian Ministry of Agriculture.'

'Vienna isn't just round the corner.'

'I know. So what?'

We left while it was still dark. In Vienna we discovered that the Austrian Minister too goes on holiday in August. Instead, we were seen by a young attaché, thirty, thirty-five perhaps, tall, blond, elegant, with just enough tan to show off his blue eyes, a warm smile, one of those characters who, in my opinion, are 'worth the journey'.

'I already have an enormous file on you,' he told us. 'Unfortunately it's not very constructive. You know, Mesdemoiselles, we have had serious problems with our livestock . . .'

He allowed us to tell him our plans, our hopes, our frustrations. Obviously he was on our side.

'I promise to speak to the veterinary service as soon as I can. If I can get you a pass, it will certainly be under the strictest health conditions.'

'Of course. But it's urgent.'

'You'll have the reply by telegram. I envy you. I don't know anything about horses, but I have a passion for navigation. I'd willingly abandon all these files to go round the world. Here's my card, if you have any other problems. Keep in touch.'

Back to Paris. Once he had the famous paper signed by Papa, Paul Winkler said we could have our fifty grand, and in exchange, we bound ourselves, Corinne and I, to keep the readers of *Le Journal de Mickey* on tenterhooks throughout our journey. As a start, the Coquet sisters would sport tee-shirts printed with *Le Journal de Mickey*—we all have our cross to bear. As for our four-footed companions, they would be incorporated into the Disney legend: Pataud as Pluto, and our two horses as Mickey and Donald. When I told my publicity friend that the whole thing was fixed, he wasn't at·all surprised.

'I was sure it would work with Winkler. Do you know what he does for relaxation? Sabre. A cavalry weapon. Perhaps that's why he's on the same wavelength as you.' And he went on: 'You haven't even bought your horses yet. And you'll be on the road for seven or eight months at least. Are you sure fifty grand will be enough?'

'Fifty grand? But it's the riches of Byzantium . . .'

As always, my values were based on the standards of my beloved Godfrey de Bouillon.

CHAPTER THREE

Choosing the Elect

For three weeks I did the rounds of half the stables and riding-clubs of France, inspecting horses of every breed and price, and receiving the most contradictory advice.

'Don't take thoroughbreds, they're too sensitive to changes of food.' 'Don't take trotters, they'll lose fifty kilos every 300 kilometres, because you won't be able to feed them properly.' 'Don't take horses that are too big, or any that are too young.' 'Choose horses registered in the stud-book, otherwise you won't be able to repatriate them.'

The choice became really limited, and Pierre, a very knowledge-able friend of mine, suggested I should visit some of the riding establishments in the south of France. Any animal that could stand up to a summer of Parisians on holiday would do for our Crusade. I decided to go, but as I didn't trust my own judgement or my bargaining powers, I needed help—but from whom? Henry! Ah, if only he'd come with me—Henry de Barrin: four years at the cavalry school at Saumur, service with the Spahis in Algeria, currently director of a first-class riding-club, who could be better?

The first thing he asked me when we met was news of Pataud, alias Pluto. When he was my instructor, Henry had given him to me. We'd been riding in the forest of Venille and met a man of the woods, a sort of down-and-out Diogenes, who lived in a barrel. This sylvan hermit had a bitch with three puppies barely three weeks old. The toughest greeted us with piercing cries, and then never left our side. Round as a ball, he could hardly stand on his huge paws, but he followed us all the way to the stables, a good fifteen kilometres away. Henry was so touched that he immediately went back to our Diogenes, bought the puppy for twenty francs and presented him to me. At first I thought he was quite hideous, but Henry looked so pleased with his present, that I didn't have the heart to refuse. I called the little mongrel Pataud (Clumsy) because of the way he walked, and ever since he'd followed me everywhere.

'You aren't thinking of taking him to Jerusalem?' asked Henry anxiously.

'Why not? I'm sure he can stand up to the trip. He can guard our gear at night. If he gets too tired, I'll send him home. But I want to try.'

Henry agreed to act as my technical adviser so, a few days later, we arrived at the address given us by Pierre: 'Louis Giordanino, club Tourne-bride, Saint-Estève-Janson, at the foot of the Lubéron'. In a landscape crushed by the sun and fragrant with pines the ranch seemed completely deserted. Cicadas were singing, horses stamping and demanding their oats. There must have been a recent intake, for several of them were tethered in full sunshine. We made a quick tour of the stables, and I objected:

'All this is very small. I don't feel we'll find much here.'

Henry was less impulsive: 'Wait a little, we'll soon see.'

An outburst from the dogs and horses finally roused the proprietor, looking a little bleary after an obviously rough night.

'Look round,' he said. 'Take your pick. They're all for sale: the season's nearly over.'

None of the horses pleased me particularly, but I had decided to let Henry choose.

'Here's one who could certainly reach Jerusalem,' Giordanino assured us. 'Allow me to introduce Ondo.'

He displayed a reasonably good-looking dark chestnut with a long mane.

'He's a provençal—a local horse—born here seven years ago. He won the last long-distance rally this year. He's got stamina and his legs are sound.'

As an expert salesman he added:

'I wouldn't part with him to just anyone. I'll sell him to you because I like the idea of your trip.'

The horse had an enlarged knee-joint, but nothing serious. Apart from a small hygroma, he had clean limbs with short shanks, which meant he could walk without tiring, and he stood well. His hoofs seemed solid, neither too dry nor too soft, with plenty of frog. He had shoes on his forefeet but not on the hind ones, and seemed to have finished his last trip without any ill-effects. He was well packed but not thin. In fact, all the horses on the ranch were in excellent condition.

Giordanino went on: 'You can pile a good load on his back. He's strongly built and well muscled.'

He was stongly built indeed, the muscles supple and rippling, the shoulders marked without being too pronounced. I pointed out a few small white marks on each shoulder. 'It's an old saddle sore. Quite cured now. All you need is to find the right saddle.'

O.K. It wasn't love at first sight, but there was no more to be said.

'He might suit us very well,' concluded Henry. 'Have you another?'

'There's this one who will pair up well with him. This is l'Enclume [The Anvil].'

A little smaller, the same dark chestnut, with a shorter back, a squarer head, a shaggy mane, reddish and bleached by the sun. His general condition appeared to be good, but I wasn't too happy about his legs. Half-way up his fetlocks he had traces of white hairs, probably the result of an old injury, perhaps caused by barbed wire. The accident didn't seem to have left any ill-effects, but on his offside hind leg, just above the fetlock joint, there seemed to be some muscular damage, probably from a fall or a kick. The deep flexor was cool, but all the same . . .

'He's been through the wars, hasn't he? At least he's thoroughly experienced,' joked Henry.

'He's a real tough guy,' replied Giordanino. 'You'll see. He can go anywhere.'

He shouted to one of the stable-lads in a stentorian voice spiced with his splendid regional accent:

'Hola, Georges, walk him up and down.'

About fifty yards away, a huge tree-trunk was split into a lop-sided V just above ground-level. Georges amused himself by making l'Enclume do gymnastics, and the horse climbed through the hollow of the V without turning a hair.

'Not bad,' admitted Henry.

'Would you like to try them,' offered Giordanino. 'Have a ride round.'

I was only half-reassured. I confessed to Henry:

'I don't trust the smaller one. Have you seen his legs?'

'They may not get worse.'

'No, but they may not get better either.'

'Listen,' said Henry, 'try him. You'll be travelling at a walk. With one horse it'll be one thing, with another, another. It's difficult to find a horse with all the right qualities. Come on, let's try them both.'

I decided to begin with the bigger of the two, Ondo. Giordanino, meanwhile, hitched l'Enclume to a chain outside the stables.

'It's the gipsies' system,' he explained. 'Their horses browse by the roadside. They can manage with very little. In an hour he'll have had his fill. That's the advantage of these Mediterranean horses. In your part of the country, the grass is too rich, it produces very big horses, but they could never stand up to a journey like yours because they need regular rations of oats and hay which you won't always be able to find. Whereas these two will scratch away the snow to nibble a blade of grass and that will do them.'

At that moment, l'Enclume was nosing at the red-hot pebbles and gravel trying to find a blade of the short, stubby, dry grass. Yet he was in fine condition.

I tried out the two horses, one after the other. They plunged about in all directions, and it was quite fun. I was less pleased with their floppiness when they walked or trotted: they seemed to be marking time without driving forward as Concorda would do. Even when they galloped they didn't cover much ground.

Henry knows Concorda well. When I compared my fantastic trotter to the two provençals, his reaction was sharp:

'How stupid can you get! You might just as well argue over the merits of a Ferrari or a 2-CV. The Ferrari will probably give you more pleasure on the motorways, but you'll do better with your 2-CV when you're stuck in the mud on a bad road in the Balkans.'

'Oh well, if you put it like that. After all, they don't have any vices, they are sound, except for l'Enclume whose hind leg worries me a little.'

'It isn't serious, you can always take him, and if anything goes wrong, ask Giordanino to change him!'

'That's not the object of the exercise. I want to prove that horses are capable of covering 6,000 kilometres. I have no intention of changing them in mid-stream.'

'Of course, but you know, it doesn't mean this one won't hold up and you can't be sure whether another who seems sounder will stay the course. You never know. In any case you'll need a lot of luck. *A priori*, these are already in condition and ready to start. In any case I'd much rather see you go off with l'Enclume than Concorda, who is absolutely mad.'

Well, do I trust Henry or not? Yes, I do. So I struck the bargain. Without too much enthusiasm. Thinking how pleased I should be when I got home to my four-legged Ferrari. Thinking too that this marriage of reason might very well in the long run turn into a love-match.

So Corinne and I would ride to Jerusalem, *inch-Allah*, on two very French horses, with ancestors from the Alps, crossed with horses from the Camargue. Two horses used to rocky ground, the cold of the Lubéron in winter and the crushing Mediterranean heat in summer: horses accustomed to living rough and putting up with bad handling by tourists, as inexperienced as demanding. Not too big, we would be able to climb into our saddles quickly if we were attacked (we must foresee everything), and in spite of their comparatively small size (15.3 hands for Ondo, 15 hands for l'Enclume), they were strong enough to carry us and our gear across half Europe.

I wasn't altogether unhappy and decided to go ahead without further delay. It was 10 September. Why shouldn't we start on the 23rd, a Sunday, which gave us almost a fortnight? The first week could be spent with Giordanino—from now on Loulou to us as to all his friends—afterwards we would have enough time to sell our *pied-à-terre* in Paris and say good-bye to our family and friends. Sometimes it's a good thing to go full speed ahead. Loulou undertook to bring Ondo (who would become Mickey) and l'Enclume (rechristened Donald) up to Paris in his box.

For one moment I hesitated: would it be wiser to get better acquainted? Perhaps. But as I was determined never to press the pace, at least during the first month, the four of us would have time to get run in. So, off we go! From the square outside Notre-Dame to the Church of the Holy Sepulchre, the demoiselles Coquet, Mickey and Donald, would have plenty of time to get to know each other as they followed in the steps of the Crusaders . . . not forgetting Pluto, of course.

CHAPTER FOUR

Excitement at Square One

Days of madness followed with mountains of papers, formalities, visits, papers and more papers. It wasn't enough to have horses, we had to know how to manage them and Loulou proved an admirable instructor. All the precautions we would have to take, all the mistakes to avoid, he listed the lot, and he also helped us to pick out our gear.

I thought I was fairly well up in matters equestrian until I tried to re-shoe Mickey. Having acquired a shoeing hammer and pincers, I enlisted Corinne as my assistant. Streaming with sweat as she held a hoof, I sweated as much, while I endeavoured to remove a piece of horn. It took us three hours. The blacksmith took three minutes. Conclusion: we would have to pray for professionals on our travels whenever we needed them.

One vital problem: the baggage. I knew that military mounts carry up to 120 kilos, but according to the experts, our loads shouldn't exceed fifty. In canvas bags attached to the backs of the saddles we had stuffed the inevitable duvets, 'mountain specials', in which we could sleep in the open at minus 15°. I hoped it wouldn't happen very often, but the duvets could be used as extra coverings for the horses. Hadn't we been assured that the Balkans and Anatolia would be like antechambers to Siberia?

We had also bought polar anoraks which we might send on to Budapest or Belgrade, for till then we wouldn't need them. But you never know. Not that their weight was a problem, but an anorak, long flannel underpants, a spare pair of jeans, two pullovers and a pair of heavy woollen socks made up into an enormous bundle which rubbed the horses' flanks and might cause serious chafing. Under each bag was a pair of very strong leather saddle-bags. Unfortunately, even empty, they weighed a ton. If you added a movie camera and lenses, with spare rolls of black-and-white and colour film, a still camera, first-aid for eight months, pincers, shoeing hammer and assorted blacksmith's nails, rubber boots, a log-book and the formidable mass of papers necessary to get the horses through customs, the weight of the saddle-bags quickly amounted to fifteen kilos. And that load had to be balanced in front by a ration of oats, just in case. The whole lot was protected by a waterproof poncho. Then there was the 'cow', a folding canvas bucket for the horses to drink out of, two water-bottles of two litres each for hot countries, and fifteen yards of fine cord, to draw water from wells if necessary. 'You always need one,' Loulou had declared. Add on the weight of the saddle and bridle—thirty kilos—and our own—fifty per sister— the limit of 100 kilos was easily reached. If Corinne and I could have slimmed down, we would have wasted, like jockeys, but we had no more to lose and whittled away at the equipment. I don't believe the NASA technicians could have worked more feverishly to lighten Apollo's cabin by a few grammes.

D-Day minus eight. Good news. Our elegant attaché from the Austrian Ministry of Agriculture had been beavering away. A telegram from Vienna gave us the green light on condition that our horses were properly vaccinated (the least we could do), that they would spend four days in quarantine at the frontier (so much the better, we'd be able to have a short rest too), and that they didn't come into contact with Austrian animals (no one would bother about that).

D-Day minus three. More good news. Also by telegram, the Turkish Government sent good wishes and the permit to enter Turkey.

In between times I had acquired exit permits for Mickey and Donald. As for repatriating them . . . In fact, assuming that we got to our journey's end without disaster, I hadn't the least intention of abandoning them.

M. Béchau La Fonta, president of the National Interprofessional Union of the Horse, wasn't very optimistic.

'If you cross into the foot-and-mouth zone, you won't be able to repatriate your horses. No horse coming from a country east of Bulgaria can enter France, except as dead meat. If you leave, you know what you'll be doing . . .'

To salve my conscience, I registered our horses with full details of their appearance. If we reached Jerusalem, I would have proof that I wanted to bring back two home-bred horses, and not pure-blooded Arabs. I might even soften up the Ministry of Agriculture by pleading that two such valorous provençals couldn't be condemned to exile.

Language was another problem. In the depths of Hungary, Yugoslavia or Turkey, our linguistics (Corinne could get on quite well in German, I in English), wouldn't be much help. Then I had an idea. I asked the tourist offices of each of the countries on our route to give us a letter of introduction explaining who we were, what we were doing and asking whomever it might concern to give us and our horses aid and assistance in finding shelter and lodging, a blacksmith or a vet. Everyone I contacted obliged. And they also sent us a phonetic vocabulary of sixty essential phrases on the lines of: 'Good evening. Which is the way to X?' 'Where can we buy hay for our horses?' 'Is there an inn, a barn, anywhere where we can spend the night?'

D-Day was Sunday, 23 September. H-Hour, 9.30. Our point of departure, the square outside Notre-Dame. By eight o'clock, in freezing weather, our fans had begun to collect. Corinne arrived to find a small crowd. Little sister was late. Her excuse: she had had to clear out the flat for the new tenants. She might have done it a little sooner. I couldn't complain because I was even later myself. My excuse: like the Crusaders, I wanted to distribute all my worldly possessions before leaving for the Holy Land. If I never returned, at least my television, my record player, my books, Concorda and the rest would be in good hands.

Lined up were those who believed in us and those who didn't. The family, of course, *en masse*: parents, brothers, uncles, aunts, cousins, the lot. My parents had brought Pataud—excuse me, Pluto. I had had to leave him in Nevers while I was busy in Paris. There was also a delegation from *Le Journal de Mickey* in a scarlet and gold minibus. And big Loulou in blue jeans and cowboy hat, who had brought the two horses up with his Land-Rover. He talked to them soothingly, in his Marseillaise accent. And there was also a crowd of friends, though I didn't know them all, and the press, the radio, TV and newsreels.

How the horses were saddled and the baggage strapped on I've no idea. What I do know is that I felt limp. Fatigue? Fever of departure? I'm afraid it was fever. Not surprising after the excitements of the last week and the series of injections pumped into us. A distinguished figure approached, holding out a paper which Corinne grabbed and stuffed unceremoniously into her pocket. Later we discovered that it was a list of extremely valuable night stops: thanks to his help we would be expected and looked after by an incredible number of exclusive riding-clubs.

Very suitably, a service had been arranged in one of the chapels of Notre-Dame. The Crusaders never started without having been duly blessed. I wanted to take Pluto with me into the cathedral but the canon taking the service stopped me: no dogs in the house of God.

'The Church has no desire to develop the folklore side of the story,' he declared. 'What is essential is that you should receive the grace of God.'

And he pronounced his prayer:

> Holy Virgin Mary, Notre Dame,
> You who knew the joyful paths
> And the grievous paths
> That led to Jerusalem,
> Be as a careful mother
> Towards your two children
> Protect them,
> Endow them with the grace
> Which was given to you
> Through your son, Jesus Christ.

Privately I considered we would certainly need it.

> They join their prayers to ours,
> Hail Mary.

The little congregation returned to the square where the sun had come out.

The two heroines were more emotional than they would like to admit. I heard one photographer exclaim:

'My word! They don't look a day over fourteen!'

It must have been our hats. We had spent hours and hours on the problem: hard hats were out because they would be too heavy and give us headaches: cowboy hats would be considered too frivolous by the French Federation of Equestrian Sports, who are dead against overseas influences. Eventually, the consensus of opinion agreed on unisex tartan school caps, with pompoms.

Once again there was a friendly scuffle while photographers and cameramen elbowed each other. Orders rapped out, punctuated by flash-bulbs.

'The two girls on the ground, the dog on horseback, look at me!' Click. 'Both girls on horseback, the dog as well, pat the horse's neck, very good, don't move.' Click. 'Raise one arm and wave so we can see the Mickey tee-shirts. . . . Perfect. The dog on the ground, one girl too, the other on horseback, smile. . . . Kiss your parents in front of Notre-Dame. Fine by me.' Click! Click!

Now a sequence for the TV. Readjust caps.

Question: 'Why Jerusalem?'

'We've always wanted to make a pilgrimage to the Holy Land.'

'Speak up, we can't hear you. . . . Don't step on the cables, for God's sake . . .'

I obeyed, happy to oblige, knowing that before long we would meet some of the countless viewers who had watched our departure on the small screen, and who might be much more likely to give us a helping hand if we asked them.

Is the happening over? Can we go now? Yes.

For the first stage of our journey we had company: a police car and two motorcycles, then behind a real convoy with the minibus from *Le Journal de Mickey*, Loulou's Land-Rover with him balancing on the roof, singing 'La Provençale' in patois at the top of his voice, and a whole procession of cars.

Our first stop was a football club on the banks of the Marne. Our supporters had brought enough oats and hay to transform an empty coach-house into a stable. Corinne and I would spend the night on camp-beds in the cloakroom.

Our motorcyclist friends left us, mission accomplished, making no secret that they would have liked to escort us as far as Jerusalem. A final dinner before the farewell scene with the parents: Papa, still anxious, Maman dropping a few tears. Everything according to plan.

The watchman in charge of ladies—*charge d'âmes*—mumbled a few words of welcome. His rhetoric seemed a little summary but he explained with a splendid regional accent:

'I can't do it in French. I'm from the Pas-de-Calais. In my dialect it'd be much easier.'

We're off to a good start, I tell Corinne. Language difficulties before getting out of Paris . . .

Next morning, the second day of the Coquet sisters' private crusade, we were left to ourselves. Objective: Meaux. From now on, we would ride alone. We had no complaints. The weather was brilliant. *La vie est belle.*

CHAPTER FIVE

The Day Continues

At the Poteau stud everyone had been up for hours. I could hear the stable-lads mucking out while daylight streamed through the curtains.

I leapt out of bed, crammed my bottom into my jeans, and my feet into my boots. The rest could wait: priority was with the horses who were hungry and expecting their oats.

I went across to the stables and looked at the horses through gaps in the planking. They were already on their feet. Mickey had sensed my presence and turned his head towards the door. So had Donald. I could see only two very round rumps and two heads under their long tangled manes, while a white blaze down their noses made them look like naughty little boys. If they'd been children they'd have been banging the table with their bowls crying: 'Where's our breakfast?'

When I opened the door, Donald neighed. Salutation or scolding because I was late? He stamped his right forefoot. It's his way of letting me know he's not pleased. He neighed again and became more insistent. He was very hungry. Donald was always hungry.

'Good morning, my darling. Sleep well?'

A friendly pat for each and a quick look at the rations, then I had to draw their water. Mickey always swallowed half the bucket in one gulp, then I made him stop for a moment because the water temperature was lower than the stable, and might bring on colic. Mickey never stopped until he'd had about a bucket and a half, about fifteen litres. After that he would dabble his nose in the water, sucking it up and spitting it out as if he were gargling. I adored this trick and from then on rinsing his teeth became his favourite game.

Then it was Donald's turn. Poor thing, he always had to wait. I'd got into the habit of looking after Mickey first, perhaps because he was *my* horse. With Donald, watering became a test of patience. Far from knocking back two-thirds of the bucket with a single gulp, he would begin by moistening his lips, as if to test the temperature of the water, raising his head and swallowing a few drops. A true comic, he would then stretch his whole body like a cat, beginning with the right leg, which he stretched backwards as far as possible. And the same again with the left. Then the neck and head, followed by a colossal yawn, which showed all his teeth and gums. He repeated this performance several times, carefully, meticulously, in the identical order, before addressing himself to the bucket. A real clown. But isn't it tricks like this that make you love one horse rather than another?

Then the oats: three kilos at night, three in the morning, the usual cavalry ration, though Mickey and Donald weren't used to as much. In Provence they ate horse nuts, but they seemed to have accepted the new regime and their droppings didn't show too many undigested grains.

'Have a good feed, enjoy yourselves. You don't know what you'll get to eat tomorrow.'

It took them about half an hour to eat, and then they would lie down again for a short digestive nap until 7.30, which gave Corinne and me more than an hour to get dressed, collect our things, pack and have breakfast, our main meal until dinner at about eight o'clock at night. It was obviously better to reach our next halt before dark, i.e. before five or six at the latest. During the day we would stop occasionally to let the horses rest and enjoy the last of the autumn sunshine, so taking delays and wrong turnings into account, we had to be on our way by eight o'clock every morning.

I woke up Corinne, as our hostess was already pouring us huge mugs of fresh milk spiced with chocolate and buttering thick slices of toasted country bread. Delicious! Then the bags had to be fastened to the saddles. We staggered under their weight, and yet, truly, we had only brought the minimum. My own fifty kilos took a lot of carrying the 150 yards from the house to the stables, particularly because I always seemed to catch my foot in the bridle or the long reins.

The horses viewed our arrival with a jaundiced eye. An energetic brush-down to remove the night droppings clinging to their coats and legs. Check-up. No swellings, no overheating: all correct. The manager of the stud arrived.

'I looked your horses over this morning. They've got good appetites. But I'm very worried about the little one.'

He pointed to Donald.

'You don't think you'll get to Jerusalem with him, do you? His tendons won't hold out for 200 kilometres. If you get as far as the German border you'll be lucky. And besides, your horses are only just fit. They'll get thinner during the next three weeks, you'll find it difficult to keep them in condition. You should have taken Percherons, at least they wouldn't have had any difficulty carrying your baggage.'

'The girls wouldn't look very pretty when they got back,' sniggered a jockey, 'they'd have hoops instead of legs.'

'You don't ride Percherons, but you can't talk,' teased one of the grooms, laughing.

In my heart of hearts, I slightly shared the director's fears. Donald's forelegs had always struck me as doubtful, but I still trusted Henry. With several hundred successes to his credit, we would be really unlucky if for once his judgement had come unstuck.

The stable-lads helped us hoist the saddle and gear on Donald's back; one lad directed by Corinne on the left, another with me on the right. At the exact moment we laid the saddle on his back, Donald kicked out with both hind legs and we beat a hasty etreat. The blanket flew off and the bags were scattered. Every morning we went through the same pantomime ten times over before the saddle and blanket were fixed. Sometimes the blanket was too far forward, sometimes too far back, sometimes longer on one side than the other, so the whole thing had to be lifted with one hand while you pulled on the blanket with the other. By the time we'd finished with Donald, I was exhausted. Fortunately Mickey was quieter, and things were a little easier. By the time we left the stud, a pale sun was beginning to show through the light mist and we were half an hour late.

We went straight back to the Marne canal. The grassy tow-path was good going for the horses and we were far away from towns, roads and noise, and had no problems of navigation. The sun gilded the leaves shining under the dew, while a thick layer of fog floated above the water like a white ribbon. Fishermen had already set up their rods. The horses didn't like the men in their funny shiny clothes and were afraid of the fishing-rods. However hard I kicked, I couldn't drive Mickey on, so I tried to tickle him up with the long reins, only succeeding in lashing the bundles.

I tried again. No good.

'O.K.,' I said to Corinne. 'There's no point in struggling. We'll have to get down and lead them.'

The path was narrow and we had to pick our way between one of the fishermen and his motorcycle which was leaning against the hedge. With me in front, Mickey wasn't afraid and followed me obediently. Pluto was sniffing about in the hedge. Suddenly a voice yelled:

'Can't you control your bloody dog? Mind my new rods!'

Pluto had flushed a pheasant which took off right between Mickey's feet. He shied, plunged sideways, and landed with all four feet on a collection of spare rods laid out carefully on the grass.

'Are they broken?'

'What a stupid question! Not one of them's usable . . .'

Corinne suggested the fisherman should claim for his rods through our insurance company, but in view of the time it would take to find the right forms, the fisherman preferred to see us depart before Donald could give a demonstration of his talents.

A few hours later, standing on the saddle, I was picking walnuts and filling the pockets of my anorak while Corinne gathered sweet ripe blackberries to be eaten on the spot.

Pluto, plunging about among the reeds, one paw raised, tail quivering and nose twitching, stared at a whirlpool marking the disappearance of a catfish. All four paws together, like a grass-hopper, he jumped into the water after his finny prey. That's how I like to see him: glad to be alive: full of ideas. He always came back dripping and waited until he was in our midst to have a good shake and shower us with water.

He must have been jealous of the horses who needed so much of our time and attention and took umbrage very easily, always using the bank opposite to the one we were on.

Pluto swam across to our bank and lay a little way off, still sulking. We took off the reins and allowed the horses to graze. I looked for a place where they could go down to the water without sinking among the reeds or falling into the canal, but couldn't find one, so I looked for a gap where I could fill the bucket. Whoops! My rubber boots skidded on the thick grass and I found myself flat on my bottom in the mud. I emerged sticky, muddy and draped with long ribbons of grass. At least I could fill the bucket. Corinne offered the water to the horses.

'They don't want it, the pigs. A ducking for nothing.'

Mickey and Donald were much too busy cropping the fresh grass to bother with the canvas bucket. All I could do was lay out my jeans in the sun, in full view of the river-men. Bad luck for them. Or good luck? We still had some *pain d'épices* and the end of a tube of condensed milk, a treat for Pluto. We must be nice to him. Corinne squeezed the tube and Pluto sucked it up and licked his lips.

How pleasant to lie out on the grass, without a care in the world, listening to the silence of the countryside. I thought of the Paris sky, saturated with carbon fumes, and all the people crushing round counters and battling for greasy sausages and luke-warm Coke. For us there would be no noise, no midday rush-hour for months and months. Corinne woke me out of my dream:

'Why don't you watch your horse?'

Mickey had been indulging in a few caprioles, until, chased by Pluto, who didn't appreciate *haute école*, he had taken refuge in the adjoining field.

'Hey—boy—gently—Mickey, come back . . .'

There's no point in running after a horse because he will always go faster than you. Mickey began to circle round a tuft of grass, sniffing.

'He's going to roll . . . My God, the baggage!'

Mickey wasted no time but knelt, and rolled over.

'Help—my camera . . . Hey, you! Get up!'

But Mickey was too far away: he stretched with obvious pleasure, carefully rubbing his side, scratching his back and turning violently, all four feet in the air, with a total disregard for the baggage. He got up at last, shaking himself voluptuously then dropped his nose into the grass as if nothing had happened. My Nikon must certainly be in smithereens. I rushed forward, half dressed, to check up on the damage. The camera, wrapped in a plastic bag, was still in one piece. The sun-shield was bent, but the case had merely been shaken. Nothing serious. When I considered that 450 kilos of flesh and bone had rolled over it, my admiration for the Japs went up about ten points. All the same, I told Corinne we should have it checked as soon as possible.

'It would be too silly to have nothing but blank films at the end of our trip. I think . . .'

Corinne will never know what I think. She yelled:

'Evelyne, look!'

I looked and it was my turn to yell: 'Stop! My trousers!'

A gipsy child of about twelve was running off with my jeans and the packet of *pain d'épices*. He ran faster than I could in bare feet over the prickly grass, so Pluto summed up the situation and came to the rescue. He set off after the thief and took a good grip of his ankle.

Terrorised the little villain didn't dare move. With his dark skin, straight black hair, sharp features and dark eyes, he was as beautiful as a fox in a trap. I didn't feel the least resentment but— to hell with morality—I thoroughly approved of the way the kid was trying to fend for himself. I made a suggestion:

'Keep the *pain d'épices* and give me back my jeans.'

When he dropped them, I ordered Pluto to let him go and the ragamuffin took to his heels and disappeared into the middle distance. As I made myself decent, Corinne burst out laughing. 'Imagine you arriving at the village this evening in see-through underpants. What a success you'd have!'

We had been threatened with thieves—in Anatolia. But we were only seventy kilometres from Paris. A promising beginning.

'Good. Now you've got your clothes back,' said Corinne, 'perhaps we could move on.'

'O.K. Let's begin by sorting out Mickey's load.'

This took half an hour.

'Don't you think we'd do better to leave the tow-path,' said Corinne. 'It's a bit overgrown. You need an axe to cut the thorns. And a lifebelt: the edge has been eaten away by musk-rats.'

'Yes, it would be quicker across the fields. The canal makes a wide loop here, and it'll give us a change of scene.'

The Brie region spread its golden fields as far as the eye could see. But Pluto was running on three legs. I dismounted to examine his pads. He must have picked up a thorn, but I could see nothing. Corinne was sorry for him.

'Let him ride,' she told me.

In principle, I didn't approve, for the horses could do without his eighteen kilos. But I couldn't expect a limping Pluto to run after us, so I balanced him in front of me on the bundle of hay, where he trembled like a leaf and leant against me with all his weight. He hated being on horseback. After five minutes, he jumped down and ran off. Without limping. Cured by fear.

A few kilometres further on, we met an electrified fence and stopped to consult the map: there might be a way round. The horses grazed while we discussed direction and detour. I called out:

'Look out, Corinne, your horse is under the electric wire.'

Donald lifted his head, got a shock which made him buck like a bronco, threw Corinne, managed to free himself and set off at a gallop, dragging about 150 yards of live wire wrapped round his neck. Eventually the wire broke, and he froze, petrified. Corinne was as white as a sheet, shaking all over, and couldn't even stand. Donald kept completely still. I didn't dare touch either of them for fear of being shocked as well. Eventually, I pulled myself together, thinking the current couldn't be all that strong. A few lumps of sugar quickly cured the casualties. Now the fence had gone, we could start again.

In another meadow, Pluto was chasing some cows.

'Look at that one,' said Corinne, 'she looks very odd.'

'She's giving birth.'

The cow in question ran towards us, obviously curious, with the hind legs of the calf already showing. She didn't seem in the least concerned and began to gallop and rush about, much more intrigued by us than her own interesting condition. She came across and stopped a few yards from the fence, just in time for us to see the blessed event. The cow tried to get rid of the calf by leaping about. A birth at full gallop: I'd never seen anything like it!

We still had about ten kilometres to go across an absolutely flat landscape and couldn't possibly reach the next village before dark.

'We might stop at that farm over there?'

'Let's see.'

We dismounted and walked, as we always did for the last half-hour. La Chaumière was more like a big suburban house than a farm, with green shutters and white-washed walls. The lawns were meticulously cut, the paths impeccable and from a neighbouring field, a grey mare called to our horses.

Two men were fiddling with a tractor in the yard. One of them, blond and bearded, with sparkling green eyes, was the master of the house, and knew nothing about our trip to Jerusalem. Had we stumbled on that rare animal, a Frenchman who didn't watch television? He was quite willing to put us up, if his wife had no objection.

When she appeared, she was quite agreeable. The stables were opened up especially, the heavy gear was unloaded, and I could almost feel the horses' relief in my own body as we patted their backs and gave them an energetic massage. I wished someone would do the same for my own stiff shoulders. The map-case hanging round my neck was definitely too heavy. The handsome farmer watched us at work. I asked:

'Can we buy a dozen kilos of oats, two bundles of hay and two bundles of straw for tonight and tomorrow morning?'

'Of course you can. Arthur,' he said to his companion, 'go and fetch the hay and straw for these young ladies.'

'Can we have two buckets of water too?'

'Arthur, fetch two buckets of water.'

The farmer's wife came to see how we were doing.

'Do you have a tent?'

'No, we can sleep on the straw.'

'Do you have any sandwiches, or a spirit stove, something you can cook on?'

'No. It would be too heavy for the horses.'

They were amazed. Finally it was agreed that we would sleep in the loft and eat with them, provided we washed and peeled the extra vegetables and mushrooms. The least we could do.

Over dinner, the hostess plied us with questions. Why Jerusalem? Why on horseback? Why not work like everyone else? Why wasn't I married and mother of two children? She could only see one possible explanation: I was going to Christ's tomb to find a husband because I couldn't find one in Paris, or else I was trying to get over a disappointment in love.

The dinner was excellent, like our appetites. I demolished two huge bowls of soup and would willingly have had a third if I hadn't been afraid of overstepping the mark. The omelette flavoured with wood- and field-mushrooms picked the same morning was quite delicious.

We lent a hand with the washing-up. And then we were treated to a film show of their last holiday and the gambollings of the newest born. We were dropping with sleep when finally we slipped into our sleeping-bags. The full moon flooding our loft with light should have inspired us with romantic dreams. Who would appear to whisper sweet nothings in our ears?

By way of whisper we soon heard an increasing Bzz . . . Bzzz . . . Flies—swarms—myriads of flies.

If I said I didn't like it, it would be an understatement. I was terrified. Knowing perfectly well that it was ridiculous, I curled up inside my sleeping-bag and didn't move, sweating like a pig in my goosefeather sauna until coming up for air, I swallowed at least two flies in a single gulp.

I wasn't at all happy and neither was Corinne, but I burst out laughing at the bottom of my sleeping-bag.

'What's the matter?' asked Corinne.

'I'm thinking how our lot would react at home if I told them I was afraid of flies.' I could just imagine.

CHAPTER SIX

Chateau and Champagne

In spite of what anyone may say, French hospitality isn't to be sneezed at. Admittedly, the publicity we had had in the press and on TV helped a great deal. When we crossed the fields or met a tractor, the peasants would stop and ask:

'Eh? Are you the ones going to Jerusalem? Saw you on the telly, Sunday night. You've got a nerve and no mistake!'

A bargee who overtook us on the Marne canal wanted to give us a lift:

'Good luck, little ladies! How about loading your horses on the barge? You'll be able to watch television . . .'

After one long day of crushing heat on the golden and treeless plain of the Brie region, we were crawling along, half-asleep, a hollow in the pit of our stomachs. Corinne asked a peasant if he knew of a farm which might put us all up.

'Just go along to the chateau, plenty of room,' was the reply.

'Shall we?' asked Corinne, delighted at the thought of spending a night in a chateau.

Why not?

A notice-board outside the main gate informed us that it belonged to the Princes de Condé. The paths and lawns were immaculate, the iron gates open, but there wasn't a living soul in sight. I didn't dare bring the horses into the courtyard: they might forget themselves on the impeccably raked gravel.

Someone emerged from the main building and came to meet us, explaining he had recognised us immediately—the telly, of course. With old-world courtesy he invited us to accompany him to a building where our animals would be treated with all the respect due to our rank. We girls would have a room—a room each—in the chateau itself, which belonged to him, since our host was none other than the Comte de Sade, descendant of the notorious marquis, and of the Princes de Condé.

After dining with the comte, his wife, his daughter and one of her girlfriends—five women to one Sade—it was nearly midnight before we were given a personally conducted tour of the chateau. Not surprisingly, by the time we got to bed, Corinne and I were slightly dazed. After all, the Coquet sisters weren't used to sleeping in rooms once occupied by Richelieu and Mazarin.

Next morning our host took the trouble to mark out a special scenic route for us and checked personally to see if the paths were practicable for the horses. In addition, he had obtained permission for us to ride through a private forest and turned up at every crossroads to make sure we hadn't lost our way.

So the famous gallantry of the French isn't such a myth after all.

Chateau-Thierry, Dormans, Saint-Martin-d'Albois, Epernay. By the sixth day we had covered only 200 kilometres, but we were entitled to our weekly day of rest. What had made Mickey and Donald so tired? Change of air and climate? Possibly. Anyway, they hadn't yet got into the rhythm of a long journey and seemed languid and uneasy.

Usually I would go in front, because as Mickey was the bigger, he could lengthen his stride a little, but by mid-afternoon I would be exhausted myself and Corinne would take over. The horses always followed each other without trouble, but we never managed to make them walk side by side: often because the paths were too narrow but mainly because Donald preferred to bury his nose in Mickey's tail. If we tried to make them walk side by side they used up all their energy quarrelling.

The horses weren't the only ones. Everything wasn't so rosy with us either.

I would harp away at my favourite subject:

'Corinne, your horse is tired: get off and give him a rest.'

'I've got blisters.'

'I've warned you. If your horse packs up after a week, it'll be your own fault.'

'If we're going to walk to Jerusalem, I don't see why we needed the horses.'

'Idiot! There's a difference between walking 6,000 kilometres and giving your bottom some air from time to time. When you've got your backside stuck to the saddle, there's no getting you off.'

'My darling big sister, kindly note that I'm not prepared to put up with your stinking bad temper for months and months. If it's going to be like this, I'm taking the first train back to Paris.'

I considered Corinne perfectly capable of carrying out her threat, so I calmed down a little:

'Of course, your horse is smaller than mine. Supposing we changed over. I don't mind walking a bit, it'll help me unwind.'

After several hours in the saddle I needed to run about, or at least stride out briskly, and it was probably because I wasn't using up enough energy that I had become so aggressive.

Everywhere we went, the fields were teeming with the most frantic activity. Obviously in Champagne they take the grape harvest seriously. The mayor of Saint-Martin had said:

'Don't have an accident in Champagne. There'll be no one in the hospitals. Everyone's out harvesting the grapes.'

No accidents. We arrived exhausted, in filthy tempers, but intact, at Epernay. While the Riding Club took charge of the horses, we were entertained by Madame Pol Roger. After a great aristocrat with a famous chateau, a great lady with a famous line of business. Sparkling. Immediately my good humour was restored. And Corinne forgot all about her train.

CHAPTER SEVEN

Marching through Lorraine and Alsace

From stud-farm to barn, from riding-club to stable, through sunshine and through rain, we proceeded slowly eastwards: Chalons, Vitry-le-François, Bar-le-Duc, Ligny-en-Barrois.

A glance at the map showed Domrémy under thirty kilometres away. If ever a woman could be considered on the same level as the Crusaders, it was Joan of Arc. When Paul Winkler gave me his patronage—and his cheque—he said: 'You look like Joan of Arc, it's a good sign.' So wouldn't a quick side trip to the Maid's birthplace be the least we could do? I hesitated. And turned down the idea. This homage to the most famous horsewoman in the history of France would take up two whole days. Never mind.

After a night in a log house which smelt deliciously of cows and hot soup, a romantic ride through the woods of Sexey brought us to the gates of Nancy, where a cavalcade was waiting for us. They were to pilot us to the blue line of the Vosges mountains, where they would hand us over to a group of pathfinders who would take us over the mountains into Alsace.

We couldn't think of anything better, but we wanted to make a halt at the Rosières stud to get new shoes for both horses. Mickey and Donald were in splendid form, as was Pluto. Corinne and I, on the other hand, were a little jaded after our third TAB jabs.

'No food, no alcohol and complete rest in bed,' the doctor had advised. Having promised to obey instructions, we tucked into an enormous breakfast and climbed into the saddle. All we had to do was trust Jean-Lou, the leader of the group, who knew the district like the back of his hand.

The hours and kilometres slipped past happily, enlivened by the military songs of our entertaining companions. But even Jean-Lou had his troubles.

'Damn it, I didn't expect this. About turn, everyone.'

A drainage ditch barred the main ride, too wide for any of the horses to jump across. Two hours later, to my great delight, we met the same ditch again. The air turned blue. So even the experts can be stumped when ordnance maps disregard the splitting up of paths and drainage work in progress. Jean-Lou wouldn't admit defeat and searched for a way round.

'Victory!' he exclaimed.

Only a minor ditch. Jean-Lou jumped first. I couldn't see through the thick leaves but heard a loud plop, then silence. He finally reappeared on the other side, brushing off the mud and laughing heartily, as amused by his accident as the rest of us.

The bells were ringing for Saturday mass when we arrived at Donjevin. It had been arranged that we would sleep in a barn with the horses, our first night roughing it.

Corinne groped for sticks, lit a camp-fire and cooked potatoes in the ashes, and Jean-Lou showed us how to make a bed in the straw.

'You choose a flat place, moving away the bales of straw if necessary, then you break open a bale and fill in the gaps, making a thick mattress and pillow. You try it to see if it's comfortable, and if you're satisfied, spread your waterproof over the pillow: that way you won't chew straw all night. And you'll be as warm as if you were in a featherbed.'

Cold, damp and daylight woke us around four o'clock. The horses were already on their feet, eating the fresh straw. But where was Donald? His halter was still tied to a stake. Mickey must have been playing with him and unfastened the buckle.

'Evelyne, if you could see what I see!' cried Corinne, smiling.

Good old Donald! Not finding his bedding comfortable enough, he had managed to climb up to a higher level, don't ask me how. There he was taking his ease, like a pasha, among the loose bales of straw. He surveyed us now, without moving, like a dog who has played truant and doesn't know whether to look pleased or put his tail between his legs.

It was too funny: how can one be angry with a coward crossed with an acrobat? While Monsieur took his ease, Corinne gave him his hay which he ate lying down, greedy and relaxed, exactly like a dog chewing a bone. Then, without being asked, he came down again to rejoin his colleagues.

An hour later, fortified by hot coffee—what a wonderful smell in the morning mists—we were back in the saddle and on our way.

At Cirey-sur-Vézouse, Jean-Lou and his friends handed us over to three new guides to take us over the col at Dinon, the highest pass in the Vosges. To my great surprise, Mickey and Donald stood up to the mountains very well. Spurred by the sharp air, they climbed up the steep paths, strewn with loose stones, without turning a hair, probably inspired by pre-natal memories of their Alpine ancestors. Pluto was bursting with joy among all the interesting smells and rolled in a puddle after dislodging a wild boar who had been having a good wallow.

All the same, the midday picnic was a welcome rest and we all drank the local white wine in turn from the same gourd. Corinne and I went at it greedily because we were very thirsty, so an hour later when our guides were cautiously preparing to negotiate a six-foot drop, Corinne and I were falling about laughing, stoned out of our minds, and singing at the tops of our voices. Our guides must have wondered what kind of state we'd be in by the time we got to Jerusalem if we couldn't behave better after a few mouthfuls of white wine.

Mickey and Donald, thank God, had only been drinking from the puddles of rain-water and maintained their self-control, making their way deliberately down the vertical wall. The other horses followed only after considerable hesitation. One jumped down violently enough to crack his hoofs, another stepped on his rider's foot, making him howl, and the last caught his legs in the reins. We continued to laugh.

'You've got bloody marvellous horses!' our companions admitted.

At Donan, the forest ranger installed the five horses in his field, where they spent the night, while our guides slept on the straw with the pigs and ducks. They were on a week-end outing and thoroughly enjoying themselves. We cheated by slipping off to a neighbouring farm where we were comfortably tucked up under lace-trimmed eiderdowns.

Next evening, two riders appeared, asking questions which we didn't understand. And for good reason: the Alsatian patois is as impenetrable as the ways of the Lord. 'Well, of course, you don't understand, you speak French,' said one of the newcomers, explaining that they were members of the riding-club of Obernai.

'We're taking over and guiding you into Alsace,' they told us. Decidedly, the great brotherhood of the saddle has a great deal to recommend it.

We had an early start next morning, for there was to be a party in our honour that evening at Obernai Town Hall. At five o'clock it was still dark, and in a fog you could cut with a knife we searched in vain for the horses.

'They must have lain down to shelter from the cold. Mickey! Donald! . . .'

The white mist muffled our voices. Nothing moved in the fog-shrouded meadow.

'Fetch the oats. Then you won't have to call.'

And at once, the five horses ran up, coats wet, legs cold and sound, nostrils wide open. They had stood up to their tough day perfectly well.

'Hurry up and dish out five rations, if not there'll be a battle.'

Corinne distributed the fodder.

'Ha . . . ha . . .'

Donald, who had finished first, let out his war-cry and attacked his victim, the guide's thoroughbred. Ears flattened, teeth bared, he hurled himself on his adversary and bit the tip of his nose (a horse's sensitive point) and gave him a violent kick on the thigh. The thoroughbred surrendered, abandoned his oats and moved away limping, leaving Donald to gobble up a second breakfast.

The guide's voice rang through the frost:

'Hey . . . come and have some hot coffee and a glass of schnapps.'

Who could refuse?

We had climbed to the top of the Vosges mountains, now we had to go down the other side.

'We're going to follow the Roman road. You'll see the ruts left by the chariots. The paving-stones aren't too easy for the horses, but the route is very pretty.'

All this was said with such a strong accent that the demoiselles Coquet forgot their manners and fell about laughing, until we got the hiccups. Why not? Not a care in the world. Freedom. Happiness. The forest. Horses in good shape. For the past three days we'd been swimming in euphoria. A euphoria fully shared by the rest of the group. Suddenly I heard a shout:

'What's happened?'

My laughter was cut short: Corinne and Donald had shot off like a couple of bullets. 'Ow!'

Our guide had just been stung on the hand. A swarm of wasps were buzzing under Donald's stomach, while the little horse plunged about like a devil in a stoup of holy water. Then Mickey collected some of the wasps in his flowing mane and I could feel them settling on my hair.

All three of us galloped off at top speed to get away from the nest we had disturbed. A few wasps circled round us until we reached the banks of a stream: Corinne jumped down and splashed everyone with water, putting the last of the wasps to flight. The horses didn't seem to have been badly stung but our guide complained long and loud. Corinne teased him:

'Do like my grandmother. Say: "Baby Jesus, cure my sting" and blow on it three times.'

At this point the guide decided to take an even shorter cut down a ravine at the steepest angle.

'Look out!' yelled Corinne.

Her horse had stumbled against I don't know what, sat down and slid down the carpet of fallen leaves. They carried away a rotten tree and fetched up fifty yards lower down in another tree which, luckily, held firm. I rushed up as quickly as I could:

'Are you all right?'

'I hit the tree with my thigh.'

'Can you walk as far as the path?'

Corinne pulled a face but said she could.

'I'll give you a hand up as soon as we're back on the road.'

Miraculously, Donald wasn't limping. All the same, I scolded the guides:

'Good heavens, don't you know any steeper paths? Are we supposed to be blazing a trail for Olympic skiers?'

How long did it take for us to recover our good humour? One minute, two perhaps? And then we realised that our tobogganing had had its useful side.

When we dismounted outside the town hall, the doorman objected:

'No dogs in the reception hall.'

'All the heroes have been invited,' retorted Corinne, picking up Pluto and marching in, holding him in her arms.

On the table in the reception hall was set out the wine (in our honour), the sponge cake (traditional) tied with a ribbon (in a bow). The mayor cut the ribbon and addressed the company:

'As an ex-cavalryman myself, I admire your courage and enterprise. The commune of Obernai is proud to welcome you and offer its specialities. I raise my glass . . .'

Until then, I had behaved very well. And then, suddenly, my laughter exploded. I couldn't help myself, but I don't think any-one held it against me. Everyone knows the effect of three days in the open washed down with the local wine.

The previous day's journey had been very short. And yet the physical effort, the wine, the many snacks of bacon, sausage and potato had been a hard test for our legs and livers. But apparently we hadn't come to the end yet, for our guide—a different one, tall and fair, riding an animal at least eighteen hands high, informed us:

'I'm taking you to lunch with a friend of mine, O.K.? He breeds fjords, the little Norwegian horses, the strongest in the world, eh? Ja, ja . . .'

It was said with such charm that I couldn't refuse. And yet, on this morning after the night before, I felt a bit limp.

'Is it far?'

'Fifteen kilometres.'

'Another three hours . . . God preserve us.'

Discouraged, I closed my eyes. Mickey trotted along. I could feel my head fall into nothingness and made a few feeble attempts to lift it, but lulled by the clip-clop of the horse's hooves, I fell asleep.

'Ho, ho! We're here!'

I woke to a marvellous island where wild duck swept the waters of the Rhine, sending up bright showers as they landed. Herons with long beaks were fishing. Three roe-deer watched us with curiosity from the opposite bank.

I was still in the saddle and Mickey was cooling his feet in the river. I had slept for more than two hours.

'We've arrived at Vogelgrun,' our guide announced. 'The ranch is over there. We crossed the canal and the first bridge over the Rhine while you were asleep. The island is a game reserve: hunting and motorcars forbidden. Tomorrow you'll see birds of all kinds and colours and the game which comes to shelter here. Even the famous Alsatian storks which you won't find anywhere else.'

Our hosts, the Schmidts, appeared, welcoming and charming. The parents did the hard work of the restaurant, while one daughter ran the bar. The two elder sons taught riding and organised excursions on horseback while the youngest, two red-cheeked ten-year-olds, ran the local pony club, with all the responsibility that that implies. A happy family which enjoyed its work, despite the demands of the German invaders who came to scatter their revalued marks in this earthly paradise.

'Why not spend a couple of days here before crossing the border so the horses can rest?' proposed Corinne. 'Papa and Maman could come and visit us. They'd be vastly relieved to see their little daughters in such excellent form.'

'Good idea. The horses will be in good shape for the vet and besides, we're on schedule. We'll cross the frontier exactly three weeks after our departure.'

Next morning at dawn, the German veterinary officer arrived to officiate and examine the horses. His verdict:

'Perfectly healthy. How about the dog?'

'He's off exploring the islands.'

'If he's not tired after six hundred kilometres it proves he's fit and well. You have your certificates?'

I held out a bundle of papers and let him get on with it. Everything in order, except . . .

'Your authorisation to cross Germany on horseback has expired.' It was all going too well. But the vet reassured us.

'I telephoned Stuttgart this morning. As far as they're concerned, everything's in order. You can cross the frontier tomorrow morning, at nine o'clock. I'll be there.'

'You can rely on us. *Danke schön.*'

A few moments later, our parents arrived, delighted to find

their offspring in fine form, cheeks pink, all smiles. They had brought large-scale maps of Germany, replacements for our first-aid kit, and expected to collect Pluto before he dropped dead with fatigue. In point of fact, Pluto was out hunting with a girlfriend and had no intention of giving up the trip.

Next morning, as agreed, we presented ourselves at the frontier, escorted by the Schmidt family in all its glory: parents in a carriage (and their best clothes) and children on horseback. Then, apart from the police and various customs officials, there were the journalists from both banks, TV cameras churning away.

'*Es geht, Gute Reise,*' said the officer in charge.

Once we set foot and horseshoe in Federal territory, I turned round for a last look at this corner of France. How long would it be before I saw it again? With a slight shiver I remembered that my chosen model, Godfrey de Bouillon, never saw his mother-land again. After all, a dozen centuries had passed, and if Corinne and I had dangers to face, they wouldn't be the same.

As for the rest, luck was with us in the shape of a French Colonel, who welcomed us and informed us that he belonged to the SHN, three letters representing the most precious of backing: la Société Hippique Nationale. He handed over a packet:

'Here are your maps. On the first is a route worked out for us by an officer from his helicopter, using minor roads as far as Karchzarten. A rider will meet you there to take you to Freiburg-im-Breisgau, which you should reach soon after lunch.'

I was very impressed at the thought that a helicopter had been enlisted to help a couple of scatty girls from Nevers. In the Bible, angels are always being sent to guide the Just . . . Germany was definitely putting on a very good show for us and our expedition.

CHAPTER EIGHT

Fantasia in the Black Forest

'What ghastly weather,' complained the Colonel. 'What a shame there's no sun, you would have seen the forest at its best . . . Now you have a choice of routes: either you go by the valley, and in view of the weather forecast, I would strongly advise you to, but it is shut in and narrow, and you'll have to follow the main road: or you can go along the crest, using a trail marked out for hikers. It's not really too dangerous, but I don't guarantee that you can follow it all the way on horseback, and with this filthy weather, you might get lost in the fog and clouds.'

I didn't hesitate for a moment:

'Forty-five kilometres being run down by lorries, no thanks. Let's try the crest.'

Hardly had we set out than a roadmender put us on our guard:

'*Nicht gut,*' he said, pointing to an inky black cloud.

The rain came down in stair-rods, while the wind filled our ponchos, which flapped and upset the horses. Mickey fidgeted behind the Colonel's quieter mount, and I tried not to step on his heels, which wasn't easy, and Corinne was having difficulty in holding Donald. With every squall she took off at a gallop across the ploughed fields, and after one gust, her poncho flew up and covered her face while her horse galloped straight at the Colonel's. Donald and the Colonel's horse collided at full speed and Donald promptly bit his military colleague's rump, making him react like a bronco at a rodeo. The Colonel fell off. Scarlet with embarrassment Corinne tried to apologise.

'You're going to Jerusalem,' snarled the Colonel, 'and you can't even control your horse.'

I preferred to keep my distance as I could feel the giggles rising.

The Colonel climbed back in the saddle and turned his horse round: it was time to get back to barracks.

Alone at last: the Black Forest was all ours. It wasn't as black as all that, anyway: in spite of the stinking weather it was resplendent with glowing, warm colours.

The hikers' paths, out of bounds to riders, have the advantage of being very clearly marked. At each crossing, and even on the paths themselves, different signs are painted on the tree-trunks: a sky-blue lozenge would take us to Hirtenwaldkopf, the highest point in the Black Forest, or a red triangle would guide us down to the plain. In this dirty weather, on a week-day, not a soul was to be seen, and we felt we were alone in the depths of some primeval forest. There was no sound, no living creature except three roe-deer who seemed to find us interesting since they followed us for a long time, and we met them on several occasions.

On the other hand, the paths had one great disadvantage: being intended for pedestrians and not for horses, they were often so narrow that our mounts could hardly put two feet side by side. Not to mention that the edges were slippery and the paths skirted precipices much too deep for my taste. I didn't dare look down, it made me giddy. In spite of all my precautions, I slipped once and if I hadn't grabbed a branch, my crusade would have ended there and then.

A little further on, we stopped short at the sight of a worm-eaten wooden stairway.

'What do we do now?' asked Corinne. 'We can't turn round, the path is too narrow.'

There was no other way, so we had to go forward. The steps were wide, but very slippery, and furthermore, there were fourteen of them. I took off my poncho and laid it over the first step, and then used Corinne's on the second. Mickey stepped on to the material, which was obviously less slippery, but he looked a little doubtful. I couldn't blame him. With a dogged patience, of which I wouldn't have believed us capable, lifting one foot at a time, we managed to get him down one step. Drops of sweat poured from my brow. Mickey's legs were as stiff as ramrods and he refused to bend his knees. He was shaking all over and throwing us looks that would have melted the hardest heart.

And Donald? Well, Donald, who was terrified of traffic, didn't know the meaning of giddiness. In a few seconds, he negotiated this obstacle without any help from us.

I closed my eyes and addressed an emotional thank-you to Loulou: 'Your horses really are extraordinary. You did tell us they'd go anywhere . . .'

Although we sheltered under the trees, the wind still billowed out our ponchos and the rain soaked through three thicknesses of pullovers. I was very cold.

The horses laboured up the steep slope, panting, soaked through. We were up in the clouds—the Colonel was right—and we couldn't see two yards in front of us. Violent squalls blew the horses sideways, and our swollen, frozen hands couldn't hold the soaking reins.

And still we climbed. Mickey and Donald looked at me reproachfully, as if asking if this little comedy would go on much longer. I had no idea. Wrapped in my poncho, I could see nothing ahead of me and was beginning to suspect we had missed our path, for I hadn't seen any blue lozenges or red triangles lately. We had to take off our ponchos so as not to take off ourselves.

'Here's something different!'

A rotten bridge spanned a stream foaming over the rocks some hundred feet below. The left-hand guardrail had disappeared, the one on the right was only half attached. Would it take the weight of a horse?

'We can't cross anywhere else,' I said to Corinne. 'If we have to turn round, we will have had this entire day for nothing. Let's see what happens!'

I threw a branch across and Pluto ran after it. The footbridge at least carried his eighteen kilos. Then it was my turn. The planks held my fifty kilos. I called:

'Now, Corinne, send me Mickey . . . Come on, Mickey, make yourself light . . .'

I didn't like the single handrail which forced the horses towards the left. Mickey gave a careful gymnastic display, placing each foot on the only possible plank. The water-skin caught in the handrail—entirely my fault, I should have taken it off. Mickey pulled, the wood broke, and we held our breath as we saw him put one forefoot into nothingness. Would he fall? Would he not? Below, the rocks. Mickey looked at me, turned his head and looked at Donald. Please God, don't let him turn round: horses are almost always inclined to go back rather than go forward. Ouf! He started again, calmly, carefully, until he was safely over. The bridge vibrated.

Then it was Donald's turn. Impatient as always to rejoin his companion, he went so fast that the planks creaked alarmingly. Panic-stricken, he broke into a gallop, carrying away the last remnants of the handrail. One of the planks almost gave way and hung by a whisker.

Alone on the bank, Corinne was afraid, and I was afraid for her myself. Suddenly I had an idea.

'Wait a minute.'

I remembered that we had a nylon cord in our saddlebags— now was the time if ever to use it. I fixed the cord to a thick branch and threw the other end to Corinne.

'Tie it firmly round your waist. Fine. Now come forward . . . Don't look down at the plank or you'll get giddy. Look at me . . .' My knees were shaking and I had to lean against a tree. I knew only too well the cord wasn't really strong enough, but it was better than nothing.

Then one of the episodes of the first Crusade came into my mind. Its setting was another mountain pass, the Taurus, in Anatolia, which we hoped to cross ourselves, if God granted us life. The paths used by the armed column of pilgrims were so narrow and steep that men and baggage-horses in their thousands fell over the precipices. None of the rest could continue on horseback and the knights were forced to throw away their armour and continue on foot. The crossing of the Taurus alone cost more lives than any battle against the Infidel.

By now, Corinne was on the bridge. I kept saying:

'Look at me. Look at me.'

It was all very fine for me to give advice. If there's one thing I'm sure of, it is that I would never have had the courage to cross myself. Corinne took one step, two, three, testing the plank each time to see if it still held. And suddenly she had the same reaction as Donald, and rushed over the last section and fell into my arms.

This was too much for the footbridge and it gave up the ghost. We watched with tremendous interest while the planks fell into the abyss.

After that we had to hope that the path would lead us somewhere.

CHAPTER NINE

A Curious Noah's Ark

We had hoped to get to Donaueschingen by nightfall, at the source of the Danube, but we had lost too much time during the day and had to look for shelter in the next village.

Fields at last, but not a cow or a farm in sight. No lights. Miracle: a tractor's headlamps. Corinne hailed the driver who didn't hold out much hope:

'The stables are full everywhere, we've just brought all the animals in from the fields.'

'All we need is a shed or a barn.'

'The barns are full too. You'll have trouble finding anything. The village is further on—go and ask at the last house, they may have room.'

We called at the last house and found a family of farmers who thought we were mad. They suggested we should ask their neighbours, three kilometres further up the road, but they wouldn't even listen to us. For two hours we searched, freezing, soaked to the skin, until we found the answer.

A huge building. Two Dobermanns gave us a warm reception. I trembled for Pluto and only just had time to leap to the ground, grab eighteen kilos of fury and hoist him up on my saddle, where he became even more valiant, growling and showing his teeth. He might have landed me in real trouble, as I was still on the ground and didn't dare try and climb up on top of the baggage for fear the enormous brutes would nip my ankles. The owners arrived in the nick of time. Two of them. The first, about fifty, his eyes hidden behind inch-thick pebble lenses, had a hangdog expression. The other was a little younger, broad-shouldered and looking like a docker, all the more because of his tee-shirt and violent red scarf. They both looked extremely odd. But what did it matter since they were prepared to shelter us all, and showed us straight to the cowshed.

A donkey brayed—a sound which always sends me into fits of laughter: a stallion pony neighed and tried to climb over the door of his loose box. A marmoset stopped scratching to scold the pony and a peacock screamed. Ducks and chickens joined in the concert. Had we stumbled on a latter-day Noah's Ark?

All this hullabaloo was much to Pluto's taste and he sniffed round everywhere. Donald was afraid and reared, or perhaps he was competing with the stallion pony who was still trying to break down the door. Definitely not a quiet night for our poor horses. A Yugoslav stable-boy was supposed to take care of them. What a character! Immediately he made it clear he would much sooner take care of us and gave us a sample of his talents. Communication was impossible as he appeared to understand only two phrases in German: '*Ich liebe dich*' [I love you] which his roving hands made even clearer, and '*Ein moment*'. Nothing in the world could make him hurry.

Indoors, things weren't much better. Nanny-goats, a he-goat and their young skipped up and down the stairs, followed everywhere by another pony. The floor was littered with droppings of all kinds. Birds flew from room to room and greyhounds sprawled in the sagging chairs.

Our hosts led us to a private bar on the first floor, lit feebly by a red lantern. A lot of drinking seemed to have been going on in the smoke-filled room. What a lot of men and animals!

Our arrival created an obvious interest, though perhaps I should say lack of interest, for in a hundred ways the gentlemen demonstrated a very special attitude towards my sex: what wasps' nest had we fallen into? But why worry? With people the exact opposite of our Yugoslav, we could relax. Their manners towards women were all the more exquisite because they expected nothing in return.

We were asked if we would like to take off our clothes, or rather, our wet sweaters, let's be honest, and have them dried. Glasses of vodka and orange scorched our gullets but warmed our insides and the master of the house offered to lend us a couple of jackets which we accepted with pleasure. Phew! They reeked of goat. I buried my nose in my vodka to hide the smell. After emptying half a bottle of gin, our saviour sat down at the piano to voice a welcome to his two young guests. One of the fraternity accompanied him on the guitar while additional accompaniment was provided by a barn-owl, a parrot, the Dobermanns and the pony. We were given a tureen of soup: a piece of pork floating in clear broth, thickened with crusts of bread. Delicious. The pony dipped his nose in my bowl. A goat climbed onto my chair to steal my bread from behind.

The party went on all night. Without us. For we took refuge as quickly as possible in the room we had been given, a charming little room, with flowered wallpaper. As always in Germany it was unheated. Tucked in among the attics of the second floor, it collected all the smells from the rest of the house. In other words, it stank of goat! Out teeth chattered for half an hour before we began to feel a little warmer under the eiderdowns. *Gute nacht!* Below, the music continued unceasingly. The singing and dancing went on until dawn.

It's hard to get out of bed at 5.30 when the eiderdowns are nice and warm. It was still dark and the cold was hardly inviting. I felt sick: was it the all-pervading smells? The vodka? Or both? I coughed. I had no desire to go outside, I was much too comfortable and warm. But the horses were hungry, I had to get up. Corinne was dead asleep beside me. I shook her:

'Up you get, fatty!'

She didn't move. I put a toe to the ground. Oh God, it was cold. And the smell. I felt sicker by the minute and staggered when I tried to stand up. My back was as bent as if I were a hundred and I couldn't straighten up. My teeth were chattering like castanets. Not surprising! The water in the jug was frozen solid and I couldn't even wash. The goats' droppings were as hard as glass balls and covered with a white film. What the hell: I snuggled back into the warmth of the bed alongside the lovely hot-water bottle called Corinne. I scolded myself: 'Evelyne, you mustn't, the horses are hungry.' I gave myself a few moments' grace and went to sleep again . . . an uneasy sleep troubled by a bad conscience: 'Get up, the horses are hungry.' I opened one eye. Just for once couldn't that lazybones Corinne stir herself to get up and feed the horses? I beat a tattoo with my feet on her bottom and back. No reaction. She is so used to getting up only after I have fed the horses. Oh well, if I must I must. I get up.

Buildings, fields, forest, everything was white. The sharp air woke me up and the dew took care of my toilet. In an instant it was as though I had been under a shower. I didn't even feel dirty any more.

As I cross to the cowshed, I wonder how our two provençals have fared on such a freezing night, particularly after their gruelling day of climbing under the rain and wind. At once I am reassured. Donald is lying in the middle of the hens, sucking an egg. Mickey is flirting with the stallion with the tip of his nose. They must have spent the night exciting each other over an impossible love affair and he'll be very tired all day. Mickey is a sentimentalist: meeting a colleague always makes him emotional and partings for him are always a cruel separation. The pump is frozen, I can't draw any water. I rummage round for some oats.

In another stable, where an impressive number of Lippizaners were installed, I stopped before a grey-mottled stallion with a silky silvery mane. He had both forefeet on the door and was trying to leap over a six-foot obstacle. What wouldn't I give to leap on his back and gallop and gallop . . . I heaved a sigh of regret. You can always dream.

In the house only the animals were awake and the oats were locked in a store-room. I couldn't feed the horses. We couldn't leave till the horses had digested their meal. We couldn't wake up the masters of the house. We couldn't do anything except wait. What was the point of getting up so early?

The goat-smell was quite unbearable and the cacophony from the animals, dominated by the peacocks, made me wonder how anyone could sleep through such a row. Even Corinne had got out of bed. I fumed because the horses hadn't been fed at the proper time, my bad humour was contagious and Corinne lost her temper too.

Eleven o'clock. Finally a door opened and a sleepy figure emerged—our Yugoslav Lothario. He explained that his masters never had breakfast before two o'clock. What curious people! Both surgeons, they had given up their clinic for the pleasure of living in the country with the animals. An attractive idea. But the results struck me as very questionable.

At last Mickey and Donald were fed and fell ravenously on their rations. Meanwhile Corinne had heated some coffee and cooked an egg, but I was so upset by the stable-boy's advances and the goat-smell I felt sicker and sicker. It really wasn't one of my good days. The stable-boy and the goat followed me everywhere, infuriatingly. If one of them went to Corinne, the other redoubled his attentions to me. I was in such a hurry to get out of the smell that we saddled up as soon as the last mouthful had been swallowed. I knew it was wrong, but after all, it was twelve o'clock.

The cold struck us almost like a blow. The landscape was marvellous, covered with frost and sparkling. Nostrils damp, tears in his eyes, Mickey embarked on his usual hesitation waltz: first movement, immobility; second movement, about turn; third movement, ear-splitting neighs. He was telling his new friends how sad he was at leaving them.

The pony, the Lippizaners and the Dobermanns answered in heart-rending accents. These farewells left Donald completely unmoved, for as far as he's concerned, only his stomach matters. He took advantage of this emotional moment to chew a few sprays of frozen leaves.

The horses broke the ice as they walked through the puddles and a clear blue sky promised a pleasant day as we plunged into the golden and flaming forest. Pluto, delightedly, barked after wild boar or roe-buck. There is very little hunting in Germany, so the animals were no more frightened by our songs than the barking of our dog. They only took off at the first squeaks of Corinne's harmonica, but I must admit they usually seemed to put up with her flute. The pure air settled my stomach very quickly and I began to feel better.

It was not quite dark when we arrived at the riding-club of the little watering place called Titisee, soaked to the skin, teeth chattering. A tall blond lad was there on his own. He didn't look very intelligent, and wasn't very talkative. Fine, he'd do the necessary for the horses, but what about us? Nothing doing. We could sleep on the straw or look for a room somewhere else. What we most wanted was a hot bath and somewhere to dry our clothes. So, off we went to the *Gasthaus*, to be met with blank astonishment.

'They don't seem to know,' says Corinne.

'Know what?'

'That we're the ones who're riding to Jerusalem.'

My sister who hates journalists, already so used to fame, was upset when nobody recognised her, in a remote corner of sylvan Germany.

'German telly's coming to interview us in the morning, and then everyone will bring out the red carpet.'

'Idiot! I don't want that. All I need is a bowl of hot soup.'

The *Gasthaus* was full, so we ended up in a neighbouring farm. The farmer's wife brought us a huge bowl of creamy milk with bread and butter, plum jam and a few slices of salami. Up jumped Pluto!

'No, no, I haven't forgotten you.'

The dinner, in fact, was traditional and had been exactly the same ever since we had crossed the Rhine. Wherever we went, breakfast began with a cup of coffee, an egg, bread and butter with ham and sausage, and finished with a bottle of white wine. At mid-day we'd nibble some kind of sandwich. Dinner, at eight o'clock, began with a bottle of white wine, continued with bread and butter, ham and sausage, followed by an egg and finished with a cup of coffee. We'd got *charcuterie* coming out of our ears. Even Pluto was getting fed up with sausage-meat, while I drooled at the thought of vegetable soup and *pot-au-feu* with marrow bones. Ah!, Maman, how we miss you . . .

Our revictualling completed, the farmer's wife installed us in a little blue-and-white bedroom, heated by a tall porcelain stove which dried our clothes in no time.

Next morning, back to the stables. No let-up in the rain. Not a soul in sight. But the horses had been meticulously groomed. Hallo! Two plastic bags tied to our saddles. Ham sandwiches and sausages in one: woollen pullovers, long flannel underpants in the other, and a note: '*Gute Reise*.' [Bon voyage!]

Our mouths fell open.

'A present from the tall blond.'

'But he never uttered. Sure they're for us?'

'They're tied to our saddles . . .'

'Sweet of him. Everything's new, and so warm. Shall I try them on?'

Corinne pulled on the underpants and a sweater.

'They fit me fine. Shall we keep them?'

'Where can we put them? We can eat the sandwiches, but the clothes weigh a ton. Pick the one you like best and leave the others. I've got all I need. The jackets are scrummy, but if we start wearing them now, we won't feel the benefit when it's really cold.'

A charming gesture, and as we rode away, I wondered what had got into the tall blond. Maybe he was sorry for us?

Donaueschingen: nothing memorable. But an important point for us, as it was the beginning of the Danube. Now all we had to do was follow the river, like the Crusaders, into Bulgaria. Sigmaringen . . . Ulm. . . .

CHAPTER TEN

Shopping in Ulm

At the riding-club in Ulm, we were met by a delegation of riders and interpreters. We turned up three hours after we were expected, so nearly all the people had gone home, and the stable-master was about to shut up shop.

'What happened?'

Could I really tell him that nothing had happened, except that we'd had plenty of sun, and after a week of solid rain, we had halted at the slightest pretext to photograph a charming land-scape, or an apple-tree covered in apples. And then we had stopped for quite a while—twice—to enjoy a meal. How lovely to dawdle along, munching cream-cakes, salami, cheese and stewed pears, one eye on the horses cropping the grass, the other on the Danube and a fantastic variety of wild life. Moorhens zigzagged across the water, using their webbed feet like water-skis. Wild swans uncurled their necks and threatened Pluto with their wicked beaks while he chased the wild duck. Pluto couldn't understand why he never caught anything, or why he couldn't take off like the birds. So he remained earth-bound, looking foolish, sniffing hopelessly after his airborne quarry.

I began to worry. There's a lot of marshy ground near Ulm, and it could be dangerous after dark.

'Better move on,' I decided. 'During the Crusades, a Turkish army was swallowed up in the marshes near Ried. Thousands of men and horses were lost and no trace of them was ever found, except a few horseshoes with the nails still in position.'

At five o'clock, as the sun was turning red, we were still twenty-five kilometres from Ulm. So we allowed the horses to trot, trying to cover as much ground as possible before dark.

My conscience was troubling me. We'd been dawdling all day, and now I was trying to make up for lost time. We'd overheat the horses who could easily catch cold if the stable was chilly.

A luxury caravan had been parked near the stables, and the president of the club invited us to tuck ourselves in.

'Hans will look after the horses. Just put out what you want them to eat in the morning and you can stay in bed a little longer.'

A kind thought.

'I've been told you want your horses to have an anti-tetanus boost,' he continued. 'I've laid on the vet for three o'clock, so if the vaccination affects them, they'll have plenty of time to recover.'

I asked if we could go shopping in Ulm in the morning, as we needed quite a lot of things for ourselves and the horses.

'Of course. I'll send Fritz, my chauffeur, and he'll take you anywhere you want. It's only about ten kilometres away. *Gute nacht.*'

'*Danke schön.*'

Charming, eh?

Next morning, Fritz appeared at the wheel of the inevitable Mercedes. His orders: to take us to the specialist shops first, and then to a charming little village and give us a taste of the finer points of German cooking.

The few cold days we'd had had made me realise that the gourds would soon freeze and we'd have no water to drink. The colder it gets, the drier my throat becomes. Therefore, first purchase, a thermos. Sounds simple, but when it comes to carrying the said thermos on a saddle, it's another matter. It has to be light, unbreakable and fit into one of the existing gourds. Poor Fritz! He must have taken us to every shop in Ulm that sold camping equipment before we found the right one.

The previous week had shown the uselessness of our ponchos, perfect in light rain, but hopeless in a storm. The rain poured in with the wind, the baggage had been soaked and the sleeping-bags were beginning to rot. Some changes had to be made. The ponchos could be used to cover the saddles and gear, but we ourselves needed waterproofs, light, strong and long, with a pleat in the back, capable of standing up to twelve hours in the pouring rain. Easy to say, impossible to find. Once again, poor Fritz! We called at every shop.

Finally we came up with a couple of canvas jump-suits, lined with waterproof, indestructible, German fisherman [*sic*] for the use of, one size only. Under these we could wear all our anoraks and climbing pants, certain of keeping our knees and backsides dry.

We certainly weren't the epitome of French elegance, but so what?

Then a trip to the saddler's. We needed some straps to tie down the saddle-bags which banged against the horses' flanks as soon as we tried to trot: eight short ones and a medium-length one to fasten Donald's military blanket. The saddler had gone to lunch, so we had to buy a bunch of cheap belts in the local chain store, and cut them down to the right size. Loulou had shown us how to knot leather thongs without using a buckle. Clever Loulou!

Oh, I nearly forgot: films, toothpaste, notebook, ballpoint pen, cod-liver oil for Pluto's chapped pads. We found just about everything and then Fritz took us to lunch, but because of our appointment with the vet, we hadn't much time. Poor, poor Fritz! If you gobble a venison steak without chewing it properly, it spoils the pleasure. Fortunately, the blueberry jelly helped it down.

The vet vaccinated the horses and gave them an international health certificate. A real passport!

He was very concerned about the weather conditions. Our carefree attitude (on the surface) and our enthusiasm (a little forced) amused him very much all the same.

'I must admit that the five members of the team are in excellent form,' he said.

While Corinne made regulation buttonholes to keep Donald's blanket in place, I rubbed, cleaned, polished and greased the saddles and all the tack. A week's rain had covered them with mud, and the leather broke at the slightest provocation. Every fold had to be carefully greased, for we wouldn't be able to repair any breakage ourselves, and you don't find harness-makers in the forest.

'Damn! We've forgotten the little plastic money-bags to hang round our necks and hide our money.'

'We won't need them between here and Vienna, because we haven't any money to hide,' Corinne pointed out calmly.

'Quite right!'

When we left Notre-Dame, we had had enough petty cash to get us to Vienna, a little more than 2,000 francs. As a precaution, we had hidden a 500-franc note inside each of our boots. At Bry-sur-Marne we had made a depressing discovery: three of the banknotes bore no resemblance to the brand-new folding money we thought we still had. Once the numbers had been washed off, they were worthless. We'd kept them all the same, for our scrapbook.

We still had the equivalent in marks of 115 francs, but we wouldn't get any more until we reached Vienna, in four weeks' time if everything went according to plan.

What to do? Ask for an advance from *Le Journal de Mickey*? Better not, as we'd need every penny later. We must manage somehow. As most of the people we were meeting were extremely rich, they usually refused to let us pay for anything, so we had a good chance of getting by.

In the meantime, we had another problem: how to transport our recent purchases without increasing our loads. Obviously, by discarding some of the things we had thought indispensable in the first place, but which?

We had two gourds, one small and one large. I decided to scrap the second in favour of the thermos. Two kilos saved. I sorted out my photographic stuff, and then there was a pocket Bible we had been given outside Notre-Dame.

'That can go,' said Corinne.

'We can't dump a Bible, it'd be sacrilege!'

'Don't make me laugh. It weighs at least five hundred grammes. Are you really expecting to read it one day?'

'Supposing we get held up for a fortnight or three months, somewhere, in a village without a single French book, at least we'd have this one. What could be more essential on a ride to Jerusalem?'

I didn't have the nerve to tell her that my grandmother taught me never to throw away anything sacred or it would bring bad luck. We kept the Bible.

'Our toilet things?' asked Corinne.

'Let's keep two toothbrushes and a minitube of toothpaste. We don't need the soap.'

'How will we wash?'

'The locals always have soap, if not, sand gets rid of the grease just as well.'

'Soap is useful and it doesn't weigh much.'

'*Everything* is useful, but if we take this and that, we'll overload the horses. Let's scrap everything ... hand-towel, face-cloth. From now on, we'll rub down with our hands.'

'You don't need to go through the bags. Just leave everything and the horses will have nothing to carry.'

Corinne began to lose her temper. We had now reached the most disputed item in the baggage: a small round box, six centimetres high, four centimetres in diameter, my sister's most treasured possession. Several head-on collisions had taught me not to bring up the subject, which could easily lead to divorce. Corinne the cool cat, ready to sleep rough without the most elementary hygiene for six to nine months had to clean her ears every morning. Without her little box of cotton-buds she was lost and bad-tempered all day. Once I had had the unfortunate inspiration of 'forgetting' the famous box at a farm. She had sulked for a week. If we hadn't finally found another in a chemist's shop, she'd have taken the train back to Nevers. After the Bible episode, I could only give in: the box weighed considerably less than the Holy Scriptures.

Hand-cream? Indispensable. Talcum powder? Unnecessary: our bottoms were tougher. A thermometer? Why? If either of us had a temperature, she'd soon know. Yes to the mercurochrome and aspirin, yes to the aluminium powder (to disinfect the horses' cuts) and the anticolic and anti-spasmodic capsules (also for the horses). All that was left was the blacksmith's bag: three kilos! Aie!

'Are you sure it's essential?' asked Corinne. 'You never use it.' Corinne obviously used her cotton-buds much more frequently than I used my shoeing-hammer.

'Suppose we don't find a blacksmith—we'll have to manage ourselves. It would be like a chauffeur throwing away his spare wheel because he's never had a puncture.'

Even so, we hadn't any spare horseshoes, and only carried an assortment of nails of different thicknesses, apart from the shoeing-hammer and pincers. It was up to us to check the nails every night, see that any missing were replaced, and hope to be lucky enough to find a blacksmith. I insisted we keep a small tool-kit: a dandy brush, a cork, a hoof-pick, 700 grammes in all.

'We aren't getting rid of much,' Corinne pointed out.

Then suddenly we each had a brilliant idea. We could send the road maps we no longer needed home, and cut the others down to the minimum. I saved two more kilos by discarding a first-aid manual for horses which, like the Bible, I'd never even opened. Corinne proposed to dump a pair of heavy boots, which hurt . . . and weighed four kilos.

Now where did we stand? Hell! Each pair of saddle-bags weighed about thirteen kilos. With the waterproof covering for the duvets and a change of clothing, we were still over the eighteen-kilos allowance. Not surprising that the horses' backs were getting rubbed.

I had another idea. We didn't need to carry a day's ration of oats until we reached the Hungarian frontier, so we emptied the feed-bags and stuffed our clothes into them. Six kilos per horse saved. A change of jeans, two sweaters, a Mickey Mouse tee-shirt, underclothes and socks in Damart thermolactic wool went in first. Then a little juggling with anoraks, sleeping-bags and the water-bottles. Check: five kilos in front, fifteen behind, plus the weight of the saddle. We'd done it.

However, we still had an apple of discord: the plexiglass mapcase which also held our passports, transit papers and two ballpoint pens. Corinne flatly refused to carry it, saying it made her neck ache. What about my neck? She wouldn't discuss it. I couldn't very well hang it on Pluto. I knew that when they lost half their horses in Anatolia, the Crusaders used their dogs as pack-animals, but Pluto had his work cut out transporting himself. Oh well, let's try and settle the problem another day: time now to groom and feed the horses, it's getting late. Our day of rest had worn me out completely. I hadn't even the strength to go down to dinner.

Five o'clock in the morning. The rain had drummed overhead all night and was still coming down in stair-rods. We got up like excited children the morning after Christmas, anxious to try on our new equipment and climb into the fishermen's jump-suits. When the Germans saw us emerge, they fell about laughing. Fritz consoled us:

'You'll be nice and dry, you won't be cold and it's very hard-wearing, I promise you!'

We were delighted with our acquisitions. Another nice surprise: the thermos had been filled with *café au lait* with sugar. Super-luxury! With our knees dry and our digestive systems taken care of, what else could the Coquet sisters require?

The ponchos covered the double humps of the baggage which made the horses look really enormous. The camels of the Near East would have nothing on our valiant little horses from Provence. We were very proud of them.

CHAPTER ELEVEN

D for Disaster

'I often wonder why that horse of yours hasn't ended up driving a tractor,' I complained bitterly.

Recently Donald had become dangerously nervous and excitable, shying at the flight of a bird, rearing when he saw farm machinery, lashing out at dogs, pirouetting at the sight of a lorry and hurling himself into ditches.

For the third time in a week, Corinne had found herself hugging an electrified fence, and I was getting tired of seeing her standing in the middle of the road, separated from her fiery steed. I allowed myself to give her some advice.

'When you see a lorry coming, instead of getting frightened and jumping off, talk to Donald and pat him. While he's listening to you he'll calm down and forget the lorry.'

'You try if you like. I don't want to be run over.'

We exchanged horses. A combination of gentleness and authority quickly calmed Donald. Aware of his change of rider, he didn't dare play up as he had done with Corinne, which proved my point that you must have confidence to be in control. All went well for a few days. Donald never put a hoof wrong, and Corinne was amazed but didn't quite dare to take him back, while I wasn't at all displeased with myself.

'There, you see! Gentle as a lamb, your terrible monster.'

We were crossing a bridge over the Danube, leading the horses. There wasn't much traffic but I was being cautious. Donald seemed a little restive, but I didn't take him seriously and I walked beside him, relaxed, holding the reins in my right hand,

Pluto's lead in my left. A car passed. Donald didn't turn a hair. I was congratulating myself when suddenly I found myself flung into the middle of the road. As my head hit the asphalt, I closed my eyes. When I opened them it was to see a horse's hoof, a worn shoe, complete with all its nails, about to land beside my face rather than on it.

Corinne rushed up. Everything had happened so quickly she had only seen the horse setting his feet down in a tangle of arms and legs.

'Did he step on your back?'

'No. My ankle . . .'

'Can you walk?'

'Let's try.'

I got up, legs shaking, head ringing, jeans torn, thigh bleeding.

'All right?' inquired Corinne anxiously.

'My right foot hurts, though it's bearable. But the left . . . Now I'm lame. What a bore!'

That wicked Donald had really done a good job. Fortunately my boots, solid leather with reinforced heels, had broken the impact.

I insisted we should go on to the proposed stop.

'Do you think you can?'

'Of course, of course . . .'

But of course not, alas. My ankle hurt so much we had to stop at the next village, Bertoldsheim. A farmer's boy showed us the way to the *Gasthaus*.

The village was unlit, and we walked down a narrow street, chatting with our guide, unconcerned about the horses. Never trust a horse. What made Donald, panic-stricken, suddenly charge blindly ahead, and why did I once again have to be in his way? I saw bloody stars. I could feel Donald crushing my feet and waited for him to roll over me. Then, total darkness. I had a vague feeling that I was being carried, screaming and struggling, and that I was afraid. I could see cows, hundreds of cows, and a farmer's wife on a three-legged stool. I don't know which hurt most, my legs or my back. Blood was pouring from my nose and mouth. A cow's head with flaming horns tipped with blue stars was bearing down on me. I heard someone say: 'Do something. She's dead.'

I came to in a huge kitchen, surrounded by an entire family, and couldn't understand a word anyone was saying. I wanted to tell them I was in agony, but my tongue was choking me. I didn't dare try and touch my nose because it felt like a boiled potato. With my right eye I could only see shadows through a thick film of gravel under the eyelid, and with the other eye, swimming in blood, I could only make out silhouettes like burning coals. The malevolent cow with golden horns gradually became recognisable as Corinne, and I heard her say: 'You really gave us a fright. If you could see what you look like!'

The doctor with her had come from Neuburg thirty-five kilometres away, so I must have been unconscious for quite a while. My eyes were bathed in warm water, my nose cleared of blood and gravel. The cartilege had been broken by a stone, but the bone was intact. Apparently my jaw wasn't broken either. I began to see and breathe a little better, and the doctor embarked on a thorough examination.

'Ow! My foot.'

I couldn't rotate or straighten out either ankle. I was given an injection and my head and feet were bandaged.

'If she's in too much pain,' said the medico, 'put on compresses, give her these tablets every three hours and don't let her get up.' I wondered how on earth I was supposed to. 'I'll come and see her tomorrow and take her to hospital to be X-rayed. There isn't a bed for her tonight.'

What a night! Because of the lump on my head, I couldn't sleep on my back, the damaged eye ruled out the right side and I couldn't lie on my stomach because of my nose, not to mention my feet which hurt me to screaming point every time I moved. Daylight at last. People came and went. Diagnosis: a fracture. I was less pessimistic and refused to entertain the idea. A fracture would mean three weeks in plaster, at least . . . or even six months. What would we do with the horses? The farmer who had taken them in would never keep them so long. They would lose the effect of their training and everything would have to start again from scratch. Perhaps I could ride with my foot in plaster? Don't be ridiculous. The additional weight would be far too much for the horse. There was only one conclusion: a fracture was out of the question.

An ambulance took me to hospital.

'Ow!' My ankles were pulled in every direction. The pain was excruciating, yet it did seem as though my toes were beginning to move. Things were looking up. I wasn't surprised. It wouldn't be right if I had broken an ankle when I had come safely through much more spectacular accidents. There was that show when my mare refused a fence, and crashed into a rope barrier. She ruptured her spleen and had to be put down. I had been flung across a steel cable. Two days in hospital showed that I was as sound as a bell.

Then there was the day when I was going flat out down a forest path, on a strange horse that had bolted. We were stopped by a plane tree. The horse didn't get up again: his skull, nose and shoulder were broken. The expensive saddle had been torn in half lengthways, as if it had been made of cardboard. I had cannoned head-first into the tree, and clung there with my arms wrapped round the trunk. When I got to my feet, I didn't even have a bruise. For a long time I didn't dare go near a horse for fear of destroying it.

The doctor returned, full of smiles.

'*Nichts gebrochen!*' [Nothing broken.]

Yippee, hurrah, fantastico. We can go on. But when? A *cavalier servant* (I've never been without one when I needed one) took me back to the *Gasthaus* where he spent his days carrying me from my bed to the dining-room and vice versa. He was very proud of me and told my story to all the locals who came to shuffle the cards and drink gigantic steins of beer.

'From Paris on horseback ... *Ja* ... If you could see their maps, all the roads, all the farms, even the barn and our inn, all of it written down ... with the names in italics ... *Ja* ... *Zwei Franzosichen Mädchen* ... They are writing a newspaper for Mickey Mouse ... *Ja* ...'

I was dying to get back to the mountains and valleys, but I still couldn't put my foot to the ground.

'I'd be all right if someone could lift me into the saddle. I wouldn't have to walk and I could follow you ...'

I could wiggle my toes reasonably well, but the difficulty was the boots. Leather ones were out of the question, and wellingtons were no good either.

'Try mine.'

Corinne's boots were two sizes larger, so by taking out two pairs of lamb's-wool soles she had stuffed inside them, and covering my bandages with a silk sock, I could just slip into them. Grimacing with pain, gritting my teeth . . .

Having given me her only pair, Corinne took mine which were a little small, but she was so anxious to leave that she was ready to suffer. Why should I be the only one?

On the eighth day I still couldn't walk very well, but I was getting better. I still looked like a corpse, had giddy spells from time to time, and even saw imaginary cows falling in front of me on to the rails of the Paris Métro.

In cold and fog we started again, without any fixed goal. We would stop when we had to. Visibility was down to two yards, and I was content to follow Corinne, my eyes on her horse's tail. There was no direct path going east, and the route was complicated. There were no signposts in the fields or forest, so we had to keep our eyes peeled for landmarks: a clump of trees, a fountain, high tension wires, a handrail, a Calvary.

I enjoyed letting Corinne do the navigating: the less responsibility I had . . . After a few hours I called 'Pax'. I wanted to dismount and stretch my ankles. From then on, I swore never to walk in front of Donald, but beside or even slightly behind him.

'Never two without three,' I said to myself, 'so watch out.' But I really believed that horse had it in for me, for he sprang forward, and with one kick sent me flying into a ditch.

Dazed, I sat up in a puddle and . . . burst into tears. Corinne, hearing the noise, turned round, surprised.

'Did you fall over?'

Rage and sobs gave me the hiccups.

'You can have your horse back, I don't want him any more!' My disaster seemed to leave Corinne unmoved. She laughed! I tried to make an inventory of my new wounds: my left hip carried the outline of a horseshoe with all seven nails: another with only three nails was imprinted on my right thigh. I didn't even feel any pain, I was so angry.

'Gentle as a lamb, your ferocious monster.'

I didn't know she had such a good memory.

CHAPTER TWELVE

We Meet the Bundeswehr

Ingolstadt, Ratisbon, were behind us ... The Austrian frontier ... This time we studied the map carefully and checked that the streams flowing into the Danube were well supplied with bridges. We had been making good time.

'We'll get there too soon!' said Corinne.

'Yes, in principle. But as every day something happens which takes an extra hour or two ...'

Suddenly, a large sign: *Verboten*. No entry.

'Evelyne! Now what?'

'Keep going. It won't be the first sign we've ignored.' It's as if all the interesting paths are '*verboten*' on purpose. The banks of the Danube are out of bounds to riders, private forests are closed to hikers, paths across cultivated fields are reserved for tractors, and with pavements, footpaths and cycle-tracks, we've had to ignore several thousand signposts.

'If anyone bothers us, just say "*Nicht verstehen*"—don't understand.'

'Just a minute, Evelyne. Look.'

Another board. 'Military zone. Danger. No entry'. To make sure no one could fail to understand, the text was decorated with a skull and crossbones. 'Who's going to believe you if you say you don't understand that?' said Corinne.

'Just go on. Haven't you seen the map? We can't make a two-hour detour just because of a no-entry sign.'

'Yes, but what about the Danger bit?'

'They've got to discourage trespassers somehow. Go ahead!'

Two hundred yards futher on, a siren wailed. Donald froze. Soldiers emerged from every bush crawling on all fours, lorries skidded to a stop, and several men loaded on stretchers were piled on board.

The Bundeswehr on manoeuvres.

'Don't stay here, we're in the middle of their firing range. Full speed ahead!' I shouted to Corinne.

That military zone went on for ever. Every hundred yards a black skull and crossbones glared at us. We couldn't see anything, but we could hear bangs. Donald put his ears back.

'That one was quite near,' I said. 'I heard it whistle.'

Corinne was a trifle green, and so was I. We quickened our pace, the horses pouring with sweat. Pluto had no time to swallow the mole he had dug up, but hung on to it. The mole struggled and squeaked.

'Look out, a man moved in that bush.' A sentry emerged from the undergrowth, his gun slung over his shoulder. All five of us stopped breathless. I had the presence of mind to sing out a loud '*Bonjour! Guten tag!*' The Federal soldier was so amazed that his mouth fell open.

'*Gruss Gott,*' he managed finally. 'How did you get here? All the gates are locked and guarded.'

'We came through the forest.'

'Didn't you see the notices and hear the firing?'

'We were already half-way through!'

'You've had a lucky escape.'

'Does the firing go on for a long way?'

'The road is clear now, you can go ahead. Ah! There's a level-crossing a little further on. You open it by pressing a button.'

Pluto swallowed his mole. I could hear it squeaking as its round fat body and short paws disappeared down his throat. After that he tried to come and lick our lips!

'That sentry was quite nice,' I said.

'You wicked thing! You won't get me to follow you down paths marked with death's heads any more.'

We found the barrier described by the soldier, but no button.

'Pull the handle,' said the instructions on a large box.

'*Ja! Was wollen sie?*' ['Well, what do you want?'] demanded a disembodied voice from a hidden loudspeaker.

Pluto barked furiously into the microphone.

'*Durch!*' said Corinne.

Unable to think of a well-turned phrase in German, Corinne had come out with 'Go through'. What could be clearer? The two gates striped with red zigs and white zags rose. Donald pulled on the reins and backed away.

'*Danke schön!*' I cried. (You should always be polite to talking boxes.)

'*Bitte schön,*' replied the disembodied voice.

But alas! The horses refused to budge.

'Pluto! Bite them! Make yourself useful!'

The dog, snarling furiously, snapped at the heels of our reluctant steeds. We had only just passed the first barrier when the second began to fall.

'Hey, hey! We can't stay here in the middle! Full speed ahead!'

I didn't want to find myself trapped in a level-crossing and shouted 'Hurry, hurry! Get a move on.'

The barrier was already half-way down. The horses hunched their backs. The cross-piece struck the baggage, tearing half of it away, bounced off Donald's rump and brushed Mickey's tail. We were through.

'High time!'

We checked the baggage. A train roared by.

We came out of a maize-field and struck a long track leading due east, which bypassed several Bavarian villages: just made for us, a sort of Paris–Jerusalem express route. It had a name on the map: the Cattle Road. What could be more tempting? Naturally it was marked 'No entry', I don't know why. Fifteen minutes later: 'Do you see what I see?' asked Corinne.

'Er . . . yes . . .'

A jeep. Two men got out. The taller wore a grey uniform, his jacket trimmed with gold braid. I didn't know if he was a game-keeper, a soldier or a police officer. The other, in civvies, was no less impressive, with an Erich von Stroheim monocle.

'*Guten Tag. Halt. Polizei!*'

Corinne replied with the agreed half-lie: '*Franzosich, nicht verstehen!*'

'Oh, you're French,' said Erich von Stroheim. 'I speak French.'

Our luck was out. He went on: 'What are your names? Where have you come from? Where are you going to?'

He made notes in a little book. He was grim and methodical.

A despairing glance from Corinne. This must be the result of our trespassing in a military zone. How stupid: to get ourselves arrested on our last day in Germany.

'An alarm call has been sent out for you,' the monocle told us. 'We picked you up last night at the Schiffer farm, but you had already left when we called there this morning. You were sighted several times today, including once inside the military zone. Is that right?'

Corinne and I looked at each other. Who on earth could be searching for us? The monocle didn't tell us, and grim as ever, continued: 'Please report to the police station this evening as soon as you arrive. *Au revoir.*'

The two characters saluted us briefly and climbed back into their jeep.

'With our system of never obeying "keep out" notices, we've got into a fine mess,' complained Corinne.

'Don't get worked up. What can they do to us? Lecture us? Fine us? The pleasure of going exactly where we please is well worth it, wouldn't you say?'

Policemen met us. Charming. Full of kindness. Wanting to know our plans. They made all kinds of suggestions.

'Keep smiling. Keep well. Take care. Good journey!'

Another intervened.

'A French lady is waiting for you,' he announced, showing us into his office.

'A French lady? Maman!'

Well, yes! No one else could have managed things like that.

'I'd had no news of you for three weeks!' she told us, once the first excitements had calmed down. 'I didn't even know if you were still in Germany or Austria. The Customs officers told me you hadn't appeared at the frontier, and no one seemed to know when to expect you, or where you were. I couldn't just go home without seeing you after driving 1,500 kilometres. Your father would have laughed at me: "I told you so. You haven't a hope of finding them. Germany is a big country, you might just as well look for two needles in a haystack." Only the police could help me.'

To persuade the authorities to help her, acting on a single piece of information (she knew we were probably travelling down the Danube), she had used a clinching argument:

'I explained that I had come to fetch the dog and take him back to Nevers before the journey became too much for him. The police thought I was absolutely right.'

'You've come all this way just to fetch Pluto—you'll have to go back without him because he's as fit as a flea and we've no intention of handing him over. Our normal mileage means nothing to him now: he spends his entire day hunting and he's enjoying himself every bit as much as we are. Look at him!'

I gazed at my mother in admiration. It was just like her to take off because she wanted to see us, and instead of trying to talk us out of our mad trip, she simply wanted to scoop up our Pataud-Pluto. She insisted: 'Are you sure you don't want me to take him home? It's going to be cold and he'll be attacked by wild dogs. They say there are wolves too. I won't come for him again, I promise you. It'd be too far. I've had to spend five days on the round trip already!'

I promised that if Pluto showed any signs of failing I would send him home.

'But how?'

'We'll cross our bridges when we come to them.'

Maman had to go home. When we said good-bye, big tears ran down our cheeks. She tried to hide hers, so as not to spoil our pleasure.

I knew that while she was waiting, she would rush to the letter-box twice a day, and very often be disappointed, for we wouldn't have much time for letter-writing. I knew she would stand the telephone on her writing desk and tape all our phone-calls so she could play them back again and again, for we had been authorised, and even ordered, to make reverse-charge calls at least twice a month. I could just see myself trying to explain this to some clerk in a Balkan village.

Maman had created such an uproar that all the frontier inhabitants had heard of us. A crowd gathered.

'The necessary arrangements have been made for you to cross

the new bridge over the Inn tomorrow,' the Customs official informed us. 'It was only opened to traffic this morning. You will spend four days in quarantine in a special stable at Schärding where a veterinary officer will make some tests. If the results are satisfactory, you may continue your journey.'

Compliments and advice followed. We accepted the first whole-heartedly, the second more cautiously.

'You're very brave. Germany, Austria, beautiful! Hungary, cold. After that, better stop. Yugoslavs, Turks, Arabs, all savages, not good people. You need a revolver to fight brigands, and wolves attack your horses. You should your dog home send: no way can you him back bring.'

I'd heard this kind of thing Wotan knows how often. Fortunately I knew enough German to answer, like a polite little French girl, *'Ja, ja, naturlich . . .'* Which, roughly translated, meant: 'Why don't you save your breath . . .' With a dazzling smile.

CHAPTER THIRTEEN

Capoue on the Inn

Schärding, Austria.

The horses were taken to a stable, recently used as a brewery storeroom. I spread out a thick carpet of straw so they could sleep away their holiday, while a vet took urine and blood samples, examined their droppings and listened to their hearts. Everything seemed all right, but we had to wait for the lab tests.

Schärding is a charming little town. The houses, several centuries old, have outside stairs, wooden beams, porches, turrets and gables, all elaborately carved, and pantiled roofs. Each house is painted a different colour. Our stable was olive-green, the Furstiner Hotel opposite was old rose, then came a periwinkle-blue patisserie which jostled a bright yellow beer-shop. Wrought-iron signs proclaimed the best wine, delicious beer or the gourmet's paradise. A curved skylight showed a patch of pale sky reflected in the Inn, almost as wide here as the Danube. Swans ruffled in the deep cold water, waiting for the scraps of bread the old ladies threw down from their windows.

Our quarantine did everyone good—including the horses. Pluto was able to explore the streets in company with a friendly boxer bitch, and we girls spent a happy time in an ultra-modern hunting lodge, fully equipped with swimming bath and sauna. Also—why not?—with attendant cavaliers, so we combined the delights of Capoue with a little light flirtation. I wondered if Corinne and I would ever have the courage to end such an enchanting interlude.

I was almost angry when the vet brought us down to earth. 'Your horses are in perfect health. You can leave whenever you like. If you'll come to my office, I can fill in your papers.' So there was nothing for it but to saddle up and move on: Nach Wien: 220 kilometres as the crow flies. Only ... Mickey and Donald weren't crows.

The Austrians, like the Germans, prefer to ride enormous horses, seventeen-and-a-half hands at least. Ours seemed very small in comparison, but everyone realised that they were very much tougher.

Up to this point, Mickey and Donald hadn't lost weight and had even gained a little. They were sporting their winter gear now, thick fur coats with long shiny chocolate-coloured hairs, and had got used to changes of stabling and foodstuffs. At night they lay down to sleep in order to rest better: Donald, particularly, would lie down as soon as he was unsaddled and knock over his bucket of oats so that he could eat lying down. I might have thought he was dangerously exhausted if every day he didn't go through his circus act of buckings, cabrioles, about-turns and runaway gallops. I found I liked him more and more, and he always knew when he was being talked about and pricked up his ears. When people saw how eager he was to lie down, they didn't think much of his chances, but the riders who escorted us would express a different opinion. Arguments would develop and bets would be made.

'If that horse gets to Jerusalem, I'll eat my hat. The other one just might ...'

'You haven't seen him in action, he's got stamina. If I had to do a trip like this, I'd take the little one, he's better built.'

'I'd take the big one, he's got better legs!'

Our gear, too, had a tremendous success.

'What kind of saddles are those?'

'Army saddles, but we've used layers of felt instead of pads underneath.'

'Don't they rub the horses?!'

'Look at them, no sign of swelling or sores. And yet they carry the saddles and bags for more than eight hours every day.'

The hackamores amazed everyone. When they saw the bridles in the tack-room they imagined we were using vicious and cruel

Arabian bits, and pitied the poor horses. Then, when they saw how the hackamore was adjusted, they understood even less.

'Nothing in the mouth? Just a strap instead of a snaffle? How can you make them stop without a bit?'

'By a slight tug. They learn very quickly and are much more obedient. If they had to wear a bit every day, for weeks and months, they might get sores at the corners of their lips. This way, they can graze whenever we stop to look at the map. We aren't asking for any fancy tricks. They don't need to be collected, we just want them to walk, and the hackamore does a very good job.'

I took care not to let on that not so long ago I hadn't heard of this system either, though it's used by the cowboys, gauchos and vaqueros of North and South America. It was Loulou who gave us the tip.

When the riders saw our stuff spread out on the ground, they wondered how on earth it all fitted onto the backs of the horses. Our knapsacks were particularly impressive, for when they weren't tied down, they expanded and blew up like balloons. Some of the riders even got up in the small hours merely to watch how we organised our gear.

As for Pluto, everyone adored him. Owing to the tremendous distances he covered through his hunting habits, we greased his pads every night with cod-liver oil. Anyone who saw this was deeply moved and there would always be some kind soul, usually a woman, who rushed off to buy him a kilo of meat. Pluto would have a good gorge, and then stretch out under a bed and go to sleep. Next morning, he would parade about among the onlookers and pick out someone with a car, nearly always the same dog-lover who had produced the meat the night before. He would stick to them like a shadow, rubbing against their legs and looking up at them adoringly. It worked every time! The sucker in question would inquire where we were going to stop that night, and offer to take our mongrel in his car. I always accepted as I considered Pluto had every right to his comforts.

And I always accepted if anyone offered to carry our bags. Never once did it enter my head that we might never see Pluto or our possessions again. We never even troubled to take the name of our kind helpers or the registration number of their cars. All we knew was that when we reached the agreed halt, we would find a gorged Pluto and our night's lodgings organised: our unknown friends had fixed everything.

Some even inquired tenderly after our backsides. No problems. Our new jeans had chafed a little to begin with, but after a fortnight the seams had softened and the problem was solved. Now, after eight hours of daily massage, our muscles were hard and our skin soft.

Everything would have been fine but for one continual discomfort. When I left Paris I had had a touch of bronchitis, with a temperature of 39°. My bronchitis never got worse, but it never got completely better either, in spite of all imaginable French, German and Austrian suppositories. I still ran a temperature at night, which delighted Corinne, as it kept her warm. She was less happy when, having used up my own supply of handkerchiefs, I borrowed hers. I tried vine-leaves once, but my nose immediately became even redder—the leaves had been sprayed with sulphates.

For fifteen years I have suffered from asthma and my coughing fits have always provoked witty inquiries of the 'Sure you'll get through the winter?' variety. But now people looked at me when I coughed with an expression I didn't care for, and as I had acute backache as well, I found myself wondering if I might not end up in a sanatorium.

Naturally I vented my fury on poor Corinne. As I couldn't say 'You get on my nerves when I cough, I hate you because I've got a cold,' I scolded her for letting her horse run away when I was as much to blame as she was. I accused her of riding when Donald was tired, or sitting too far back, of not getting up on time in the morning, etc. In short, I needed to hurt somebody, and as she was the only person I had handy . . .

She annoyed me when she met my complaints with: 'It's nothing, you must be very tired'; she annoyed me when she cried; she annoyed me when she took umbrage and a quarrel sometimes lasted for several hours.

'I'm not sitting any further back than you are,' she would protest. 'Look at yourself.'

'You're not going to teach me how to ride?'

But we always made it up and never did we argue in front of

other people and always appeared to be in complete accord. I know why, and so does Corinne. Because we are.

Ried, Wels, Linz . . . A message from the Schmidt parents to say they were waiting for us at Melk. Remember that Alsatian family who spoilt us so just before we crossed the Rhine? We were so glad to think we would see them again.

Yes, there they both were, arms outstretched, smiles dazzling.

'Well, hallo!' said M. Schmidt. 'How did you get on in Germany and Austria? You had pretty bad weather, didn't you?'

How his Alsatian accent warmed my heart.

'And the horses? The mountains and the rain must have tired them a little. But now you've come down to the plains again, they can rest.'

'And besides, you know,' continued Madame Schmidt, deeply moved, with tears in her eyes, 'the war is over. There has been a cease-fire.'

Soon after our departure, hostilities had broken out in the Near East, and there had been a fierce battle on the Golan Heights, close beside the route we intended to take.

'It's much quieter now,' Madame Schmidt reassured us. 'But all the same, when you're crossing the Arab countries, don't tell people you're going to Jerusalem, they might make trouble for you.'

'Don't worry, Madame Schmidt. Our star will protect us.'

'You know, every morning when I get up, I think of you and I look to see what the weather's like.'

'When it rains, she never stops worrying about you,' said M. Schmidt.

We were very touched. These people who took us into their home, without knowing us, had crossed Germany and half Austria to come and see how we were.

Time to say good-bye.

'Look after yourselves. *Au revoir*. And don't forget to write.'

CHAPTER FOURTEEN

Guardian Angels

The farmer's wife in whose home we spent the night had been to Nevers on pilgrimage, like so many Austrian Catholics. She was delighted to reminisce emotionally over the processions in honour of St Bernadette who rests in peace at the Convent of St Gildard.

The previous night we had arrived, fairly early, in an apocalyptic storm. At Saint-Jean-de-Maurienne, where I used to spend my holidays in a children's camp, the Mother Superior used to say 'It's the angels playing bowls', so I've never been afraid of storms. I've always been convinced the lightning would strike anyone else but not me. However, I couldn't pass my conviction on to the horses: Mickey shied at every flash of lightning, and Donald didn't behave very much better.

A farmer had seen us and insisted we should shelter at his farm, and as there was no sign of a break in the weather, we stayed the night there. Without a moment's hesitation he had moved a lorry full of corn out of his barn to make room for the horses. Even after covering it with a tarpaulin, he ran the risk—and for whom? for what reason?—of ruining part of his harvest.

Having served in the cavalry in the old days, he insisted on giving us a sample of his talents and obviously knew his stuff since he warmed the water before he gave it to the horses. I would have preferred to do the rest myself, as I knew from experience that our hosts would either try and overfeed them ('They've come such a long way, they've such a long way to go'), or else not give them enough ('They're so little'). But nothing doing: he and his wife sent us off to dry out and rest beside the fire. So be it! I knew I could check up later to see if the ex-huzzar (or dragoon, or lancer) had done his job properly.

Now for the rest of the scenario. In a few moments there would be a procession of neighbours, alerted that the Xs had visitors not-at-all-like-other-people. For the nth time, we would have to tell them the story of our lives, smile politely at their admiration and thank them when they congratulated us on our courage.

The previous night, while Corinne and I were being the centre of attraction, I had had an attack of the blues, though it didn't last very long. I suddenly began to envy the women we saw as we rode through the villages. While we dragged along under the rain, they were in their snug kitchens, beside a bright fire, sometimes with a baby in their arms, or sipping a cup of tea while they gossiped with a neighbour. And I, what was I doing all that time? Up to the neck in our Great Adventure. Well, really! Was it such a Great Adventure to cover forty kilometres a day, forty hours a week? I was nothing but a long-distance rider.

The blue's faded very quickly. After ten days of continuous wind and rain, I suppose it was to be expected. And I swore I wouldn't change places with anyone.

Next morning the sky seemed to have cleared a little.

'You may have some bright intervals today,' my farmer told me.

I looked at him and his wife. How could anyone be so kind? They would have reconciled me if I had had any particular quarrel with humanity.

'Be careful,' said the farmer's wife. 'There's rabies in the woods. Don't let your dog wander about, and if you're bitten by a fox, go straight to hospital.'

'We promise. *Au revoir!*'

'*Au revoir!* God bless!'

I turned round to wave to our guardian angels, I could have sworn they had wings.

The horses were stiff and tired. The saddle covers never had time to dry out and had to be put back while they were still damp. My cough got steadily worse, and I had a slight temperature which was tiring, but I preferred bronchitis to the attacks of asthma which never stopped and really exhausted me. If only we could have had a few days of sun, everything would have been much better.

Mickey was sniffing too. If he caught flu, it would really be the end, but Corinne and Pluto seemed to cope quite happily with the appalling weather.

The Danube shimmered at our feet, sometimes shut in by high cliffs. We kept to the banks as much as possible, but when we found ourselves on giddy overhangs, we would have to scramble up on to higher ground. Pluto would arrive cheerfully at the end of these short climbs, whereas the four of us would all be out of breath. And often he would disappear into the undergrowth. Monsieur was hunting.

Suddenly, anguished yelps.

'Corinne, listen, it isn't his hunting cry. Pluto is hurt. He's caught in a trap or been attacked by a fox.'

The yelps were redoubled.

'We must stop—I'll go and find him!'

I hurried to save Pluto—for he must be in a bad way—dropping the reins and abandoning Mickey. It wasn't long before I saw my mongrel, half-buried under a thick carpet of dead leaves, standing on three legs. And the fourth? I didn't know if he was hurt, but at least his leg hadn't been broken by a fox-trap.

Pluto didn't move, but watched me, looking guilty and unhappy, holding up one paw, which he didn't seem able to move. I examined it. He growled, as he always does when I look at his paws, and I stretched the damaged leg out to its fullest extent. He turned as if to bite me. I didn't think he would, but you can't be too careful, and I moved the tip of my nose out of danger. There didn't seem to be anything broken, nor even any sign of a wound, and I couldn't imagine what had happened. Pluto was still growling and limped away on three legs. I had visions of putting him on Mickey's back, which he would hate, but it seemed the only solution.

While all this was going on, the horses had moved a little way away. As we came back to them, Donald gave the signal and they both set off at a canter into the next meadow. Two horses thoroughly exhausted after covering 1,500 kilometres.

Pluto hates disobedience, so he chased them. Without limping. So there he was, fully restored to health, when a few moments earlier he had been yelling blue murder and running on three legs. He galloped after the horses, but changed his mind and began to dig furiously: he must have scented a mole.

That day, he had been giving us a series of heart-attacks. To begin with, he had driven a herd of cows out of the field where they were enclosed by an electrified fence; frightened a flock of sheep who scattered, terrified, all over the landscape; and chased a pig out of its sty. He had driven the pig into a lane leading to a barn and attacked it furiously among the tractors and farm machinery. Later we heard the pig's heart-rending squeals, and by evening he had probably been turned into sausages.

When the marvellous not-so-blue Danube wasn't hollowing out its channel among the rocks, it slipped through the plain between marshes and lakes. A network of streams flowed into it and created problems for us. Foot-bridges were marked on our map, but in practice, either they were hidden among reeds, they had collapsed or a narrow flight of steps would make them obstacles for us. On one occasion, we were floundering among the reeds along a bank which crumbled under the horses' weight, and to avoid a dive into the Danube, I tried to climb a path full of old iron, at the risk of spraining a foot or leg. Corinne even began to climb a barbed wire fence, hoping to dismantle an electrified wire.

'What's the point? If it's closed here, it'll be closed the other end.'

While we searched, Mickey managed to catch himself in the barbed wire and cut his knee, not very deeply, but as a precaution we had to get out the aluminium powder spray. As Mickey didn't like the *pschitt* of the spray, we had to go through a complete corrida before we got the powder on the right spot. So, there was only one thing to be done: get off the soft ground and on to the main road.

Once on the tarred surface, I decided to dismount and lead the procession, holding Mickey with one hand and Pluto's lead with the other, for I preferred not to have him dash about among the traffic.

We still had two kilometres to go before the next group of houses, when I heard something which didn't sound quite right.

'Listen! Mickey is about to cast a shoe. A back one. What a time to choose!'

I knew what had happened. I hadn't been able to stop the last blacksmith from oiling his feet to make them look pretty. This was the result. I had been warned: never oil a horse's feet after he has been newly shod: the oil will seep in under the nails and they will begin to move. On this marshy ground, the mud had dragged at the shoes and pulled the nails out one by one. It was partly my fault, as Mickey must have lost several nails the day before and I hadn't noticed.

There was nothing to be done but go on. Besides, the village was in sight. Yes, but . . . after a moment I realised it wasn't one shoe that seemed to be loose, but two. Both back shoes.

We decided to press on, hoping we might find a blacksmith who could fasten them back rather more firmly. If not, we would have to do it ourselves, though I would have much preferred to hand the job over to a professional. Provided we could find one. At home, there was only one blacksmith within a radius of 150 kilometres, and you have to make an appointment three weeks in advance, I knew that here the situation wasn't much better and the first blacksmith worthy of the name was four or five days' march away. And not necessarily on the way to Jerusalem. Not to mention that the horse couldn't walk without shoes, or his feet would soon be very sore.

The rhythmic music of the clattering shoes rang in our ears. Soon it stopped: Mickey had cast both back shoes when he jumped a ditch. Corinne picked up the shoes. We reached the village.

At the first turning I had a heart-attack. I only know a few words of German, but on an enormous board, staring me in the face, what did I read? 'Romer *Schmiede*'.

'Corinne, what's the German for blacksmith?'

'*Schmiede.*'

Several welders were at work, protective masks in place, showers of sparks scattering in all directions. A garage-workshop.

'I'm a mechanic, not a blacksmith,' one of the welders told us. 'There is a blacksmith next door, but it's his day off, and he's gone into town.'

'Damn!'

'You have problems?'

'Two shoes that need replacing!'

'I can't help you . . . Oh, I say, you are in luck . . . He's coming back.'

The man had forgotten his wallet. He wasn't best pleased to see us, and wasn't sure if he was prepared to go to work in his city suit and white shirt. But when we told him our story . . .

'You can count yourselves lucky,' he said, 'because you haven't a hope of finding a blacksmith where you're going. And it's my day off. I shouldn't even be here.'

Whereupon he took off his jacket, rolled up his shirt-sleeves and fastened on his leather apron to protect his trousers. He tied the horse to the forge, took a hind foot and trimmed a quite unnecessary piece off the hoof. When I gave him the two shoes, he looked surprised and pleased: 'It'll be much quicker.' He heated the shoes, adjusted them, cooled them and drove home very firmly seven brand-new nails. The whole thing took less than five minutes. Mickey never moved.

'How much do I owe you?'

'Nothing. It'll be my way of sharing in your crusade.'

I had already managed to run out of petrol at the entrance to a service station, and puncture a tyre outside a garage, but I know no one else who has lost a shoe, much less two, within hailing distance of the local blacksmith.

But after all, why shouldn't a guardian angel know how to use a shoeing-hammer and anvil?

CHAPTER FIFTEEN

Gschwendhof: 'Luxury, Peace and Delight'

It had been raining cats and dogs all day. I'd been stupid enough to leave off my waterproof poncho, so my jeans were wringing wet, my legs freezing, my shoulders damp, my fingers dead white and I was shivering from head to foot. Corinne had dismounted, hoping to get warm by walking, and I could hear 'squelch . . . squelch . . .' as she paddled along in her boots.

So we were a sorry pair when finally we reached Maria Anzbach's stud, one of the outstanding international establishments in Europe. Among others, they look after the horses of the Spanish Riding-School in Vienna.

Stallions were playing in the bright green fields, providing a unique, marvellous and enchanting performance—and I am choosing my words carefully. They weren't just enjoying their love of freedom, or love—it was sheer choreography, and all the more perfect because it was purely instinctive. They would rear, arch their necks, toss their silky manes and bite each other, strike out with their forefeet, then spinning round sharply, gallop off at full speed, an astonishing ballet full of grace and elegance. I wanted to applaud.

Behind the wrought-iron gate surmounted by the name Gschwendhof in Gothic lettering, stood a magnificent house, its paintwork a little faded, surrounded by scattered farm buildings, a little like Schönbrunn. Hidden among the greenery, we came to a riding-ring, and then a sand-strewn jumping arena, finally a line of loose boxes. Dogs barked. A superb Great Dane sniffed at Pluto's button nose, while the latter dropped his usual swagger and cringed ingratiatingly. Our horses dilated their nostrils and steamed under the rain. Mickey hailed his new friends, and at the friendly French neigh, all the horses popped their heads out of their boxes, in spite of the fact that they were munching their oats.

A tall blond boy emerged from a loose box. He was wearing canvas overalls but was so elegant he might have been chosen specially to fit the décor. Tall and handsome, his blue eyes matched his jeans, and he welcomed us smilingly:

'My name is Miloš. Would you like to bring your horses under cover? The stable is over here.'

In the stable, not a straw out of place, not a trace of manure, not a speck of mud. Clinical cleanliness. Miloš showed us a luxurious loose box where we could leave the horses free if we liked. I preferred to tie them up as otherwise Donald would eat Mickey's food. The floor was spread with wood shavings which were vacuumed up once a week, so there was no dirt, a minimum of work and the horses could sleep on cushions as soft as straw but much drier.

A series of buckets of water had been lined up which wouldn't be given to the horses until it was the same temperature as the air in the stables: one of the precautions I always insist on. A scientifically calculated menu had been laid on: only four litres of oats for the three days of rest, half a bucket of bran mash (to replace volume and clear out their intestines), a cup of vitamins and a cup of calcium. The horses were tired, but after a few days' rest in this Eden, they would quickly recover. When I said good-night, I took Mickey's head in both hands and kissed the tip of his nose. (If Donald was jealous, he only had to ask Corinne to do the same.)

Rub-downs, massage, grooming . . . Miloš had to leave us, as he still had plenty to do.

'There you are, my beauties, you'll do fine here. It's clean, it smells good and you've got plenty of new friends.'

I forgot to mention the hay. Mickey would have been furious if it hadn't been included, delicious clover, rich in vitamins.

'Have a good rest.'

I was so happy that I forgot my rheumatics, and embarked on a tour of the stables, out of curiosity, and also in the hope of meeting the duty Apollo. I couldn't decide which to admire most:

the English thoroughbreds; the Irish cobs, dappled grey, black and white, with chests like barrels; or the tall German mares feeding their foals in the boxes. Only the Germans go in for such huge animals, and I wondered all over again how on earth they were able to mount without a step-ladder.

Eventually I found Miloš. 'Have you finished?' he asked. 'Then come with me and I'll show you my favourite horse. He's in the other stable with a bunch I've just brought back from Czechoslovakia. I'm a Czechoslovak myself.'

He proudly led out a fully grown stallion, a bay Arab, strong and well-muscled. His square head was half-hidden under a long silky mane, and his tail swept the ground. He sniffed the air, blew out his nostrils, smelt the two strangers and let out a shattering challenge. He was absolutely splendid.

When the stallion had calmed down a little, Miloš patted his forehead gently and ran his fingers through the silky mane. Obviously he was in love with his horse, and I couldn't blame him.

'Fine horse,' he remarked. 'He's called Monseigneur. There, there, my lovely! Now, I'll show you to your room. You'd probably like to change.'

The guest room, above the stables, was enormous, with a beamed ceiling and a polished wooden floor strewn with animal skins. A white fur rug was thrown over the bed. It seemed much too beautiful for the pair of us, who stood, dripping wet and dirty, in the midst of all this luxury. Pluto had already left a trail of muddy paws on the mirror-like floor. However, his natural delicacy did restrain him just as he was about to jump up onto the bed.

'There's a shower next door and a stove to dry your clothes. As soon as you're ready, come and have a cup of tea with me at my house.'

In no time at all, the room was festooned with washing. We dug out our best trousers, though they were a little mildewed from having been left in the bags for several days: still, we were clean, though a quick touch with a hot iron wouldn't have come amiss. Usually I wouldn't give a damn, but today I wondered what Miloš would think.

Corinne rang the bell and Miloš opened the door. He had

changed into black velvet trousers with fine pink patent-leather boots, and a pullover to match. On anyone else it might have been a bit much, but on him it looked great.

'Have some tea, do sit down. I must cook the dinner before my mother and brother get back from Vienna.'

The room was very much turn-of-the-century with heavy curtains, fringed lampshades, vases of flowers and family photographs. Miloš gave us tea in fine china cups.

His mother arrived, charming, smiling with Miloš's brother, quite a bit older, with greying hair and great charm.

After dinner we talked, and obviously there was music, for we were in the land of Mozart, Schubert and Haydn. The elder brother, a complete intellectual, told us old Austrian stories and all about life in Vienna. He was terrific. So was Miloš. Could I have fallen in love?

'*Es war primat!*' declared the elder brother as we said goodnight. In France he would have said 'Extra', and in England 'Super'. I absolutely agreed.

I hoped next day would be even more '*primat*' because we had been invited to the Hofburg to a performance of the Spanish Riding-School.

Why, I asked, was the school still called Spanish? As we bowled along, the elder brother explained that the ancestor of the Lippizaners who work there had been a Spanish stallion, so for 400 years the Hofburg had remained faithful to the breed.

The winter riding-school where the stallions perform every Sunday is a magnificent rococo building. Huge crystal chandeliers hang from a ceiling with white and gold mouldings. Soft music fills the hall as the lights in the boxes go out one by one, leaving only the two chandeliers above the working area still lit.

A glass door opened and the procession entered, slowly and majestically. The riders wore the traditional cocked hat, long, black, double-breasted coat split up the back, white leather breeches and long boots.

The young stallions showed no sign of nerves when they were greeted by thunderous applause and continued on their stately round. Our Donald obviously still had a great deal to learn. Then it was the turn of four more highly skilled horses, keeping time to a waltz. Suppleness, grace, natural obedience, it all looked so easy. I was absolutely fascinated and wanted to pull Miloš down to the arena with me, and waltz with him like the riders with their horses.

Then came six more stallions, each held on a long rein for a display of *haute école*. The first, attached to two pillars, demonstrated the piaffe. Another, standing on his hind legs, executed a levade. A third sprang into the air like a great white bird, seemed to float in the air for a moment, and gave a tremendous backward kick with both hind legs before landing. This was the capriole. The audience held its breath until the end of each movement, then broke into rapturous applause.

The sixth horse had no saddle, only a small square of red velvet embroidered in gold with an eagle. His cavalier held him on the same long rein, and he broke into a spirited trot, though the horseman didn't seem to be issuing any commands. The horse obeyed him and they embarked on a little dancing canter, pirouette to the left, pirouette to the right, the most difficult figures merely seemed to amuse them both.

There was a flourish of trumpets, and six more stallions pranced onto the sawdust. Two of them had their tails plaited and tied up out of the way. By executing a capriole they showed how an armed knight could leap out of a circle of attackers: a lesson we might find useful if a quarter of what we'd been told about Turks and female tourists was true.

Each stallion executed all three figures, and then they all took a general bow. Frenzied applause, a final tour of the ring and the six glorious beasts cantered away. They seemed to have enjoyed themselves and tossed their heads as if thanking the audience. A quadrille to music from Bizet's *L'Arlésienne* suite performed by eight stallions rounded off the performance.

On the last day of our Austrian halt we really had to attend to business. First stop: the French Embassy to collect our mail, and it was great to hear from so many friends and well-wishers. One envelope was addressed:

Attention to Mrs Evelyne Coquet
French Embassy
Beograd, Austria

It was from an old friend, a sculptor living in San Francisco. Viewed from California, Vienna and Belgrade might seem to be interchangeable, but even so . . .

Second call: the bank. The 3,000 francs we were expecting from *Le Journal de Mickey* was waiting, and it was very satisfactory to collect money earned by the sweat of our brows, if I might put it like that, especially because, after losing our 500-franc notes we had had to cut things pretty fine. If we hadn't been offered so much hospitality, we might have been in dead trouble. And when I say 'trouble', it's because I like understatements . . .

Next day, a dazzling sun was melting the white powder snow. A fresh sparkling morning, the kind I like. Yet for the first time I took to the road again with a lump in my throat.

Ah, Gschwendhof! I would like to have each letter of your name fastened to my heart with blacksmith's nails. Number 8s, naturally, the strongest of all.

CHAPTER SIXTEEN

The Priest and the Pilgrim

Wienerwald, the Vienna woods—never once did I feel in the least like whistling Strauss's famous waltz, and for very good reason. We hadn't a hope of sticking to our planned route, since for every road marked on our large-scale map, in practice I found at least three. What on earth could we do? Although the forest seemed perfectly laid out for Sunday walks, it was hopeless for riders. I followed a path marked with arrows, hoping it might bring us out into the open, but alas, it had been created as a circular promenade and after three hours we found ourselves back where we started.

So I put the map away and steered by the sun and the compass. The horses panted when they climbed up and panicked when they came down, skidding on the thick carpet of fallen leaves which an icy wind sent swirling around us. Frightened squirrels hid in hollow trees and the horses listened uneasily to these strange sounds. At last we came out onto an abrupt cliff as the sun was setting behind a village crowned by a cluster of belfries. A monastery or convent.

'Let's hurry and get there before we're completely lost in the dark,' said Corinne.

It was indeed a monastery where, thank God, they did occasionally receive benighted travellers of the feminine sex.

The father who welcomed us had a very highly developed sense of hospitality. He took the horses into a barn where we looked after them, and then the worthy ecclesiastic made the

kitchens open up again and invited us to dine in a small refectory
reserved for guests.

'Today at least we won't be forced to sing and drink and we
can bring our letter-writing up to date,' said Corinne.

She was absolutely delighted with her surroundings which
breathed piety and meditation. There wasn't a sound except the
tapping of our boots as we walked through the cloisters. The
reverend father sat beside us, and while the serving brother
waited on us, he discovered with delight that we were pilgrims
going to Jerusalem by means other than an airline.

'How delighted I am! You're Catholics, of course.'

'Born in a Catholic country, baptised into our holy mother
Church, brought up in a practising family, in a centre of pilgrim-
age, educated at a religious school and purified by masses at the
Convent of Saint-Gildard.'

I added that for several years the part of Bernadette in the
school playlets had become mine by right: Bernadette the
shepherdess, Bernadette listening to the Virgin, Bernadette at the
convent, Bernadette ill, Bernadette dying, Bernadette canonised,
I had played the lot. Once I was standing on a bench, dressed as a
nun, my hands clasped on the Mother Superior's rosary, when the
Blessed Virgin who was standing on the other end of the bench
got down too soon, and the bench overturned. In falling I broke
the rosary. The Mother Superior saw it as an omen:

'Evelyne may be our next Saint Bernadette!'

'No, no, Reverend Mother,' the nun in charge of studies
protested, 'she's much too dissipated.'

'The little Soubirous girl wasn't the best child in the world
either,' the Mother Superior retorted, fully aware of the impenetrable ways of God. 'Our Lord will decide.'

My story seemed to make a great impression on our host.

'Ah, my children, you are living through a fascinating adventure,' he exclaimed, clasping our hands in his own, soft, white
and unctuous; then with a fatherly gesture he smoothed our
rumpled hair, teasing us gently about our red cheeks and pressing
us against his shoulder. He spoke to us as if we were small girls,
each sentence punctuated with a tender *'Meine Kinder'* ['My
children']. However, his way of sitting much too close to me, knee
to knee, made me feel a little uneasy. The more I shrank into my

corner, the nearer he came. I began to imagine that his intentions weren't 100 per cent pure ... Really, really, Evelyne, I said to myself, you're losing your mind.

Full of excitement, the reverend father departed to collect a jug of wine to celebrate properly. He returned armed with several ampullae. I may not be particularly religious, but all the same, to drink to the success of our ride in Communion wine didn't seem in very good taste. If my grandmother could have seen me!

The father raised his glass. '*Prosit! Prosit!* Your good health! But you aren't drinking! Drink up, there's plenty more. You're tired? I'll take you to your room.'

He put out the lights, locked the doors and led us into a labyrinth of pitch-dark corridors. Not a Christian in sight. The monks were probably at their devotions, and I might almost have been afraid if we hadn't been under the protection of a member of a contemplative order.

You can never rely on anything ... While Corinne was a few paces ahead of us with Pluto, I suddenly found myself pinned against a marble column and wrapped in the folds of a long black cassock. The cold of the column, the agitation of the cassock, the eagerness of the hands moving unerringly to their target, all made me shiver from head to foot.

But Pluto came to the rescue, growling ferociously. He doesn't like it when men put their arms round me, and while my companion fought off my bodyguard, I clung to my pillar.

'*Böse?* Angry?' inquired the enterprising father.

Angry? Well, I can't really say I was. I was much too surprised. My attacker was about thirty and I suppose several years of chastity had been too much for him.

Next morning the room was full of sunlight and the bells were ringing. My head still felt heavy, full of sleep and outlandish dreams.

Two taps at the door. The father entered and kissed each of us on the forehead.

'Good morning, my children, I hope you slept well. Your breakfast will be ready in a moment.'

'Thank you, father.'

'Aren't you coming to feed the horses?' demanded Corinne, dragging me from my stupor. 'We're late.'

'Come back soon,' said the father, 'I'll show you round the monastery.'

The morning freshness quickly cleared my head. Donald and Mickey did full honour to their rations, as did Pluto, and so did we, after which we visited the monastery. A vestige of Norman, a touch of Gothic, a sprinkling of Renaissance, an avalanche of baroque, and yet the overall effect was harmonious and restful.

The priest invited us to attend mass. In the chapel, apart from ourselves, there was no one. I watched him moving about in front of the altar, then he knelt to pray for grace and turned to us: 'In the name of the Father, the Son and the Holy Ghost, I bless you.'

He kissed the cross, wiped it and offered it to me. I remembered a snatch of the service in Notre-Dame the day we left Paris:

'Go forth, bold and adventurous, Heaven grant that on your way you may meet only kindness and care, and that you will return enriched by wonder, friendship, the grace of God, and in health and in joy, reach the heavenly Jerusalem at the end of your earthly pilgrimage.'

I was thinking that I ought to write a short moral fable called 'The priest and the pilgrim', but decided not to. In this modern version of the temptation of St Anthony, I should have to play the part of the devil, and I wouldn't care for that at all.

CHAPTER SEVENTEEN

Our Graceful Travelling Companions

'Yippee!' I yelled at the top of my lungs. I was so happy I had to let off steam or bust, for three deer were following us, stepping proudly, antlers high, flirting their stumpy tails and flaunting their white bottoms, Three deer, but not just any deer. These were old friends.

We hadn't seen them for several days, and how on earth they had found a way through the built-up areas, river barrages, motorways and railway tracks we had had to negotiate, or why they had followed us, we will never know.

It had all started when we were climbing the Vosges mountains. Three elegant shapes had burst out of one thicket and plunged into another. Pluto had chased them, barking furiously, but as he was quickly outdistanced and was probably tired, he had come back, panting, as soon as I whistled. Two or three minutes later, our three new friends reappeared and watched us from a respectful distance, obviously intrigued by our strange caravan.

The little mongrel was definitely not a hunting dog, the two girls carried no whips, horns or hunting knives, and seemed to be perfectly harmless. On the other hand the horses, humped and distorted by enormous bundles, as tall as camels, were unlike anything they had ever seen before.

They took up station at the corner of a clearing and watched us. Pluto yelped with joy when he saw them and they disappeared in a flash. From then on they would reappear at the most unexpected moments, teasing and tormenting him, all four playing a game they obviously enjoyed.

When we halted for the last time in France, we mentally said good-bye to them, for with the canal and the concrete banks of the river we would have to cross, we fully expected we would lose our graceful travelling companions and yet . . .

Several days later in the Black Forest, I thought I was seeing things. Three little white bottoms were wriggling among the branches.

Our deer!

Corinne didn't share my enthusiasm, still less my faith.

'Why do you imagine they're the same ones? There must be thousands of deer in France and Germany. These belong to this forest.'

'We'll see . . .'

Pluto had been doing some illegal hunting again, happily indulging in his favourite sport, though all he ever did was drive the game towards us so that we could see it too.

'Look over there,' I said.

Three animals had just jumped up onto a bank. I recognised the smallest, more lightly built and always hanging back behind the others, with horns not more than ten centimetres long. The second had no horns, was a deeper brown with rounded curves and obviously a female. The third had long legs and carried his head high, displaying well-branched antlers with more points on the left, always leading the other two.

'It is them,' I declared delightedly.

'Pooh,' said Corinne, shrugging her shoulders. 'All deer look alike.'

But my uncle had taught me to recognise the forest animals and to read their tracks. He had shown me the large round marks left by the wild pig, the stag's long slots, the lighter, more pointed and narrower tracks of the roe-deer, helping me to find the lairs of the wild boar or the scratches the stags had made on the trees. In September we would go into the woods at night to listen to the stags belling.

'I may be wrong,' I said, 'but we must look a little closer.'

I dismounted and examined the slots. It had been raining all week and they were clearly printed on the soft ground. Two cloven hoofs slightly spread, a little more than usual, perhaps a sign of fatigue, leaving two sharp marks, the right toe deformed and foreshortened, and I was certain I recognised the footprint of the one I had called St Hubert. We found that particular mark nearly every day wherever we went.

I always wondered how the deer had crossed the Rhine. Had they swum across or found a ford? And why not? I was more and more convinced that they had taken a liking to the horses who always knew they were there long before we did. They dazzled us with their agility and grace, or they would stop and wait for us, totally unafraid, though St Hubert was the least shy. With a few bounds, a single spring, they could cross streams, ditches, walls, fences and barbed wire and never seemed to flounder among the marshes the way we did. At least we never saw them in difficulties. They would watch us, horns arrogantly high, heads tilted ironically.

I was sure we would lose them at the Austrian frontier, during our four days' halt at Schärding, and that they would give up the expedition and turn back, and I knew I would miss them for I loved them dearly. And then one day . . .

We were travelling along the Danube embankment, our turbulent little Black Forest stream now as wide as an arm of the sea, placid and calm, except where it was ruffled by a string of barges. Low wooded hills edged its bed, and the water was tinted Indian pink by the reflection of the setting sun. Pluto flushed a couple of pheasants which flew off with a great beating of wings and that was when I let out my triumphant cry.

'What's up?' asked Corinne.

'There they are.'

'Where? I can't see them.'

'They've just gone back into the woods. But maybe they aren't our ones.'

'These look younger.'

I swung off Mickey's back and ran to the place where I had seen the deer leaping, but the slots were regular and I didn't think St Hubert had been with them.

'They must be native deer, I expect.'

By this time it was dark, and suddenly I saw a white splodge—Pluto—running and heard his joyful bark. Five brown silhouettes stood out in a clearing at the edge of the water feebly lit by the first rays of the moon. They disappeared at once, three first, then the other two afterwards.

'It's St Hubert and two Austrian deer,' I cried. 'They have found us again. They're still with us!'

Mad with joy, I flung my arms round Mickey's neck and kissed him before embarking on a mad supposition.

'Supposing they came with us all the way, what a wonderful story. D'you think they know where we're going? Animal instinct is really marvellous. You know, once at Tronçais we roused a ten-pointer that was a legend in the district. He was quite old and people said experience had made him the most cunning beast in the world. In spite of his huge horns he could go where no dog, horse or man could follow. They said he had come from the far north. Just imagine, if St Hubert followed us to the Holy Sepulchre.'

'Oh, really ... don't you think you're going too far? You've read too many fairy-tales. I'm quite prepared to admit that these deer have manged to cross the Rhine, the Inn and the Danube, but what about the Bosporus? Are you going to buy them tickets on the ferry-boat?'

I preferred to call off the argument and admire the moonlight. Several days later ...

'Look!' I exclaimed, impenitently. 'Pluto is following a scent.'

It was the deer again. The two younger ones were chewing beetroot leaves a few hundred yards away, and with their dun-coloured coats, were almost invisible. Three others had been lying among the crops and took off at top speed as soon as they saw us. Hop, hop ... A few bounds took them across the field, with one leap they cleared the railway, two more and they were over the motorway.

'Look out! Pluto's going to follow them. Pluto, come back!'

But Pluto was deaf to all reason and plunged after the deer in the midst of a stream of cars travelling at 100 miles an hour. We stood frozen with horror, wondering how long it would be before he was nothing but a smear of scarlet on the asphalt.

'Pluto, stop! Come back, come back!' we yelled in vain.

Thank God, the five deer split into two groups, the three French to the right, the two Austrians to the left, and immediately Pluto, like Buridan's ass, was faced with the problem of which group to follow and stopped dead. I whistled as loudly as I could (which isn't very loud), but Corinne put two fingers in her mouth

and let out a whistle that could be heard above the roar of
the engines. Pluto lifted his head and after surveying us for a
moment, deigned to return to our side of the motorway, panting
like a marathon runner and looking at us reproachfully. The
wretch obviously didn't know how close we had come to losing
him and that it was only by the merest whisker that he had
failed to cross his last frontier.

For Hungary was not far away. The landscape had changed, the
wooded valleys of the Wienerwald melting into a wide plain, flat
and featureless, foreshadowing the *puszta*.

Next morning, at dawn, we set off across frozen ploughed fields
with never a soul in sight. Covered with a fine film of ice, the
ground was criss-crossed with the tracks of hundreds of deer. It
looked as though a general assembly had been held during the
night, as if all the deer in the world had congregated in this one
spot, like the gipsies at Saintes-Maries-de-la-Mer in July.

I examined the slots and through sheer bloody-minded per-
severance finally discovered the distinctive marks left by St
Hubert, a little apart from the rest.

'He *was* with them!'

Mickey came to an abrupt halt, and, even though I drove my
heels into his side, remained glued to the spot. Holding his head
high, his ears pricked forward, he stared at something I couldn't
see.

Pluto gave tongue and plunged into a thicket. A hundred
terrified deer exploded out of it, scattering at top speed in all
directions, then formed into groups again and leaped and played
all round us.

It was an apotheosis, a final tableau, a tremendous outburst of
pure joy. I am absolutely convinced that it was St Hubert and his
friends saying good-bye.

We never saw them again.

CHAPTER EIGHTEEN

En Route for the Land of the Magyars

We were guided through the Burgenland by Mr Welde, the world champion long-distance rider, who covered 13,000 kilometres in thirteen months. On the way, he managed to beat several speed records, and sometimes clocked up 100 kilometres a day. It's true that he only went through countries where he could be sure of finding proper fodder and stabling and that his wife went on ahead with their suitcases and set up the overnight stops. I always tried to average 1,000 kilometres a month without cantering, of course, as our horses were much too heavily loaded, but by trotting now and then.

'Your speed isn't important, always stick to a walk,' Loulou had insisted. 'Go by the clock, not by your speed.'

Various professionals had had very different ideas. 'If you keep to the same pace,' they argued, 'the horses will be using the same muscles all the time, which will get tired very quickly, while the others will relax and stiffen. Vary your pace with a little trotting.'

I wouldn't have minded following this advice: the muscles of my backside wouldn't have been at all sorry, and the horses would have found the exercise relaxing. But Loulou's personality was so strong that every time I tried to break into a trot, I heard his voice repeating with a splendid garlic-scented accent 'Stick to a walk ... Walk ... walk ...', which doesn't mean that I never gave way to temptation, and who could blame me?

As we went along, Mr Welde explained that he always let his horse break into a trot of its own accord. Bully for him! If we did the same with Mickey and Donald, we'd never leave the stable, or rather, we'd leave them to spend the day with their noses glued to the grass. Mickey, in particular, being by nature sluggish, not to say lazy, never broke into anything like a brisk pace unless he was urged on by a willow wand applied to his rump (if I could find a spot not covered by baggage), or attracted by an apple. The carrot theory only works in comic strips.

As we rode through the vineyards, Mr Welde said 'I've been through this region so many times that I know it like the back of my hand. It takes forty minutes to get to Gols, but it's up to you to set the pace. Walk if you like, but we can trot if you prefer. I'll do whatever you say. You know how your horses work. I never allow myself to be influenced by guides. The decision is yours, I'm entirely at your service.'

So it was up to me to set the pace, slowly at first, then I decided to trot a little on the good going. My tired backside was very grateful.

At Gols a blacksmith reshod the horses. It wasn't absolutely necessary, but I thought it was just as well, for we had no idea what we might find behind the Iron Curtain. Although we could manage more or less in German, Hungarian would be quite a different kettle of fish, especially when it came to technicalities.

A final lunch, washed down by the local wine, and then a last smiling photo for a local journalist who had offered to take our baggage as far as the last Austrian Customs post.

Our distinguished guide could go no further, but handed us over to three girls, who would escort us as far as Mickelsdorf. Often enough (for the Austrian press had done its stuff), we were recognised, and the peasants cried '*Vive la France*' as we rode by.

'Spend the night here,' a farmer advised us.

As the Hungarian Customs post was five kilometres away, and if the formalities took any time at all, we wouldn't be able to reach our next stop-over until very late, it might have been wise.

I remembered too our parent's advice: 'Never travel at night.' We had promised, but we wouldn't be what we are if our impatience hadn't got the better of us. Enough messing about. On to the Austrian Customs post.

'Passports,' the Customs officer demanded.

'We're the two French riders. Our passports are in the bags the journalist brought you this morning.'

'What bags? What journalist?'

And as our faces must have been a study, he added hastily 'Wait here. I'll go and ask my colleagues.'

He disappeared and returned, shaking his head. No one had seen any journalist or any bags. 'Do you know the name of this character?'

He had told us vaguely that he worked for a paper in the Burgenland and obviously it had never occurred to us to check. I was furious with myself. Supposing he wasn't a journalist at all? Supposing he had decamped with our bags? What a fool I was: no one should be so naïve at my age.

Confronted by fans on foot, in cars or on horseback, the demoiselles Coquet put up a fine show. A prayer rose to my lips: 'Saint Anthony of Padua, please let us find our bags. You're still in charge of lost property, aren't you?'

'Go and inquire at the Hungarian Customs,' our Austrian officer suggested more practically. 'It's five kilometres further on, and your gentleman may have left them there.'

'Couldn't we telephone?'

'Telephone across the border? It's not so easy. You have to go through Budapest and ask for an official interpreter. It's much too late. Hungary isn't Austria.'

'I had forgotten. I'm sorry.'

We prepared to ride on. It would take us an hour, and darkness had already fallen.

'Come back if you don't find your things and we'll look after you,' suggested a couple of mounted supporters.

I forced myself to smile. Optimism reigned. I was sure our bags would be on the other side of the frontier. So:

'*Auf wiedersehen Österreich!*'

A light. A red and white barrier. A man in a green uniform:

'Pass?'

I asked if he spoke German.

'Pass?' he repeated.

I tried to explain the situation, but not only did he not understand, I got the impression that his knowledge of Hungarian was limited to the word 'Pass', which he repeated louder and louder, until I began to lose my temper and the situation hotted up.

A guard came across to see what the row was about. Oh, joy! He knew a little German and ended up by raising the barrier, whereupon a dozen individuals, guards and Customs men, surrounded us, all trying to out-shout each other:

'Passport? Visa?'

We explained our situation yet again.

The German linguist translated for his colleagues, and everyone exclaimed at once. Said one of the officers:

'We have seen neither journalist nor baggage, and without your passports, I cannot let you through.'

I had the nerve to say that he might be mistaken, and if he would go back to the office to see if by any chance . . . And to my great surprise I heard him say 'Come and look for yourself.'

He showed me round the building. Nothing.

We had no option but to ride back to Austria, not at all certain that the Austrians would allow us to re-enter, and in that case, what would become of us? Would we be forced to spend the night in that no-man's-land—excuse me, no-person's-land. We were tired and frustrated, but we hadn't gone a hundred yards when a small van came to a halt alongside.

'It's the Austrian Customs officer,' exclaimed Corinne.

And so it was. He was bringing our gear which our journalist friend had just delivered.

It had been a narrow squeak, but I wasn't at all sure we had come to the last of our troubles.

We rode back to Hungary, and while Corinne looked after the horses, I confronted the inspector.

'Passports, visas, formal authorisations, ministerial authorisations, traveller's cheques?'

By a stroke of luck, everything was in order.

'So may we pass, please?'

'Not yet. Wait in there.'

I sat down in an overheated room, and considering I was dressed for a temperature of minus 10° the Customs officers were soon laughing at my red nose and astronaut's anorak.

After a very long hour's wait, the inspector returned.

'I'm calling up a vet. We've had instructions from the Ministry about you. If the veterinary examination is all right, you can go ahead.'

He dialled a number, spoke to someone and then said:

'The vet is free, but he has no car. He lives about eight kilometres away. Can you pay for a taxi to bring him and take him
home?'

In such circumstances could anyone count the cost?

'*Naturlich!*'

An hour later, the vet arrived. I was worried about the horses
which had been in the open through all this and must have been
cold and hungry.

I liked the vet for two reasons. Firstly because he was very
attractive, and secondly because he spoke German. He stamped
our passports without going into details, and wrote out our pass.
He didn't even bother to glance at the horses, he was far more
worried about us.

'Where will you sleep tonight?'

'We don't know yet. Do you know of a farm near here?'

'A farm! In Hungary! Ha-ha!'

He burst out laughing.

'There've been no farms in Hungary for more than fifty years.'

'A riding-club, then? We've been told Hungary is full of
horses.'

'There used to be ... twenty years ago, but it's different now.
Listen, you could go to Masonmagyarovar tonight. D'you have
a map? There's an agricultural college there where they breed
riding horses. It's sixteen kilometres away.'

'It'll take us three hours to get there. It's dark, and the horses
are already tired by a day's journey. We must find a stable or a
barn as soon as possible.'

'In that case, go to Hegyelshalom. I know an inn there, and I'll
try and get you a room. Wait for me at the first crossroads.'

'Can we get hay and oats?'

Fresh laughter, then more seriously:

'Oats, in Hungary? Ha-ha-ha ... Ladies, there are no oats in
Hungary.'

I found it hard to believe, remembering all the posters I had
seen, printed in four colours, showing the herds of wild horses
galloping across the limitless *puszta*! I had never imagined that
those horses were fed on anything but the finest oats. My in-
grained capitalist thinking habits ...

It was a dark night and very cold. The lights of the town seemed very far away and I wasn't in a merry mood, but after all, there was nothing so surprising about the situation. When I started, I had divided my journey into four stages. In France, it would be a breeze; in Germany and Austria a long trek; and in Hungary Phase III would begin, a tough business, not for amateurs or holiday-makers. I had expected this phase would take us as far as Turkey and the Near East, where we would be faced with barbarism and war.

The crossroads to Hegyelshalom at last. The vet was waiting for us.

'There's no room anywhere,' he announced. 'I'll go on looking. Tie up the horses here and come home with me for a meal, you must be cold and hungry.'

'We can't leave our horses in the open, it's really much too cold. We must find them a stable as quickly as possible.'

'You're right. Wait here. I'll come back as soon as I've found something.'

Grass was growing on the pavements, and the horses crunched the frozen blades. The temperature must have dropped to minus 10° or 12° and Corinne and I were congealed. Men and women strolled past, chatting, in no hurry, ignoring the cold. They looked at us without any surprise, and it was obvious they preferred not to meddle with something that was no concern of theirs.

It was past eleven o'clock when the vet reappeared and our horses had had time to pull up all the grass in the street.

'I've found a good stable!'

We followed him and it was indeed a good stable, but twenty-odd horses occupied it already. They were squeezed up to make room for our two, and the vet returned to his hearth and home, having done far more than his duty as far as we were concerned.

We found ourselves with people with whom we could communicate only by gestures, so I mimed that the horses were hungry. Someone brought me a pan of corn on the cob, the usual ration for a Hungarian horse. No oats, the vet had said. I pulled a face and tried to find some barley. Someone else scraped the bottom of a wooden box and collected a kind of powder, which they called *coucouroutz*. Does that mean anything to you? Nor me.

Corinne sniffed it and thought it might be ground maize, but it was much too late to find anything else.

At last it was our turn. I mimed that we wanted something to eat before we went to bed, and one of the lads beckoned to us to follow him. First stop: a cheap café. The owner was about to close and didn't want to serve us, but finally agreed to sell us some take-away food: dumplings made with some mysterious substance, and herrings which I suspected had been smoked, but which were very dry, and some not very fresh bread.

Second stop: a hotel, two kilometres from the stable, and therefore two kilometres on foot, which in our present state was quite something. We were asked to pay for the room before we had even seen it, and it proved to be a rabbit-hutch with barely room for two small iron beds. Rough sheets, torn but clean. Inadequate woollen blankets. Stiflingly hot. No window. Next door, a bathroom with no water.

Corinne and I were too exhausted to be affected by aesthetic and hygienic considerations, but as I fell into bed, I translated into French money what I had paid for the room. It worked out at about two francs per person. We certainly weren't being overcharged.

Until we reached the Austro-Hungarian frontier, we had been treated rather like film starlets. Sometimes we were even rather bored at having to give up so much time to the gentlemen of the press. Here, only one representative of the fourth estate came to see us, but he alone was responsible for distributing everything that could decently be said concerning us, text, pictures and sound, in newspapers, on radio, and TV, throughout the Hungarian People's Republic. We couldn't imagine a more efficient public relations system. We knew that publicity could only be helpful, since it would mean that we wouldn't have to explain who we were and what we needed.

There was only one small inconvenience: the fans. They were kind but tiring, and we really didn't have time to have a drink with all our admirers.

After Masonmagyarovar, on the way to Györ, we tried to take a path through the vineyards. The snow was deep and we sank in up to our knees, and where the wind had blown it away, the path was icy. As the snow balled under the horses' feet, we kept slipping and falling without making much progress. A blacksmith had given me several pairs of studs but they didn't match the thread on our mortices and I couldn't fix them on.

Finally we gave up and stuck to a minor road, which wouldn't have been so bad, if it hadn't been a Sunday. Everyone made a point of stopping to congratulate us in Hungarian. What could we say except '*Koszonom!*', one of the very few words we were able to remember, which means 'Thank you!'

Just once the conversation did go a bit further. From one car came a hearty '*Bonjour, ça va?*'

There were three of them, father, mother and daughter, and they all spoke French.

'We saw you on the telly. Welcome to Hungary. Can we do anything for you?'

'Oh yes, please. If you could go to the riding-club at Györ, and ask if they've got room for us . . .'

An hour later the car returned.

'The groom is waiting for you and will take you to the club. By the way, we live in Budapest, here's our address. Come whenever you like. Why not tomorrow? It's very quick by train.'

And off they went. Corinne and I looked at each other. It so happened that we had decided to make a detour, because at that point the Danube takes a wide swing round and Budapest wasn't on the direct route to Jerusalem. As Mickey, Donald and Pluto didn't need to come with us, owing to their total lack of interest in sightseeing, they could wait for twenty-four hours until we could all set out on Godfrey de Bouillon's route for Yugoslavia.

The stables at Györ sheltered about thirty horses who had been squeezed up shoulder-to-shoulder to leave two stalls for our pair. Still no oats or barley, naturally, as even in the riding-clubs the horses eat maize. However, Mickey and Donald didn't mind, so we could relax. The man in charge seemed to know his business.

CHAPTER NINETEEN

Goulash and Pork Fat

At Györ Station, the waiting room was spangled with red stars on the caps of Russian soldiers, and after so many weeks in the saddle, the thought of taking the train (a stopping steam locomotive) filled us with excitement.

Budapest. Our new friends received us with open arms. He was a doctor, she a sculptress, while their daughter was still at school. All three of them bent over backwards to make sure we'd have an unforgettable day.

The town itself is wonderful, quiet, very grand and yet full of charm. I expected to hear music coming from each palace, or historic building. There were shops too. As our tartan caps were much too light, we wanted to buy Russian fur hats with flaps, which can be pulled down over the ears, the back of the neck or the forehead, but they were impossible to find. The women were much too conscious of their elegance and the fur hats they wore were very smart, but didn't have ear-flaps. When they saw us coming with our thick mountain anoraks, one salesgirl even asked if we were planning to go to Siberia. We had to be satisfied with fur hats, without ear-flaps, tied under the chin.

We did have time for a hot bath in an underground thermal establishment and a meal in a 'typical' restaurant: fish soup spiced with paprika, goulash, sugared pancakes stuffed with cream cheese, all set off by Tokay and gipsy music. I won't say too much about that wonderful hour, or I might sound like a travel guide.

When we got to the stable at six o'clock next morning we were a touch worried, as it was the first time we had been away for so long. The guardian had been equal to his task and brought our gear from the safe where it had been shut up under double lock. We found Pluto busy lapping up his soup, whereas Mickey and Donald had already swallowed their rations. They had even been artistically groomed. Their tails had been carefully plaited, and looped up to stop them dragging in the mud, and even their manes had been plaited. Their rumps were ornamented with a sort of chequer-board of lozenges created with a drop of beer or sugared water, while our boots were neatly set out, side by side, beautifully polished, just like a parade. All we needed were the stirring strains of the Rakoszy March to set us on our way to Székesféhervár.

Székesféhervár . . . I repeated the name twenty-five times before I could ask the way correctly, and yet the Hungarians all got it right the first time. I thought they were all very clever, but then, I told myself that the Hungarians think we're clever because we can toss off names like La Foulée de Castelnaudary, la Charité-sur-Loire, or Colombey-les-Deux-Eglises without batting an eyelid.

That night luck was with us, relatively speaking, for it took only two hours to find a stable with the help of several local fans. One of them even offered to put a sofa in his prefab at our disposal.

Something to eat wouldn't come amiss either, so he opened his store cupboard. There was nothing in it but pork fat and a few pieces of stale bread. Pork fat, as we had already noticed, is the steak and chips of the Magyar proletariat. We swallowed it, holding our noses, closing our eyes, gritting our teeth and slipping most of it under the table to Pluto.

As dawn was breaking, I wiped the steam away from the window panes. Snow was falling heavily. People wrapped up to the eyebrows were already going to work through the dazzlingly white streets where the cars were moving at a walking pace. The first real cold! How would our Mediterranean horses stand up to it, I wondered. Ten minutes later, the snow had stopped and was even beginning to melt. One problem less.

A few moments later, the stable owner appeared, flanked by a jockey. As he had to exercise a big black horse, the jockey planned to show us the local scenic route.

After less than two kilometres, there was an unexpected hitch, for the splendid pasture we were crossing was cut by an irrigation ditch, nine feet wide and twelve feet deep. There was no way our two country-bred, overburdened horses could jump such an obstacle. As for going round it . . .

I didn't despair. From the beginning of our adventure, as in all good self-respecting romances, there has always been a *deus ex machina* who arrived to rescue us in the nick of time. This time it took the form of a squad of soldiers who offered to build us a bridge. Just leave it to them. They placed two thick planks, rather less than five feet apart across the ditch, and then laid more planks across them. All we had to do was ride over.

The jockey and his big black horse turned back and left us. I don't ever remember having faced such a violent wind. It must have been blowing at least 100 miles an hour, straight from the north. We were travelling, or rather, we were trying to travel east, and I could feel the horses heeling like dinghies.

We had to cross a bridge, a real one this time, over a railway. The wind threatened to snatch us from our saddles, so we dismounted, or we might have been blown on to the tracks. I could feel my reins flying away as if I was holding not a horse but a kite, and then a fresh gust, even more violent, flung us against the parapet.

The horses fluffed up their coats, dropped their heads and allowed themselves to be rocked by the wind as it whistled in their ears, while we were held pinned to the parapet until the storm abated a little and we were able to cross to the other side.

I felt it would be better to go due south, planning to go due east next day when the weather had improved. I let myself be driven by the wind.

I began to feel completely groggy. It was difficult to keep one's balance. I didn't know which was land or which was sky, and every now and then I bumped into my horse. We trod on each other's feet, and when I leant against his shoulder, I could feel Mickey staggering.

Around midday the wind dropped a little and we could rest. None of us could have gone a step further, and I stood still while the land, sky and sun gradually returned to their original positions. We took a short breather before starting again, for the day's trip had been set at fifty-three kilometres, and as we hadn't made much progress, once again we would have to go on after dark.

At four o'clock the cold enveloped us quite suddenly. There were patches of snow lying on the dyke we were travelling along, and the snow froze into solid balls under the horses' feet. I felt Mickey's right forefoot slip, then the left, and finally all four together, giving me just time to jump off before he fell to his knees. My little horse was less than graceful when it came to figure skating, and it wasn't easy to chip away the ice with the hoof-pick.

A few yards further on, the same pantomime had to be gone through again in a field, but this time with frozen mud. I panted: 'If we've got to scrape their feet every three yards, we'll never make it. We've still got fifteen kilometres to go.'

As soon as it was dark, the wind began to blow again, but this time it was freezing in good earnest. Even our fur hats weren't enough, so we wrapped our heads in everything we could find in the way of scarves and mufflers, though we were beginning to feel nervous in open country—and open, believe me, was the right word. If we had been able to sing, it might have cheered us up a little, but we hadn't the heart, and we didn't even feel like talking.

However, all things come to an end, and finally a few pale lights began to show through the dark: Medina, our objective for the night. In view of the cold, there was nobody to be seen in the streets. But what's this? A barber shop still open: the local Figaro busy shaving a client, and while he didn't understand a word of our jargon, he understood instinctively that we wanted shelter. He abandoned his client's half-shaved chin and ran off to rouse some peasants who took our horses in at the state farm. I tied a red, white and blue flag to their manger, just in case some peasant might harness them to his plough next morning and take them off to work in the fields, thinking they were new recruits for the co-operative farm.

We ourselves were lodged with the local manager, as it turned out, a kind, hospitable old woman. We were immediately presented with a bowl of pork fat and crusts of dry bread, and when Corinne pulled a terrible face, the kindly grandmother decided she had better cook us an egg. She even produced a piece of cheese, some nuts and a glass of wine, which made us exchange glances and burst out laughing. Pluto could have the fat, but we enjoyed a really good meal.

The grandmother was so delighted to see us suddenly restored to good humour that she even opened a tin of cherries in *eau-de-vie* which made us laugh all the more and drink her health, repeating over and over again the few polite words we had learned as we went along, which made her laugh and laugh. She didn't hold back either when it came to lifting the elbow, though she had been asleep when we arrived and certainly hadn't expected a party. We were exhausted ourselves until the cherries gave us a new lease of life.

Far into the night, we could hear the grandmother hiccuping away happily: yet another respectable matron led astray by the evil example set by the Coquet sisters.

Szekszárd, Bataszék . . . Day followed day, each as alike as the *coucouroutz* which Mickey and Donald had got quite used to, and the pork fat which Corinne and I had to stomach to keep us warm, especially if it was washed down with a drop of *eau-de-vie*. We could nearly always ride along the levees, the dykes built to hold back the floods, which made perfect paths for the horses.

For hours and hours we were quite alone, hearing nothing except the wildfowl sliding on the frozen river, or flitting among the frosty reeds.

The cold made my head ache, and I had to keep my fingers moving, or I sucked them to keep the circulation going.

At Bataszék we met Spartan conditions. At the pig farm where the horses had been stabled, we had to ask several times before they got enough to eat. They had got so much thinner since we had been in Hungary, and as our host would neither give nor sell me any more for them (he considered they had had quite enough), I used the ancient pilgrim's right. In other words, I stole two kilos of maize from the storeroom. My justification: 'They work very hard, they've been on the move since eight o'clock this morning, and they didn't have anything to eat at midday.' But the Hungarian horses work very hard too; they pull enormous carts, and when they get home, all they are given are a few corn-cobs and a small bowl of maize.

Corinne and I lodged with a grandmother (a different one). When I appeared in the kitchen with Pluto, the grandmother let out a series of terrible screams. She knew a few words of German and yelled 'Dog outside! No dogs in the house!'

'He's walked all the way from Paris. He has to rest and eat where it's warm.'

'Oh? What's he going to eat?'

'Meat.'

I knew what her reaction would be, but if I didn't try, Pluto would never get proper food and he needed it badly.

'Meat? For a dog?'

She was so amazed that she embarked on a passionate tirade. 'What an idea to bring a dog with you. You French are the most extraordinary people. Can't you afford to buy a car? You can go faster in a car than on a horse. The tourists always come by car.'

All the same, she threw Pluto a small piece of sausage. It was kind, but it wasn't enough, so I tried to compromise: 'Couldn't he have some milk?'

I hardly expected an uproar, as I had seen dozens of churns in the yard.

'Milk!'

The grandmother stared at us incredulously, while I offered to buy two whole sausages and half a loaf for Pluto, a reasonable meal for a dog who had covered fifty kilometres, and laid the money on the table. The old woman stuffed the notes back in my pocket, as apparently that wasn't the problem.

'We never give milk to dogs!'

Her tone was quite unanswerable, though as a concession she threw Pluto a piece of pork fat, exactly the same as the stuff she gave us. I sometimes wondered what Pluto thought of the regime—gastronomic, of course, as I refuse to get involved in politics. I wondered if it would be the same once we passed Mohács and reached Yugoslavia . . . I wasn't very hopeful.

Mohàcs was almost a small town, with even a few shops. We had crossed Hungary in ten days, very economically, so we had quite a few florints left. As Christmas was only three weeks away we thought we might send off a few gifts. We found some very good records and sent all our friends gipsy music.

I didn't forget Corinne and she didn't forget me. I bought a charming embroidered blouse for her, the local speciality, and she brought a charming embroidered blouse for me. When we exchanged gifts, we had a good giggle, for not only were the blouses identical, they were wrapped in identical boxes and coloured paper. We had both gone into the same 'fashion' shop (there was only one) at different times.

We had contacted 'the other side', giving them full details of our arrival, and the message seemed to have got through, for a Yugoslav vet arrived to examine the horses. Thank God, there were no problems, but there seemed to be something wrong with Corinne and me. Just as we were about to cross the frontier, the local police realised we hadn't completed a most important formality: we should have signed on at a police station every night. Of course we knew this perfectly well, but who on earth would be so punctilious? No one had ever queried the position, and surely, just as we were leaving Hungary, no one would arrive from Germany to make a fuss.

The captain of the frontier post began to laugh, and soon his men were laughing too. He telephoned Budapest, just to make sure everything was all right, before announcing 'It's all right this time, because you are on horseback. But next time, you mustn't forget to report every night.'

'Don't worry. We won't.'

CHAPTER TWENTY

Donald's Illness

When we were in Austria, we were told Hungary was a poor, filthy country where everything we had would be stolen by gipsies (which didn't happen). The Hungarians told us that they were a rich capitalist island surrounded by starving Communists and we would have a terrible time in Yugoslavia where the people were primitive, barbarous and cruel. Furthermore, this was nothing compared to what we could expect in Bulgaria. In point of fact, once we got through Yugoslav Customs, where the guards were dour and uncompromising, unlike their good-natured Hungarian colleagues, life appeared to be somewhat easier than it had been the other side of the Iron Curtain. Even the houses seemed more solid.

Beli Manastir was our first stop. We had been given the address of a vet who spoke German, and if only we had been able to cross Yugoslavia from vet to vet, everything would have been easy. He was able to take us in, but couldn't put up the horses, so he and I knocked at every door in the village, but all the stables were full. After three hours we finally found one, which was very small, but it would have to do for one night.

While the vet and I made the rounds, Corinne and the horses had had to wait in the open with the temperature dropping to minus 15°. I found it interesting that as soon as it became really cold my asthma, snuffles and bronchitis practically disappeared, and the horses didn't sniff either. The cold was definitely much healthier than the rain.

Mickey and Donald just fitted into the stable, side by side, and although I was afraid they might kick each other during the night, I couldn't find a bar to keep them apart. I consoled myself by reflecting that a bar wouldn't stop them fighting if they wanted to. Again, they had to be satisfied with corn on the cob. Pluto, too, had to sleep in the stable, for dogs weren't allowed in the house. He looked quite sad at not being able to go with us, and I was sad too at having to leave him.

The vet had killed a pig that afternoon and it provided the *plat de résistance* at the dinner we shared with his wife and daughter, a most delightful family meal, eaten quickly as everyone wanted to go to bed early.

I decided to take a shower first, since for once there was a shower, but when I emerged from the bathroom, who should be waiting for me on the landing, in the semi-darkness, but my respectable friend the vet. He considered it his duty to push me up against the stairs, two steps from the bedrooms where his wife and daughter were sleeping. Because I don't like family rows, and because he was pot-bellied and I was annoyed with him for keeping Pluto in the stables, I sent him packing—he could rumple his own wife's hair-curlers. The stable-lad we met with the two queer Black Forest surgeons had shown me what to expect from Serbo-Croats, but I hadn't expected to find a middle-aged Yugoslav determined to maintain his compatriots' hot-blooded reputation the moment we set foot in his country.

Next morning it was still freezing discouragingly, and our host was worried when we told him that it would take more—or less—to make us stay.

'It's mad to go on,' he declared, 'you'll all die of cold. It's only twelve degrees below here, and it's still quite bearable, but nearer Belgrade, it'll be twenty degrees below and later it'll be worse. Listen, give the whole thing up, sell your horses and take the next plane home. I'll pay for your tickets myself, if you haven't enough money . . .'

Could anything be more paternal? As he watched us swing up onto our horses, I swear he had tears in his eyes.

The horses struggled along, sinking into snow up to their hocks. We panted even on the easiest going, and the biting wind which stung our faces and chapped our lips made me wonder if we wouldn't have done better to follow the vet's advice and go home. I was feeling warmer under the layers of clothing I had piled on until I felt like an artichoke, but the flying snow blinded me and made me keep my head down. Nor could I make out the edges of the fields and it was only after falling several times into ditches that I began to recognise the meaning of a slightly higher mound where the snow lay white and soft.

I couldn't see roads, houses or any living soul, apart from Corinne who was the colour of an over-cooked beetroot, Donald and Mickey covered with a lacy film of snow, or Pluto, shivering like a leaf. Did nothing inhabit this region? The frozen wastes of the Antarctic could hardly be more forlorn.

Suddenly, Corinne, who has eyes like a lynx, cried: 'Look over there: it looks like the top of a pylon.'

'You're right. Let's make for it. It must lead to a village. Perhaps there's a road as well.'

It wasn't very far to the pylon, 500 metres perhaps, but 500 metres of stumbling, pitching and skidding in the powder snow, walking in wet boots filled with little pieces of ice, was hard work. Our legs felt as though they were stuck full of needles for our trousers were stiff with frozen sweat.

God was on our side. We came out onto a minor road which had just been cleared by a snow-plough, and we had to hurry for in another two hours it would disappear again. I suggested 'Just for once, let's trot, if not, we'll get bogged down.'

After a few minutes, Corinne, who was behind me, called 'Stop, my horse is limping.'

'Keep trotting.'

I looked and listened and realised that Donald was coming down more heavily on his left hind leg, which meant he was limping badly with the right. We both dismounted and I examined Donald. His stifle was covered in dried blood and there was a very deep, clean hole.

'He must have bumped into a stone buried in the snow,' suggested Corinne.

'Possibly, but I don't think so. The cut isn't fresh. Perhaps he's been limping all morning but on this rough ground we haven't noticed. Perhaps he's had it since he left the stable. The hard work he's had to put in today hasn't helped, and now he's tired and in pain.'

I pressed the wound and the inside of the thigh gently.

'Is it serious?' asked Corinne, anxiously.

'I don't know. He's certainly suffering more from the bruising of the muscle and ligaments than from the cut itself. We can clean it with snow and disinfect it.'

'What makes you think he cut himself in the stable?'

'I found them both in a very odd position this morning when I gave them their maize. Donald was right across the stall, and they had managed to change places without breaking their tethers. His legs weren't hot, but I didn't look at his thighs. It's quite probable that Mickey climbed over Donald while he was lying down and stepped on his thigh with his ice-stud. Or else they had another fight, and Donald got kicked. Just on the joint itself, it's really bad luck.'

'What'll we do?'

'We've no choice. As we can't build an igloo and wait for the snow to melt, we have to go on. The next village must be Osijek.'

'How far is it?'

'About twelve kilometres. We can ride Mickey turn and turn about, that'll be six kilometres each. O.K.?'

By the time we reached Osijek, Donald was limping even more. A café was still open.

'There's a riding-club six kilometres away,' said the café-owner in German.

'Too far, one of our horses is hurt.'

'No stables in this town.'

Whereupon an elegant apparition appeared, totally unexpected, to say the least, in this village where pigs wandered about in the muddy gutters: nipped-in waist, exquisitely cut trousers, immaculate shirt, tie in perfect taste and fine patent-leather shoes. To crown everything the apparition spoke fluent German. The café-owner was in no doubt as to what should happen next.

'Take them to Pépé,' he advised. 'He'll find somewhere for the horses as well.'

The fashion-plate agreed. I couldn't imagine where he was off to in that get-up, but he took us to a village, just outside the town, and into an ancient building. A few minutes later he emerged with a tall ungainly individual with white hair, a weather-beaten face half-hidden by a week-old beard, but looking reasonably helpful. In spite of his age he was not without dignity. This was Pépé. He beckoned to us to follow him, and pushed open the door of another building. The stench choked us, which wasn't surprising, it was a pigsty, in the filthiest meaning of the word.

The dandy who had followed us in, helped to chase the pigs into a corner and cleared a few square yards for the horses. His beautiful shoes kicked at rumps, his impeccably creased flared trousers trailed in the yellow, disgusting puddles.

There were spiders'-webs everywhere, but with a great deal of straw, some lucerne and some of the famous *coucouroutz*, the horses were much better off than out in the snow.

'O.K.?'

'O.K.'

'Pépé will show you your room ... I'll be off now. Good-night.'

And the fashion-plate departed. Not once had his expression or voice shown the least disgust and yet he had had every reason. It was quite obvious that if he had meant to call on his girlfriend, he would have to change from head to toe, and probably give himself a good squirt of after-shave. He definitely sent the stock of Yugoslav youth several points up in my estimation.

Mickey and Donald were so tired that they didn't even jib when they were led into the most disgusting stable they had ever seen.

I explained to Pépé that we would have to take our damaged horse to the vet.

'Not worth it,' he replied. 'I know what he'll tell you. Take my advice, I know all about horses. Disinfect the cut with slivovitz, rub the sore part well and put on a hot compress.'

After all, why not? The locals know their horses as well as we do, and their old wives' remedies have been proved often enough. We put on the hot bandages, without the massage, as there was no point in hurting the horse unnecessarily. We would be able to see the results next morning and then decide whether we should take him to the vet or not.

Our room was an absolute ice-box, as obviously no one in that neck of the woods had ever heard of heating. It must have been minus 18° or 20° and I couldn't pull off my gloves. The cuffs had frozen so hard that not even our activities or the heat of the pigsty had melted them. Corinne was clamped into a sort of medieval armour by her polo-neck sweater, which she couldn't get over her head.

'Don't you think we'd better sleep with the pigs? At least they'll keep us warm.'

'The pigs stink.'

Corinne agreed. However, having found there was water in the taps she had the extraordinary idea of washing her hair. It froze immediately into spiky stalactites, which wasn't at all comfortable on the pillow.

'You're quite mad to wash your hair when it's freezing so hard,' I told her.

'It was wet anyway and I thought I might just as well. We haven't had a wash for over a fortnight.'

'Dirt keeps the heat in. As long as we don't frighten the pigs we aren't any dirtier than the peasants, and it doesn't kill them, does it? You're going the right way about to catch pneumonia.'

Next morning, in the pigsty, the first thing I saw were the bandages Donald had managed to get rid of, dyed bright yellow by the urine which lay in puddles everywhere. He could hardly put any weight on the damaged leg, though his stiffness was probably the normal result of standing all night and I wasn't particularly alarmed. If he had been kicked it would take several days for the bruise to be absorbed, but just in case, I sent for the vet. His diagnosis: nothing broken, and his advice was exactly the same as Pépé's: rest and fomentations of hot slivovitz. I soon discovered that slivovitz is the Yugoslavians' panacea, and used mouthfuls of it to deaden a raging toothache. Later, Corinne gargled with it when she had a sore throat. Our host, on the other hand, swigged it happily from morning till night, for sheer enjoyment.

As for Donald, as a result of the alcoholic treatment, his cut soon began to heal, whereas Mickey seemed to be perfectly well, thank God, though he got very bored with being shut up inside four walls with a ceiling low enough for him to sweep away the cobwebs every time he moved his head. Not to mention the grunting of the pigs in their corner, and the universal stench. Corinne and I mucked out as best we could and tried to dry the ground, but the poor-quality straw used for bedding had quickly become soiled again and within a very short time Donald and Mickey were rolling in urine and their own droppings that were semi-liquid due to drinking cold water.

The slivovitz didn't produce the miraculous results we had all expected and Donald used his bad leg less and less. He hardly ever stood up and ate very little.

By now, everyone in the village knew us. Every time we met a local man or woman, child or old-age pensioner, they would mime an elaborate limp, which was their way of inquiring after Donald. It all became very tiresome, while the weather was perfect and the thermometer had climbed up to zero.

No snow had fallen for two days, and conditions would have been ideal, but alas, Donald was in no state to take the road again. He was off his food too, though we had cut it down considerably because of his lack of exercise.

Pépé did nothing to keep up our spirits: 'Your horse sick, a few kilometres more, and then kaput! No good for anything but salami. He won't get far, I tell you. Buy yourself another.'

I got the feeling he'd be quite ready to buy our Donald at a knock-down price, but nothing doing: I wouldn't for the world have let my little provençal end up as a sausage outside a Serbo-Croat pork butcher's. I wanted to get back on the road and sent for the vet for another opinion. Verdict:

'He needs another week's rest. If you start now, you'll kill him. Take this lotion and put on compresses three times a day. First a hot compress, then a dry bandage, then wrap it round with waterproof nylon and fix it with an elastic band.'

He also gave Donald an injection to improve his circulation, as the blood had thickened due to his enforced idleness. The thought of spending yet another week with that family didn't fill us with any kind of enthusiasm. Not that they weren't welcoming enough, but it wasn't all that funny to be squashed into a kitchen nine feet by nine feet, where Pépé's wife minced her pork in a cloud of greasy steam, watching over a fat baby and a clutch of newly hatched chickens. Then there were the women who came to buy a chicken or some milk, and stopped to gossip over a cup of thick black coffee, or the men who sat all over the place and drank sweet white wine. The quietest place was the stable when the pigs were taking their siesta, unless it got into Pluto's head to go and tickle them up.

The morning's programme was always the same: rub down the horses, followed by a short constitutional for Mickey who certainly needed fresh air. He pretended he was a stallion and lashed out in all directions so often and so efficiently that all the villagers shut their gates when they saw me coming. Then compresses had to be heated and reheated, bandages unwound and wound and finally applied from the hock to the loin. That idiot Donald had hurt himself in the most difficult spot of all to bandage. Fortunately, our friend Pépé was a man of infinite resource and managed with the help of some string to create a system which kept the bandage in place, let's say, on every other occasion.

Pépé was a curious character, sometimes kind, sometimes extremely gritty, which made me wonder if he too wasn't beginning to feel we were outstaying our welcome. I had the uncomfortable feeling that he wasn't too happy at seeing his barns gradually emptied of lucerne, even though we were paying the earth for what we used. I managed to thaw him out occasionally by drinking with him, and repeating the first word of Serbo-Croat I had learned, which was '*Jivél*'.

On one occasion we had an incident, caused by Pluto, who had gradually acquired permission to tiptoe into the kitchen, where he would enjoy himself with the carcass of the chicken which figured daily on our menu. He had been completely accepted the day he had allowed baby Suzanne to amuse herself by pulling his tail and ears. I have to admit I was somewhat uneasy, for I knew that Pluto wasn't exactly fond of children and their teasings. One evening he lost his temper, showed his teeth at the child and even nipped her arm, whereupon she yelled blue murder. It wasn't serious, but Pépé who had been there had turned grey with rage, and pointed his finger at me and the door, not to turn me out, but to remind me of the order to tie the dog up in the stable. I couldn't bear to leave him on a stinking pile of straw in pitch-darkness, and smuggled him up to our room and hid him under the eiderdown, where he promptly went to sleep.

A few minutes later, the door opened, and as I lay on the bed, Corinne came in with Pépé's very pretty young niece, Dubrovka, a delightful girl who provided us with a rare bonus, for she was learning French.

Dubrovka sat down on the end of the bed and I said to myself: 'Please God she doesn't discover that Pluto-the-Wicked is here, nice and warm, otherwise there'll be a drama, and we'll all be out on our ears with Donald hobbling on three legs.' The girl decided to read me a page of her textbook so I could correct her pronunciation.

'*Bonjour, mesdames, messieurs,*' she chanted, stressing every syllable.

Corinne was already half-asleep beside me. Pluto, lying between us, soothed by the reading, let out a couple of gentle snuffles which I tried to cut short by kicking him under the covers. Then a sonorous snore roused the little Yugoslav from her book, and she stared at me with wide eyes:

'Was that Corinne? Does she snore?'

'Yes, yes, it was Corinne. She snores.'

The matter would have rested there if Corinne hadn't opened one eye and sat up. While Dubrovka teased her, Pluto started to snore even louder and Dubrovka hunted all round the room, at one stage even looking under the bed.

'It sounds just like Pluto, but I can't see him anywhere.'

I pushed him a little further under the eiderdown while Dubrovka left the room. She came back a moment later, holding a dictionary. She was obsolutely transfixed. She looked at Corinne's stomach, opened the dictionary and exclaimed:

'Corinne ... snrr ... snrr ... Vaine ... tri ... lou ... qvist?'

I nodded vehemently.

'Yes, Corinne ventriloquist ... yes, oui, da, da ...'

For once Corinne had been able to stifle her giggles: what weren't we both capable of doing when it came to rescuing our Pluto from an awkward situation?

Whereupon Dubrovka rushed away to announce at the top of her voice that one of the two French girls possessed wonderful hidden talents, and next morning the entire village marched round to Pépé's to view the phenomenon.

Next day was Sunday, and we'd been stuck in Osijek for nearly a week, so we attempted an operation which we knew might take a very long time: put through a call to Nevers and give our parents the news. The post office most likely to help us was about three kilometres away. On the way we stopped at the café whose *patron* had so sweetly helped us find board and lodging and told him about our telecommunications project. One of his customers offered to take us in his car. Better still, he was even prepared to wait for us and bring us back. So much disinterested kindness didn't surprise us in the least, for our whole trip had been strewn with similar men of goodwill. The three of us therefore climbed into the car, Corinne, Pluto and I. Outside the post office I got out alone to ask for the call.

It took half an hour for the telephonist to inform me that there would be a three-hour delay. Corinne and our benevolent chauffeur rejoined me at this point to find out what was happening.

'In that case,' our driver said, 'I'll go and get some petrol.' He hadn't been gone thirty seconds when my sister pointed out casually that Pluto and our things were in the car: 'our things' being our bags with our money and all our cameras. I said 'Rush off and get them, or stay in the car with that character. If you like, go back without me, I can walk.'

Corinne reappeared alone, empty-handed: the character had disappeared. There was nothing to be done but wait and hope.

Time passed. We were put through to Nevers; highly emotional conversation with the parents. We went on waiting: our motorist still never showed up. I knew that we were having a petrol crisis, that there were queues at all the petrol pumps, but all the same . . . I gave Corinne a piece of my mind: she didn't know the man's name, she didn't even remember the number of the car. She didn't take kindly to the remarks I made regarding the level of her I.Q., and as her reactions merely fanned my fury, when the post office closed at nine o'clock, we were still standing on the pavement exchanging unflattering remarks.

There was nothing for it but to walk back, stopping at the café where we had met our thief. The *patron* didn't know him and had never set eyes on him before. Then Corinne remembered something which might put us on his trail: the individual had mentioned the name of the village where his mother lived. Perhaps he'd been speaking the truth, it was always possible. Next morning we rushed off to the village in question and found it quite easy to locate a mother whose son drove about in a German car, only she hadn't seen him for ages and had no idea where he could possibly be.

By the end of the afternoon the *patron* (who considered himself slightly responsible for what had happened), decided it was time to contact the police, who roared up and took us to the central Commissariat. The officer in charge began to take a considerable interest in us when he discovered that we had been in Osijek for some time and had omitted to register our presence in his district, a formality which we had thought we could quite easily ignore.

Fortunately the officer wasn't too much of a stickler. 'You mustn't forget to obey these instructions,' he said. 'I can't guarantee that all my colleagues will be so indulgent.'

'Thanks very much. But about this theft . . .'

'Yes, of course. Listen, go back and look after your sick horse. Come back tomorrow. We'll make some inquiries, get in touch with all the commissariats and the frontier posts. You haven't given us very much to go on, but we'll do our best.'

Two days went by and still there was no news. I was more and more worried about Pluto. Even supposing he was alive, what kind of miserable future would he have if our thief had really appropriated him? Poor Pluto, used to wall-to-wall carpeting, would he ever be able to live like his Balkan colleagues?

I had reached that point when I heard a scratch at the door in the middle of the night. I shook Corinne. 'Wake up—listen . . .'

'What's the matter? Another thief?'

'Listen. It sounds like a dog scratching.'

A dog barked. The Coquet sisters were on their feet in a flash, leaping downstairs to open the door. Pluto ran round in circles, yapping, dancing with joy. Dear creature. We were mad with excitement. The most important part of our belongings had been restored.

Early next afternoon we were told that our thief had been arrested and our cameras recovered, so if we would like to go to the police station at Darda for the necessary formalities . . .

An officer explained what had happened.

'Your thief was involved in a car crash and taken to hospital in a coma. His belongings, and yours, were handed over to us. Here they are. Will you sign this receipt, please? Thank you. Just one thing: will you come with me to identify the man . . .'

We went to see him and found him in a very bad way. Just as we were leaving, the officer told us how sorry he was that Pluto should have disappeared so completely.

'At the time of the accident,' he stated, 'someone saw him jump out of the car and take off, but we don't know what has become of him. There's not much hope of finding him again, you know; the accident happened fifty kilometres from here.'

Corinne and I looked at each other, winked and produced two enormous grins. The officer must have thought our Pluto's fate had left us very unmoved, but we quickly reassured him.

'He came home all by himself.'

'Incredible animals, these French dogs.'

CHAPTER TWENTY-ONE

Panic-Stricken

A few days later Donald had stopped limping, the damaged leg was cool and clean and we were able to start again. The prospect of a change of air cheered us up no end, but Pépé shook his head and made it quite clear he thought we were mad to be riding about at this time of year. Why couldn't we stay a little longer . . . as if ten days of coexistence hadn't been enough for him.

When I turned for a last look, Pépé was still there, a fantastic silhouette behind his gate. He had even forgotten his pigs and waved a friendly good-bye, so perhaps he wasn't such a villain after all.

I drew in great gulps of fresh air, and watched the Drava, a little river we would follow for quite a long way, where tiny icebergs in surrealistic shapes drifted slowly by.

In the main square at Bovota, on the way to Šid, a fine old man was waiting for God knows who or God knows what, but seemed friendly enough. I thrust my letter from the Yugoslavian Travel Bureau under his nose, and by a lucky chance he could read. He proceeded to declaim the letter aloud to a crowd of peasants attracted by our caravan. The revelation that we were French created tremendous enthusiasm among the spectators, including several children, and everyone started shouting joyfully:

'*Frantzouski! Frantzouski!*'

The old man was the only one who looked sad, for although he would have liked to put us up, he had no room. However, he grabbed a likely-looking lad and spoke to him rapidly.

'Branco will take you to a nearby farm,' he explained. 'They used to have horses in the old days.'

I was rather alarmed at the thought of having to go from door to door again in search of lodgings, but we could only follow Branco. By now it was pitch-dark and when he pointed to a house I could hardly make it out. All the rivers were dry, which meant the turbines couldn't function, so everyone used petrol lamps or candles. From 4.30 onwards, Yugoslavia was completely blacked out.

Branco called out the farmer, who couldn't put us up, but was willing to find room for the horses in his very fine stable. Unfortunately it was packed to the roof with bales of straw and hay. Without a murmur he cleared everything out, leaving his hay and straw in the open at the mercy of the wind, quite prepared to shovel it all back next morning. I wondered how many farmers in France would have done as much.

Fortunately a dozen kids formed a chain and gave him a hand, and once the stable had been cleared, with Mickey and Donald comfortably bedded down, they helped us unload our gear and stow it away. I asked if there were any oats. One of the boys said there were some in the next village, five kilometres away, and it wouldn't take him long on his bicycle.

Then we had to settle our own lodgings and another lad, Ivo, offered to give us dinner and put us up. His mother gave us a warm welcome, and a cream cheese I'm not likely to forget in a hurry. The young man was all over us, collecting ice which he melted and heated for our water-jug, and then rushing off to buy soap. We had barely had time to wash our hands when the candle gave up the ghost, and no one dreamed of lighting another, for it was already eight o'clock and I had the feeling only dyed-in-the-wool night-birds stayed up after that hour.

Ivo took our hands and led us to our room which was, in fact, his own. Naturally it was freezing cold, but we had got used to sleeping in four sweaters.

'*Dobro notché*,' he wished us before stretching out on four chairs against the wall. I wondered if he would be as good as he was kind, and the answer was yes.

The sun was hardly up when he brought us hot water, towels and soap, watching in amazement as we brushed our teeth:

apparently toothpaste was something unheard of in those parts. What a charmer he was! He never left us for a moment, escorting us to the lavatory and back again to the kitchen. In fact, he was so attentive that it became a trifle embarrassing: we could hardly carry out the more intimate side of our toilet while he was still there. Not that it mattered, for we could easily finish the rest with a handful of snow when we were out in the country again. War is war. Godfrey's soldiers couldn't have had much in the way of mod cons either.

By four o'clock the sun was setting over Devorac, a little village with a good many large barns, a sign they went in for big animals. We would probably be able to find lodgings without too much trouble, so we decided to spend the night there. Seeing our horses slipping on the ice, a peasant hailed us, and having been shown the famous letter of introduction, lifted his cap to show he had room for everyone.

The locals immediately pressed round, watching us unsaddle and rub down the horses. Then, without a word of invitation, they followed us into the house, where the peasant's wife produced slivovitz and Turkish coffee without a word—or a smile. This was by way of starters, for pork sausages and paprika salad quickly followed. We congratulated her on the excellence of her dinner by saying '*Dobro*', '*Dobro*', '*Fino!*' so often that we finally thawed her out.

By the time dessert appeared we had become her little girls, and she clasped us to her heart, explaining she had seven children, one daughter in Canada, a son in Austria and the others . . . I don't remember where. She brought a candle to show us the family album, and as a supreme mark of friendship, although he was muddied and filthy, Pluto was allowed to sit on the sofa.

The peasant didn't waste any time either: he told us that his eldest son was nearly nineteen, would soon have left the *lycée*, and looking from Corinne to me, said 'You should stay here in Yugoslavia and one of you could marry him. He's very good-looking, you know, and he has a fine farm. Why bother to go to Jerusalem?'

No sooner had the first batch departed than a second crowd arrived to bombard us with questions, which we did our best to answer, using gestures and mime when words ran out. As the room wasn't exactly a cinema, our host changed the audience every ten minutes, so that everyone had a good view. Only fifteen at a time, no need to push: the programme is continuous: and we had to do the whole thing over and over again, which was tiring, but excellent practice for our Serbo-Croat. On the stroke of eleven I began to yawn, and everyone was sent home.

When we came down to breakfast, another group was already sitting with glasses of slivovitz to see 'the two young French girls who are going round the world on horseback'—our ultimate goal having become somewhat exaggerated.

Our host owned a magnificent black stallion with a superb arching neck, and when I asked him to ride with us for part of the way, he slipped in the bit and sprang on to his enormous horse and sat comfortably bareback. Nervous and without studs, the horse skidded on the ice, but his rider kept his balance marvellously.

'*Dobro*,' I said, and added a whistle of admiration.

When we rode past the school, all the children rushed out of their classrooms yelling and shouting '*Frantzouski! Frantzouski!*' at the tops of their lungs. We couldn't get on until the teachers had beaten them back to their benches, and as they had never seen a tourist before, I imagine we'll be talked about in that village for at least a generation.

We found we were not alone on the road. A small skinny horse, with a moth-eaten coat, was pulling a cart loaded with two miserable cows, each flanked by her calf: another, equally rachitic, was hauling a load of coal: a wagon, with a horse and an ox yoked together, was sinking under the contents of an entire household: tucked away in another cart a shivering family huddled under a pile of torn skins, peeping at us through the rents. A peasant was dragging a reluctant cow by the horns and a woman and her children took up the entire width of the road as they drove a herd of black pigs along with yells and blows. The richest villagers rode past on fine stallions with silky coats, plaited tails and manes done up with pompons.

'It's probably fair-day in Šid,' I said to Corinne. 'How about it?'

I adore markets, and we hoped we might find some fur-lined

boots and warm gloves which we needed badly. Corinne was all for it. 'Let's tag along,' she agreed.

Riders overtook us at a smart trot, but no sooner had they passed than they stopped to take a closer look. If horses are the usual means of transport in Yugoslavia, riders are rarer and our scarlet and bright blue anoraks produced their usual effect. Corinne's was particularly startling, for having been torn by various branches it had been repaired with strips of lemon-yellow plastic, so she now sported two large asymmetrical crosses on her back. Godfrey de Bouillon's Crusaders frightened the natives, but looking as we did like Martians tumbled from the sky, we seemed to make everyone laugh. We had piled all the baggage on to Mickey to relieve Donald, and we were both on foot, so a peasant waved to us to climb onto the back of his cart where a woman, a young girl and a boy were already perched. There were a few small barrels piled in one corner.

'*Polako*,' I said. 'You'll go gently, won't you? Our horses can't go very fast.'

'*Isvolté*.' ['Just as you like.']

I climbed up and hitched Donald to the back of the cart, as they do to the colts in those parts to get them used to the road. He rebelled a little at first, but soon Corinne came to join me, and Mickey's company helped him to settle down.

The driver brought out a bottle of cider, passed it round, and each of us took a good swig: it took the skin off our teeth and burnt our throats as it went down. I astonished the noble company by using a piece of newspaper instead of a handkerchief, for I had a streaming cold. The driver demonstrated a better method of clearing your nose: pinch your nostrils between finger and thumb and breathe out sharply. You wipe off any excess on your clothes or the sides of the cart. It didn't look very difficult, and with a little practice I may be able to do it myself one of these days. Once the demonstration was over, we were offered dry bread and goat's cheese. As the cider had loosened all tongues, the women came out from under the pile of skins and soon we knew everyone's life story. The cow was being taken to be served by the bull: in the same spirit the girl was being shown to a farmer, for it was high time for her to have a husband, and the boy was planning to sell his barrels of plum brandy.

When we arrived, the market was in full swing. Empty carts were going home, their owners all smiles: everything had found a buyer. Drinks all round celebrated the sale of a cow. Voices were loud, laughter unrestrained. Taken out of the shafts, tied to a stake or grouped under a tree, a potato sack thrown over their withers, the horses were waiting. They seemed quite happy, munching the barley and chopped straw in their canvas nosebags but sometimes a fight would break out between the stallions and mares. A stallion would rear, another would lunge, there would be kicks, nips or a large piece of skin would be torn off bodily.

We jumped down and walked along the main alley between pigs, chickens and goats. We had to make ourselves as small as possible to let the carts go past between the leather goods, pots and such like. As we appeared, hands about to strike a bargain were suspended and tongues fell silent. Every eye followed us, rather too insistently, I thought, and I began to feel uneasy. The entire market population was soon packed round us, and Mickey in particular attracted the connoisseurs.

'I'll buy your horse for 1,000.'

'I'll give you 1,200.'

'1,500, cash in hand.'

I told them that in France he was worth 5,000.

'He comes from France?'

Whistles of admiration.

'He's got good legs. Three thousand, and I'll take the French horse.'

'He's not for sale. We just want to buy some boots!'

We were surrounded on all sides, mainly by men. Unable to move, I was really scared, yet there was no real reason to be worried and nothing about the men to suggest that they might be unfriendly. All the same, I was nervous of their bright eyes, and full-throated laughter. I said to Corinne 'Let's get out of here.'

'Yes, I agree.'

A little further on, we pulled ourselves together, and wondered what had got into us.

Anyway, as a result, we didn't buy any boots or fur-gloves, and our fingers and toes continued to freeze.

*

A church steeple. A steeple is always reassuring, even in Yugo-slavia, where the churches are filled with so many superb icons that they are always locked and double-locked. No priests ever seem to live near them, but by steering towards the house of God, we always seemed to find someone to help us. The village was called Martinci, and a man with a pepper-and-salt moustache was taking a walk. In that out-of-the-way spot where elegance and cleanliness were fairly rare, this gentleman was wearing a white shirt under his thick woollen sweater and sported a bow-tie.

'Let's ask him the way. He looks friendly enough.'

Alas, he spoke neither French, German nor English, and to crown everything, when we waved the letter from the Tourist Office at him, he seemed to be either short-sighted or illiterate.

A woman came past, carrying a muffled-up baby. She was wearing a long flowered dress with a black shawl over her shoul-ders, all that everyone in that Siberian climate seemed to wear, though they all went in for embroidered waistcoats (perhaps because it was as cold indoors as out). She spoke German, and said there was no stable to be had, but gave us directions as to where to find the local vet, three kilometres further on. A few minutes later, the vet in question arrived on his bicycle. Yes, he could look after Mickey and Donald and would we both like to go home with him?

When we got there, a nice surprise: a bathroom, proper plumb-ing and even hot water. This was a rare treat indeed, but I was considerably alarmed when in the middle of a nice wallow I saw two of the vet's friends arrive, then a third, and a fourth. Before the fifth could appear I pulled on my jeans, and half an hour later, the vet's living-room was crammed with all the lads of the village. We were used to that sort of thing, and as long as it was *en famille*, it might be boring to be treated like a circus act, but it wasn't alarming. In a bachelor establishment, it was a little nerve-racking, to say the least. Before long there were at least thirty of them, and as we watched vast quantities of beer and slivovitz disappearing, I became a little abstracted. I realised that Corinne was as nervous as I, and I began to feel anxious.

'Let's get away before anything goes wrong,' hissed Corinne.

'Where can we go? We can't just rush off into the night.'

'Listen, there may be another way. Look at that lad over there, he's got a kind face. Why don't we try and get him to look after us?'

Our chosen protector got the message immediately and carried us off to dine with him. Around eleven we came back with some food for Pluto, who we had left to guard our gear. The bags were still there, but no sign of Pluto. I called and whistled, thinking he might have been shut in somewhere and couldn't get out, but no sign. We hunted through every street in the village, still nothing.

'I'm tired and I'm giving up,' I said to Corinne. 'He'll come back when he's had enough. I'm going to sleep.'

I had hardly climbed into bed when someone knocked at the door and told Corinne he had seen a man drive off with Pluto in his car. He said the man was completely drunk, and the vet said he was one of his friends. He and Corinne set off after him, and to reassure me he said, 'I'll lock the windows and shutters and double-lock the door. Then nobody will bother you.'

'You mean somebody might try?'

He shoved an enormous dagger into my hand:

'Here, put this under your pillow. It will protect you.'

I found myself alone, and all the more nervous because the dagger was much too heavy for me to use.

A few moments went by—then a sound made me react like a heroine of a horror film. My hair stood on end and my eyes started out of my head, for what I heard was a key turning in the lock. The door opened, and I didn't quite know what to think when I saw our protector, Dara, come in. He closed the door and locked it, putting the key in his pocket.

'I'll stay here, it'll be safer,' he said and pulled out another huge dagger. So there I was, locked up alone in a room with a young man, calmly sharpening the blade of his dagger. Oh God, I prayed, how will this end? Where's Corinne? Struggling with the vet? And Pluto? Struggling with the drunk? My face must have been a study, for Dara felt he should reassure me. He showed me his dagger.

'You needn't be afraid. We can look after ourselves.'

I registered the 'We', since the only person I was really afraid of was the character in front of me playing with his knife.

'Besides,' he added, 'I've got something better here.'

He opened a drawer and showed me a kind of cosh mounted on a spring.

'What's that?'

He mimed the movement of chopping my neck. 'You can kill a man with one blow.'

'Really?'

'But this is even better,' he went on, returning to the drawer. 'No one can face it. It's very frightening, though it isn't always lethal. It makes no noise, and it's easy to carry.'

What he showed me, opening it solemnly, was a cut-throat razor and he rubbed it voluptuously against his finger. Perhaps he took my terrified stare for tiredness, for he pointed the dagger like an accusing finger at the bed and ordered: '*Spat!*' ['Sleep!']

He settled in an armchair and went back to polishing his dagger. What could I do but obey? I fell asleep, but not for long. Corinne came back, empty-handed, but with a whole host of new friends, determined to polish off the last of the vet's beer and spirits. I was so worn out by my various emotions that I fell asleep again. Afterwards I was told that the boys had made an appalling din all night, but I hadn't heard a thing. Nothing can disturb the sleep of the just.

Next morning we set off on our search. Corinne, the vet and I visited Pluto's presumed abductor, ten kilometres away and found our mongrel tied to the steering wheel of an elderly motor car. He must have been very cold in the night, but I wasn't in the least sorry for him.

'That'll teach you to get into just any old car with a complete stranger.'

We had all been scared to death, but no one had intended to harm a hair of our heads.

CHAPTER TWENTY-TWO

To Hell with the Militia

Impossible to stick to Godfrey all the time. If we followed the Danube until just north of Belgrade, we would have met a road which wasn't paved in his day, but which certainly is now, and it would have been very bad for the horses. So we preferred to tackle the first Balkan mountains via the river Sava. Unfortunately, although probably very pleasant in fine weather the roads were frozen and icy, without a single signpost and we landed up stuck in a marsh among six-foot reeds.

Eventually we crossed the Sava on a bridge of boats which was so odd-looking that I started to take pictures, but a dozen peasants shouted that it was forbidden. I took no notice. They insisted that it would get me into trouble with the militia (the local police), so I put away the camera. I still can't believe a bridge of boats could be important strategically.

By the time we got to Debrc, it was dark, but one café was still open. We showed our letter of introduction to an old man who took us to see his son. But the son had no room for the horses, so there we were back in the street, if it could be called a street, in a freezing snowstorm. The horses dropped their heads and went to sleep, backs to the wind, while huge snowflakes fell and melted on their coats.

A man came up, wearing an unidentifiable uniform, and made an incomprehensible speech, which he interrupted by asking 'Parlez-vous français?' Without waiting for an answer he burst out laughing, and then brandished a golden star and shouted 'Tito! Tito!' at the top of his voice.

As we continued to ignore him, he addressed a bystander. '*Parlez-vous français?*' he said, shaking with insane laughter. 'Communist! Communist! Tito! Tito!', and the golden star flashed in the darkness.

Aroused by the commotion the man who had had no room for us came back to see what was happening. The two Yugoslavs exchanged a few words. As far as I could make out, the character with the star was telling the other off for his disregard of the laws of hospitality. Words turned to blows, and Pluto joined in, barking until the militia appeared and after separating the combatants, demanded to see our papers. I produced our letter of introduction and our passports.

'Very good,' said the captain. 'Come with us. We'll look after you.'

They took us into a half-finished house where the horses would be under cover. They produced some maize and—who would believe it—some oats. Top marks for the militia.

We girls were handed over to an old woman who peered at us through thick glasses with filthy lenses. Grimly, without a word, she showed us into her house and proceeded to heat up something—I could swear it was stewed cat—on a filthy stove black with accumulated fat. She cleaned two plates by rubbing them between finger and thumb, and the fork she gave me was so greasy that I had to wipe it on my trousers to stop it slipping out of my fingers.

The animal remains she threw onto my plate weren't exactly appetising, but I tried heroically to swallow a mouthful. It was no good and yet I was very hungry. Well, Pluto could have it, but Pluto couldn't swallow it either. Perhaps the remains of a loaf might be edible, I thought, even if it was covered in black ink from being wrapped in newspaper. I cut a slice, and a long black hair came away with it, which put paid to my appetite.

There was nothing for it but to go to bed, not on the dusty pile the old woman showed me—I was too afraid of fleas—but thanking heaven for my sleeping-bag.

Next morning, we passed peasants on foot (though one or two were pushing bicycles), each holding a dog on a leash, or more exactly, a string. In Yugoslavia the dogs are chained up in backyards, or run about freely, but we'd never before seen any of them being taken for a walk.

What was happening? Perhaps they were all going to be vaccinated, for several cases of rabies had been reported in the district.

In one village square, dozens of men, each with stick in hand, were waiting with their dogs. They couldn't be going hunting for none of them had guns, and my curiosity finally got the better of me.

'*Chto éto?*' ['What's happening?']

Apparently a wolf in the forest had been eating chickens and had killed several pigs. He had to be tracked down and every available man and dog in the village had been called in to join the hunt. They didn't seem at all afraid, though all they had were sticks. In France everyone had said Pluto would be gobbled up by ferocious Dobermanns in Yugoslavia, but I never saw anything larger than a fox-terrier.

All day I kept one eye firmly fixed on him, and wouldn't let him flit off into the woods. He wouldn't last long if he did meet the big bad wolf.

Jabucje (pronounced Yaboutch): two syllables that make my mouth water, for it reminds me of a charming little village perched on a mountain, where sitting in the doorway of a big house we saw a handsome old man with an impressive white handlebar moustache. His white shirt was immaculate and he seemed very friendly. If his house was like its owner, and if we could stay with him, it would be ideal.

We showed him our passport-letter but he indicated he hadn't got his glasses and called another man out of the house, who spelled out the text with some difficulty. After a moment he asked: 'Italian?'

Obviously he hadn't understood a word.

'Not Italian, French! *Frantzouski.*'

'*Frantzouski? Dobro, dobro.*'

For two French girls they were ready to do anything. The rest of the family rushed up, barriers were pushed aside, the cows moved out and the cowshed disinfected. Finely embroidered cloths were spread on the table and sideboard while someone ran off to fetch a girl student who spoke a little French, the professor who taught English and the doctor who spoke German. A big dish of the Yugoslav speciality was passed around, a very sweet kind of preserve, accompanied by glasses of water. In case you ever find yourself in a similar situation, grab as much as you can the first time round, for it is delicious and you don't get a second chance. To wash down the jam a neighbour brought in Turkish coffee, followed by ratakiza, a liqueur which clears your throat and takes away the gritty taste of the coffee.

The hospitable peasants needed convincing that we had to look after the horses before we had our own dinner, but once the stable-work was over, the old man with the white shirt invited us in. His wife had cooked roast potatoes (our favourite food), roast chicken and apple fritters which I enjoy. What am I saying? When Maman cooked fritters at home I never touched them, so was it because I was homesick that I liked everything that reminded me of France? After our unhappy experience the previous night we were immediately reconciled to Yugoslav cooking.

The entire village fought for the privilege of giving us breakfast, and the girl student came to collect us on behalf of the professor.

'He thought you were so pretty with your pink cheeks, and you're so young and brave!' she told us. 'He wants to marry one of you, though he didn't say which! Do come along! He's only twenty-five, but he's a professor already.'

She was all excitement, but at that time of the morning we weren't feeling romantic and offers of marriage could wait. For the moment we were perfectly happy with our surroundings. I didn't feel in the least like flirting. To crown everything there was hot water in the house so we could really clean ourselves up.

A village woman begged us so insistently to come to her for a coffee that we finally gave in, in spite of the inevitable delay. The coffee was only a pretext.

'These are for you,' she said, giving us each a parcel, 'a souvenir from Jabucje.'

There was a charming mauve scarf for Corinne, and a nightdress for me.

Yugoslavia is really wonderful—sometimes!

*

With every step our escort increased, and by the time we started loading the horses at least 200 pairs of eyes were watching us, from behind the fence. Just when everything was ready—horses saddled, baggage safely tied, thanks and farewells completed, an individual arrived to inform us that we had been summoned to appear at the police station.

Corinne went first, and in the friendly confusion didn't really understand the situation, so when she reached the officer in charge, she asked for some stamps for her postcards. When I arrived a few minutes later, holding our passports at the ready, I realised that he wasn't best pleased. I handed over our letter of introduction, which he read, and re-read, and then read all over again. He inspected it in every direction, turning it over and over. Something seemed to worry him and yet that same letter from the Yugoslav Tourist Office in Paris was perfectly explicit and up until then had been our most useful possession. Eventually I gathered the reason for his suspicions: there was no stamp over the signature and he thought the letter was a forgery.

'How much did you pay for this letter?' he asked.

No luck: we hadn't paid anything.

Next he examined our passports and couldn't find the stamp from the Yugoslav Consulate. I pointed it out.

Then he lingered over the American visa on my passport which he didn't seem to like for he frowned heavily.

'You've been to America?'

'As you can see.'

'When did you leave Paris?'

'It's written in the letter.'

'When did you enter Yugoslavia?'

'That's written under the stamp of the frontier post.'

He re-examined the passports and seemed to spend as much time on the blank pages as over the others. He became more and more irritated—and irritating.

'Where are you going now?'

'To Bulgaria.'

'Where are the authorisation papers for the horses?'

It was the first time anyone had asked for the papers in the middle of a country. As I hadn't got them on me, I had to go back and fetch them from one of the saddle-bags. We had already wasted two hours, and I began to feel I'd had enough and started to lose my temper.

Outside, the entire village were gathered, 300 people at least. Had a rumour started that we were spies? Had the authorities got wind of our crime, in other words, our attempt to photograph the bridge of boats? I pushed my way through with the greatest difficulty.

When he had to admit that the horses' 'passports' were as much in order as our own, the officer embarked on another tack, apparently unable to understand the reasons for this long trip on horseback.

'Haven't you enough money to buy a car?'

Poor man! How could we explain that with the current price of horses in France, we could have afforded a car each.

With tightened lips he turned once more to a study of our passports. 'How much money have you?'

'Enough.'

'Meaning?'

How maddening he was! I showed him a few Yugoslav notes and when he counted them they added up to about 200 dinars.

'Not much for such a long journey,' he announced.

'We shall be picking up some more in Sofia.'

'It's very little, even to get you through Yugoslavia.'

I laid before him a folder of traveller's cheques.

'Will that be enough?'

'What are they?'

I had to go into a long explanation as to their use and as they were payable in Deutschmarks he was very impressed.

Would he let us go after that? No.

Do you have any photographic equipment? Yes. Have you taken any photographs in Yugoslavia?

If I said no, he wouldn't have believed me. If I said yes, the monster was quite capable of confiscating my films. It would be a pity, but what could I say?

'Yes, I have taken some pictures.'

'What of?'

Before I had time to reply, one of the peasants piped up: 'This morning she took pictures of our pigs and turkeys.'

Everyone, including me—but not our officer—burst out

laughing. Whereupon I lost my temper completely. I pointed out that all our papers were in order, that we'd done nothing wrong, that he could telephone our embassy if he had any doubts, and finally, that he'd wasted enough of our time already.

When I stopped screaming at him, he looked at me blandly and replied '*Né resoumé*' ['I don't understand'], and added, completely unmoved, 'there is a woman in the next town who speaks French very well. I'll send for her and then we'll understand each other better.'

The interpreter in question arrived an hour later and did indeed speak French very well. Through her the officer asked all the same questions and got the same replies. There was one more, all the same: 'How can you go off on such a long trip? You must be very rich.'

'No, no, we're not. The club is paying our expenses.'

My apologies to *Le Journal de Mickey*, but I didn't want to explain that we were being subsidised by a newspaper and were to some extent journalists. I was afraid that in those parts 'journalist' might be a synonym for spy.

But immediately our inquisitor relaxed.

'The club,' he said, 'ah, the club . . .'

I will never know why that word had the effect of an 'open sesame', but he immediately handed over our documents.

'That's O.K., you can go. Have a good journey.'

'You aren't angry?' asked the interpreter. 'Here it's normal, you know, we always have to answer when the police question us.'

I couldn't exactly tell her we were only too delighted to spend a whole morning at the police station.

It was twelve o'clock already, which meant we'd have to travel for four hours in the dark if we were to keep up our daily average of forty-five kilometres, so we followed a track reserved for ox-carts, which motor vehicles normally never used. And yet a small Fiat overtook us, hooting imperiously. A large 'M' and a red star told its own story—once again it was the militia. What on earth did they want this time?

The officers saluted us smilingly—they were just on a routine tour of inspection. Quite obviously they were keeping an eye on us.

It was eight o'clock when we called a halt at Kruševac, and it had been dark for two hours. In such a village we always found a café open and someone who could read our letter of introduction. This time everything was normal, except that our chosen reader took half an hour to read ten lines to the assembled company. But alas, try as they might, the Kruševacians couldn't think of any suitable place for us to stay. Then one of them had a brilliant idea. 'We must ask the militia: they'll know what to do.'

I protested vehemently. 'The militia? Never! No, no . . .'

But a small boy had already darted off and returned within five minutes with a gentleman in the uniform I was sick and tired of seeing. The officer asked what the trouble was and everyone answered him at once. Then he turned to us:

'*Dokoument?* Passport?'

That was the only thing he could think of when our horses had spent all day in the snow and it was time they were fed and relieved of the weight they had been carrying since 7.30 that morning. I'd had the militia in a big way—to hell with them all, and as the man in question understood German, I began to storm at him with Corinne's able support. It was a major tirade, compared to which my reactions that morning were a bunch of compliments. I screamed at him that if our horses dropped dead it would be his fault, and I wound up by declaring: 'Stable first, passports afterwards.'

He thought for a moment, and I wondered if he was about to cast me into the deepest of his dungeons for insulting an officer in the exercise of his functions, but after a moment he said, 'Come with me.'

I wasn't going to compromise. I insisted: '*Stalle?* Stable?'

'*Ja, stalle.*'

But the one he showed us was too small, as even he agreed, so we went back to the café where in the interval of finding a solution to the problem he offered us a drink. Better still, he spoke to an elderly customer, who could apparently provide us with something, though it was four kilometres further away, up in the mountains. We had no choice, so off we went, climbing after our new host.

We had barely covered half the distance when I felt my legs going limp, my head began to spin and I clung to Mickey's mane as he climbed on happily as if he knew the road to the stable. I slipped, fell off and found myself sitting in the snow. I wanted to laugh and laugh, and realised I was stoned out of my mind! The wine on an empty stomach, tired as I was, had proved too much for me.

Corinne was clinging to her own horse, but when she saw me, she, too, rolled off into the snow and we both laughed till we cried. Our guide laughed too, but the horses plodded on. We couldn't catch up with them, and ran along, slipping and stumbling, still laughing like idiots.

Under a full moon, the landscape was out of a fairy-tale, but all I could do was laugh.

The horses had stopped of their own accord outside the warm stable, but it was occupied by some cows that had to be brought out and put into a cowshed. There were three of them, so our host took one and left us to cope with the other two, but grabbing a cow by the horns when you aren't used to it, and pulling it along an icy path isn't all that easy, and when you're high as kites and your dog joins in the fun, it can be extremely dangerous.

My cow took on Pluto and plunged round furiously, trying to get at him. I clung firmly to her horns but she swung me round and with a toss of her head flung me into a ditch full of liquid manure.

Corinne, dragged along by her cow and chased by mine, grabbed the branch of an apple-tree and hung on to it, while the old fellow was knocked down by his own cows as they rushed into the cowshed. Talk about laugh! Eventually I managed to climb out of the ditch.

Grandpa even had some oats hidden in his attic, a small consolation for our horses, and when he wanted to know what we would like to eat ourselves, we settled for some meat and a kind of cottage cheese which is delicious when it is fresh. Alas, the meat reminded us of the unappetising mess at Debrc, and the cheese, which must have been at least three weeks old, hadn't aged gracefully. Besides, the smell of the manure was becoming too much for me, and the laughter had quite died in my throat. I began to feel very cold and wasn't even hungry. I nibbled a little so as not to upset Grandpa, and the smell of the manure got worse and worse. However, there was no way of washing it off, for the pump was frozen solid.

Grandpa fired questions at us all the time, and we grew tired of telling him we didn't understand a word he said, which was at least three-parts true. Corinne began to lose her temper. '*Né resoumé! Né resoumé,*' she repeated.

I tried to soothe her as I began to suspect he wasn't quite right in the head.

'Be careful, don't upset him,' I advised her. 'We're alone with this lunatic in the depths of the country. Do take care: let's talk to him in French. He'll get bored with it before we do.'

The tactics proved successful. Surprised and annoyed at not being able to understand, the old man showed us to our beds. It was midnight.

I was fast asleep when he shook me awake.

'Passport?' he asked.

I couldn't believe it. Everyone seemed to have the same obsession.

I asked him why he wanted our passports.

'I must know who you are. Perhaps you're bad people!'

For heaven's sake, here was this grandfather unable to sleep because he was afraid of us. But I hadn't the energy to get out of bed and no intention of showing him our passports. I snapped at him: '*Passeport soutra!* Passports tomorrow!'

Once more he retired to bed, but an hour later, the light was switched on again.

'I'm going to water the horses!' the idiot announced.

Why couldn't he leave the horses in peace?

At two o'clock, a fresh disturbance. This time he said nothing, but wanted to take Pluto outside, whereas the poor dog was dead to the world and growled ferociously because he doesn't like being disturbed in the night. The old man finally left Pluto where he was.

We'd scarcely got back to sleep when loud music rang through the house and woke us again.

'There'll be some news soon,' he explained. 'I always listen to the early morning bulletin.'

It was three o'clock. At four, he finally rose and got dressed.

'I'll go and feed the horses!'

'No, no. The horses need to sleep. They don't eat as early as this!'

At five, the idiot tried again to get Pluto to go out, but on the other hand, having asked him to wake us at six, he left us to sleep. He must have thought we needed it. I was finally roused by daylight.

By nine o'clock we were on our way down the mountain, late again, but I suppose it could have been worse. We hoped to catch up on our schedule, unless . . .

At the entrance to the village there were two cars, four militiamen and several onlookers barring the way.

'*Dobroyoutro*. Good day. Passports?'

A road-block, just for us. What an honour. I brought out the passports and could feel myself getting ready to explode. The militiamen gave our documents a cursory glance, handed them back, waved to us to proceed and saluted. The whole thing hadn't taken more than a minute, and I had barely had time to get worked up. But I imagined it was merely a deferred pleasure.

CHAPTER TWENTY-THREE

Surprise, Surprise

At the outskirts of Lapovo—we had bypassed Belgrade to the west and moved into Morava—my horse balked, sniffed, snorted and refused to move on.

A stretcher-cart drawn by two huge white oxen was coming towards us. The corpse wasn't even covered with a shroud, and in the cart, standing or kneeling, were women dressed in black, screaming hysterically and beating their breasts frenziedly. An incredible sight to meet at dusk.

At a grocery shop which was still open we asked for a stable, and they agreed to find us one, but first we must show our passports to the militia—of course. Afterwards we were sent to spend the night with a lad who spoke French reasonably well, and for very good reason: normally he lived in the République district in Paris and had only returned to Yugoslavia for a few days' holiday with his family. He expressed his pleasure at being of service to semi-compatriots.

We settled into the room he showed us, though it stank to high heaven of a mixture of dry rot, damp rot and stale air, with bouquets of plastic flowers all round the bed. In addition, the sheets were filthy, but too tired to care we stretched out, closed our eyes and fell asleep—until a violent uproar woke us up.

I recognised the old woman in a shawl whom we had seen in the cart with the body, and indeed she had seemed to be the leader of the mourners' chorus.

'Hey, hey, what are these girls doing here, Branko?' she demanded, hiccuping.

'Maman, they are two French girls who have ridden here from Paris on horseback,' her son replied.

'My poor husband ... dead ... in this very bed ... he lay there for a week, waiting for my son to come home from Paris ... Oh ... oh ... his very room ... oh ... oh ... he died of gangrene ... one leg had already been taken off, but the infection spread all over his body ... oh ... oh ...'

Immediately I identified the smell in the room which hadn't been aired since the departure of the late owner for his final resting place. I daren't move for fear of breathing in the dead man's dust. I could feel the gangrene infecting my own body, but how could I find another room? It was very late, and I was exhausted. The old woman and her Parisian son departed and I fell immediately into a heavy sleep, full of appalling dreams. The cart and the oxen came in through the window, bringing back the ghastly, pallid old man. He rose slowly and floating silently across the room, took one of my legs, leaving me one of his, and departed, fully restored to health, standing in his cart and whipping up the oxen, like a cross between Hippolytus and Ben-Hur.

The leg stiff with gangrene hurt me horribly and I opened my eyes to discover Pluto using it as a pillow, his eighteen kilos being quite enough to explain my nightmare.

Corinne hadn't batted an eyelid, even when the old woman's funeral oration reached its climax, and she'd slept through everything. Her sense of smell, normally very sensitive, hadn't been upset by the odours from beyond the grave.

A few days later it was Saturday. Our horses were entitled to their weekly rest, and we could make a quick trip to Belgrade to pick up mail and packages, which we knew would be waiting for us at the Embassy.

A quick trip, yes, but how? By train? There was only one, which left at 11.30 and arrived at five o'clock: five and a half hours to cover 100 kilometres. No, thanks, as there'd certainly be no one at the Embassy by that time. What about a bus? We checked at the coach station. A crowd gathered and fifty people simultaneously offered advice. There was only one point on which everyone was in agreement: we had no chance whatever of getting to the capital before lunch, and yet it was barely nine o'clock. I showed my surprise.

'I was told there was a bus every hour.'

'In principle, yes. In fact, one day yes, one day no. This isn't Paris. The bus either comes or it doesn't. You have to stand here and wait. Who can say?'

I must specify that Lapovo, where that scene took place, isn't a forgotten spot in the mountains: it is a town of about 30,000 on one of the busiest roads in Europe. But once more the gods were with us. Round the corner came a bus, which stopped.

'Quick, quick, get in,' everyone said, pushing us towards the door.

But the conductor intervened.

'No room!'

Our supporters burst into a single cry: '*Frantzouski! Beograda ambassada!*'

Confronted by these arguments, the conductor relented and beckoned us in, but only us. The thirty people who had been waiting ahead of us were left to wait for the next bus—if there was one.

When I say there was no room, the conductor wasn't exaggerating. People were sitting on each other's laps, while others were trying to balance precariously among packages and crates from which a chicken or a goose occasionally escaped.

As always, we were given the VIP treatment, for when two passengers got out we were immediately given their seats, but even so, we could hardly breathe. One man of about forty, bald and pot-bellied, began by leaning against my head-rest, and then more and more, on me. The more I squeezed up alongside Corinne, the more he bent over.

So many others had pestered me that I decided to teach this character a lesson and without a word of warning drove my elbow violently into his bread-basket, and sent him reeling back on to the lap of a peasant sitting on the opposite side of the gangway. After that, Baldy left me in peace. It was a trick I had seen used in the United States by disciples of Women's Lib, so I had at least learnt something during my time there.

The journey would have been almost bearable if the driver hadn't stopped every ten minutes at a café, to chat with a pal, or let the engine cool. I began to wonder how we would get to Belgrade by noon, as the timetable had promised, when a final hissing shattered my illusions. A puncture!

Everyone had to get out. Geese and chickens strolled about the main highway without anyone seeming to care. As the spare wheel was punctured as well, there was nothing for it, but to wait for the next bus, which appeared eventually, packed to the roof; but no matter, solidarity in Tito's country isn't a meaningless word. We would have to squeeze up a little more, that was all. Up I got with Corinne, and believed I should have to spend the rest of the journey on the step, but the pressure built up behind me so successfully that I found myself standing on a crate occupied by a squealing sucking-pig. Only one foot was actually on the crate as I clung desperately to the bar, bending my head so as not to keep hitting the roof. At every bump I was hurled against my long-suffering neighbours.

But what was this? Once again Serbian manhood asserted itself and a hand began to feel me in a tender spot. Once, twice . . . it couldn't possibly be the pot-holes but a sign of admiration from the young man directly beside me. The new offender had to learn *his* lesson, and a good kick from a French boot landed right in his stomach. The hand didn't return. The Yugoslavs can't have appreciated my cowboy behaviour.

Terminus. Everybody out.

At the Embassy we climbed an imposing staircase just as a group of distinguished-looking men came down. Closing time. The diplomats recognised us immediately, although we had thought we were wearing city clothes, but perhaps the smell of horse-flesh was more penetrating than we imagined.

Clarisse, the Ambassador's secretary, greeted us. She was a charming young woman, very dynamic and direct, and took us straight to her flat.

'I have a bathroom . . .'

For three weeks we had only been able to wash our hands and faces in icy water, and I imagine it was painfully obvious.

'Besides,' she added, 'I have a parcel for you.'

The parcel was really enormous, and we knew what was in it, for Maman had already told us that a manufacturer of warm underclothes would be sending us a selection of his products. He had been more than generous and there was no question of our being able to take all the waistcoats, long pants and other garments.

The trying-on session after our baths was fairly picturesque. I fixed my choice—among other things—on a body-stocking in ultra-fine lace, paper-thin, which would keep out the wind and keep in the warmth. It was absolutely ideal, for it left me complete freedom of movement. Corinne's favourite was some long flannel underwear which clung to her curves lovingly. What were we to do with the rest? Clarisse benefited from a selection, as she was an expert skier, and the remainder was packed up and sent home.

Five o'clock: time to get back to Lapovo. At the bus-stop there was a depressingly long queue, and even the Coquet sisters couldn't hope that so many people would allow them priority. Fortunately there was a train at six, but unfortunately it arrived three and a half hours late and left from a different platform from the one announced, so there we were, out of temper and exhausted, stuck in a kind of aeroplane hangar, swept by the most penetrating of icy blasts.

Back to the bus-stop. The next was due to leave at midnight, and better still, there were two seats available. I reckoned that at night, on a fairly good road, with no traffic, the trip shouldn't take more than two to two and a half hours at most. When we got to Lapovo, four o'clock had long since rung out from the church clock.

And to think that as far as we were concerned, this was a day of rest.

CHAPTER TWENTY-FOUR

An Unusual Christmas

On Christmas Day we were anxious to find somewhere with a station, for Clarisse had invited us to a party at the Embassy and we also wanted to go to midnight mass in Belgrade. We would have to stop earlier than usual and find a stable, arrange our night's lodging and change. We could try and catch a train, always remembering that we had to be back early enough to start again next morning at eight o'clock. After our experience on the Lapovo–Belgrade trip, I knew it was asking a good deal, but 'there's no harm in trying', as my New York friends were fond of saying.

Alas, the Morava, along whose banks we had been travelling for fifteen kilometres, suddenly became extremely tortuous, and from Stalać onwards it ran through deep gorges. The levee road stopped abruptly at the foot of a cliff, so we followed some cattle that were climbing up to a cluster of cave dwellings cut out of the rock, and then we found a very steep goat-track, which seemed to go up and up.

'This isn't Christmas,' joked Corinne wittily, 'it's Ascension Day.'

At three we reached the top. What a view! We could see the winding curves of the Morava, which flows north as far as Belgrade, and the dark masses of the Balkans to the east.

A few hundred yards below, there was a village on the bank with a railway track and a building: obviously a station. A glance at the map showed that the village was called Braljina, and I reckoned we could get down to it in about half an hour, after which it would be the devil's own luck if we couldn't catch a train for Belgrade.

There was only one small problem: the goat-track had stopped, and the slope was so steep that I wouldn't have attempted it, even on foot. To the left, the ground seemed to fall away less steeply, but could I risk taking two heavily loaded horses down it? On the grassy part it might just be possible, but after that it was bare rock. However, we had to try.

With the first step, Mickey dislodged a loose stone and slipped at least two yards down the slope, I snatched at the pommel and called back to Corinne, 'Stay there, it's too dangerous. I'll try and get back up. See if you can't find another way.'

Corinne, who had been gazing at the slope with a certain uneasiness was entirely in agreement. For once . . .

Now I had to turn round. I was afraid that Mickey might fall over backwards. He is very sure-footed, but when it came to imitating a goat . . . It might have been wiser to unload him to give him more freedom of movement, but how could we hoist the saddle and gear up a steep slope when I could barely lift the saddle on level ground? I didn't dare go down, or climb up again—it was a really alarming situation. Finally I decided to try and climb up again and began by making sure I was balanced myself, then put a stone behind one of Mickey's hind feet. Immediately he sprang forward, gained a few inches and slipped back until he was checked by a jutting rock. However, he had made some progress, but by the time we got to the top, his legs were covered in scratches, he had bumped his knee, my own knees were bleeding and we were both out of breath. I looked at my watch: we had been struggling for half an hour and we were still equally far from our station.

I began to be afraid we should have to spend Christmas in the open, as there was only half an hour of daylight left, and we couldn't possibly go on after dark, as it would be too dangerous.

Corinne explored the plateau. 'There isn't a road anywhere!'

'There was at least the one we came by. We must have gone wrong somewhere. It probably carried on round the mountain.'

A few kilometres further back we came to a fork in the road, which split into several paths. The first petered out; the second was overgrown with thorns; the third took us a little further, went round the mountain, growing narrower and narrower, and finally disappeared into the undergrowth. But we were still going downhill. Branches whipped our saddle-bags, thorns tore our clothes; a briar scratched Corinne's face. Stones rolled under the horses' hoofs. Still we pressed on. The sun sank. We had made good progress, but were brought up short again when the slope became too steep. Can't be helped: try again further east.

This time we came out onto meadows still lit by the last rays of the sun and followed a stream which flowed down into the Morava.

It ran through a wood, but as there was very little water we were able to use it as a path, and the cold water soothed Mickey's scratched legs. By the time we reached the foot of the mountain it was pitch-dark.

'Let's follow the evening star,' I said, 'perhaps it will guide us to a stable.'

At the first house we were given a warm welcome. No room for us or our horses? What did it matter: the cows were brought out of the cowshed and sent round to lodge with some neighbours. So were the children. So the two travellers and their faithful mounts were comfortably installed and I was even given a bottle of vinegar and some flannel to make compresses for Mickey's poor legs.

I asked if there was a train for Belgrade and was met with great curiosity. What did we want in Belgrade at that time of night? I explained that it was Christmas. Our hosts shook their heads: they were orthodox, of course, and would only be celebrating the nativity (if indeed they intended to) in thirteen days' time.

Frankly, we weren't very upset at the thought of missing the party, for we were utterly exhausted and in any case we would be too late for midnight mass. Was it really worth making a round trip of 300 kilometres to eat Christmas cake with complete strangers? All the same, it had been very kind of Clarisse to invite us.

I thought of what would be happening at home, at Nevers; the Christmas tree, the presents, with Maman very sad because her two daughters weren't with her.

'Why don't we ring up Maman?' I suggested.

'Provided there's a telephone in the village.'

Yes, there was one, in a tailor's shop which was also the village post office. We waited for four hours to be put through and then: 'Hallo, Maman? Hallo, Maman?'

Garglings and gurglings ... I hoped this extraordinary call wouldn't upset her. I kept yelling: 'Hallo, Maman? Hallo, Maman?'

Miracle. I could hear. 'Hallo, Maman, happy Christmas! Happy Christmas!'

Maman was delighted. So were we. Who cares about presents?

All the same we did get a present, and a splendid one. For some days we had been enduring cold, wind and rain with a courage worthy of a better cause, and the peasants had assured us that soon the mercury would fall to minus 30°. Well, on Christmas morning, it was 15° above. Thirty degrees higher than the previous day. Thank you very much, Father Christmas.

CHAPTER TWENTY-FIVE

Terror on the Motorway

In spite of their adventures the horses didn't seem to have suffered too much, and our farming friends showed us a pleasant route they normally took with their ox-carts. For the first time I noticed that the oxen wore shoes: two thin plates fastened on with dozens of tiny spikes, which leave odd prints on the ground.

'It's not so strange,' Corinne told me, 'they do exactly the same thing at home in the Lozère.'

It was a new experience for me, as I had never seen anyone shoeing an ox.

The rocky landscape towering above the Morava is really magnificent and very impressive when you travel through it on a path so narrow you risk your life at every step.

From path to road, from road to street, we reached the centre of Aleksinac: a fairly large town, modern and prosperous, judging by the television aerials sprouting from every roof and the number of factory chimneys polluting the sky. We asked for information, but the idea that there might be a riding-club or stabling in this industrial city made our informants smile.

'Suppose we asked the militia to help us out?' suggested Corinne.

Why not? The central bureau wasn't far away and I put together a mass of papers which I was quite sure would be conscientiously examined. In the meantime the locals behaved like any Parisian crowd: hundreds of them pressed round us, so that when I entered the office of the forces of law and order, the chief must have wondered why a riot appeared imminent under his window. Naturally he took his time—and ours— to test the 'passports' and '*dokouments*', then removed his cap and scratched his head.

'I really don't know how I am to find a stable,' he complained, then suddenly murmured, as if to himself; 'Just a moment . . .'

He dialled one number, then another and then a third. Then he sent a car off to reconnoitre. The driver came back barely ten minutes later and said a few words. His superior broke into a dazzling smile. What we required was less than 150 yards away, and he instructed one of his subordinates to take us—to the municipal slaughterhouse. Maybe the local police weren't so stupid after all.

Our horses were received royally and looked after by experts. Pluto wasn't forgotten either and was offered a chunk of meat which he gorged on to the point of indigestion.

Corinne and I were supposed to go to the local hotel but I was a little worried at leaving our companions in a slaughterhouse, for mistakes can easily happen. The butchers might in good faith knock off the occupants of stalls numbers forty-two and forty-three without realising they were the bravest equine heroes of our time. I asked if I could be allowed to sleep in the straw with Mickey and Donald, but the militiaman wouldn't hear of it.

'No way!' he said with a knowing smile. 'A girl on her own with all those butchers!'

Quite! But as an alternative, couldn't we lock the door? Yes, that was possible, and off I went, a trifle reassured.

That militiaman was really charming. Before taking us to the hotel he asked us out to dinner, and then escorted us back and up to our very room, which he entered with us, and then locked the door behind him.

It didn't take long to discover the reason for such devotion and any misunderstanding was completely dispelled because he kept repeating in English: 'Sleep with me . . . Sleep with me . . .'

In the language of Shakespeare I explained that impossible means the same in French, particularly when used by a woman, and he seemed very embarrassed.

'You really don't want to?'

'Really not.'

He still insisted, very surprised, as if what he wanted was understood, as if we were expected to tip him in kind. You never can tell with these volcanic Balkans.

And then abruptly he turned, opened the door and departed in a most dignified manner. Just before he disappeared I had time to call after him: 'Thanks very much for the dinner.'

So we came at last to the outskirts of Niš, in a sector which I knew particularly well as a result of my readings. Apparently after behaving like vandals during part of their journey (they had pillaged and burned Belgrade on the way) the Crusaders had received a friendly welcome in Niš. In fact, the governor representing the Emperor of Byzantium had revictualled the ragged hordes while he waited for instructions from Constantinople. One interesting detail: it took the couriers of the time five or six days to cover the distance between Niš and Constantinople: about 1,000 kilometres, while I expected it would take us at least a month. It was quite understandable: the couriers in the old days galloped at top speed in relays, changing horses frequently. We had no particular reason to hurry.

Our problem for the moment was to discover if we would be as well received in Niš as our pilgrim ancestors, for through our Embassy in Belgrade we had been told they had one of the rare riding-schools in Yugoslavia and the club was all set to offer us hospitality.

First problem: find the club. First surprise: a motorcyclist, whom we asked for directions in our personal jargon, replied in French. Like the son of the corpse in Lapovo he had lived in Paris, also in the République district. How many others could there possibly be? He advised us not to go to the club, firstly because it would undoubtedly be closed, and secondly because it was five or six kilometres outside the town over very bad roads, and finally because it was dangerous to go there at night: 'There are stray dogs and soldiers who will shoot you at the drop of a hat!'

It was obvious he wasn't absolutely mad about the idea of taking us there and furthermore he considered our whole scheme a direct challenge to common sense. During the discussion he shot out a fairly startling question:

'You French say you like horses, so why do you eat them?'

Eventually he agreed to show us the way down a muddy path, full of puddles where motorcycle and horses slipped as if on a carpet of glue. You wouldn't think the circumstances were ideal for flirtation, but undoubtedly the young man considered that if he was travelling at night with two French girls, good manners required that he should at least make the attempt. He went through the usual motions, though obviously without much conviction, and when he realised we weren't co-operating, he gave up and may even have been relieved. This nocturnal promenade in mud up to the knees obviously wasn't his idea of fun.

'The club is over there. You see those lights? It's straight ahead, you can't go wrong.'

And he turned back, without a twinge of conscience, for after all, hadn't he done his duty?

The motorcyclist was right on one point at least: the club was shut. I raised the barrier, and in we went, making for a light at the end of a courtyard. Through the window I could see two women and a baby, so I knocked. The man in charge of the club was away and at first the women didn't want to take the responsibility of letting us spend the night, but I saw a telephone in a corner and suggested they should ring up the President of the club, as we had been given his name by the Embassy.

One of the women agreed to call him and read him our letter of introduction. Apparently he knew nothing about two French riders who had dropped from the skies, so decided to come out in person and investigate. An hour later he arrived, glanced at our certificates, introductions, recommendations and attestations, and mentally flung open his arms.

'Consider yourselves our guests.'

So we were all taken in: the mongrel, the horses and the girls. In Niš at least the tradition which demands that pilgrims should be well treated was respected.

My head sunk between my hunched shoulders, I huddled in my saddle: trying to make myself as small as possible. I was very afraid, and to crown everything I was giddy. On one side was a perpendicular rocky wall, and on the other, a sheer drop down to a ravine with a foaming torrent. There was no shoulder at all on the horrible motorway, a section of the great link between Paris and Istanbul. Heavy lorries of all makes and nationalities overtook and passed each other with suicidal courage. I saw a Turkish tanker-lorry try to pass an articulated German truck with loud blasts on his horn and the driver must have been under the special protection of Allah; at one point the tanker had its near-side wheels almost over the edge of the precipice.

These infernal machines were making us all run the same risk, three or four times a minute, for if Mickey took one false step, horse and rider, like an equestrian statue, would plunge into the Yugoslavian abyss, as the only barrier was a thin rail that barely reached the horses' knees.

In any event, what the hell were we doing on a motorway? Normally even we would never have had the nerve to use a main artery plastered with notices forbidding horse-drawn vehicles, pedestrians, cyclists and riders. Not that we'd regarded such notices as absolute taboos, but we knew that Mickey and Donald didn't take kindly to petrol-driven projectiles.

If we found ourselves where we were, the fault lay with the Cultural Attaché of the Franco-Yugoslav Riding Association. He had very kindly come to see us at the Niš Club and tried to make himself useful by helping to arrange our itinerary. I had picked out on my map one of those delightful minor roads marked in yellow and meant for horses or shepherds and their flocks. During the three weeks since we had crossed the Hungarian frontier we had used many of them for preference.

'You can't go over the mountains,' the President of the Club had exclaimed. 'There is six feet of snow in that area.'

'And besides,' chimed in the Cultural Attaché, 'that track hasn't been used for ages. You'll never be able to find it in the snow, you'll get lost and tire the horses out climbing up to eight thousand feet, and then you'll have to come down again the same day as there's nowhere to stay. It'll all add up to at least fifty or sixty kilometres. You haven't the slightest chance of getting through and I wouldn't enjoy having to send a helicopter to find you. Go this way, it's the only possible route through the Balkans at this time of year: it's quite flat and it's always clear of snow.'

And he pointed to a broad red line on the map. I nearly fell over backwards.

'The motorway? You're joking!'

'No, no . . .'

'It's much too dangerous. The horses would be frightened. We'd rather face a snowstorm in the mountains and we'd have a much better chance of getting out alive. Besides, asphalt is very bad for the horses' legs, it wears out their shoes, and that road is out of bounds to animals.'

'The out of bounds bit isn't a serious offence,' he replied. 'You simply need a special dispensation from the highway police.'

He made a few phone calls and came back, triumphant.

'Permission granted. The police are absolutely against the mountain route, and they'll help you through the tunnels.'

As soon as the police were involved we had no choice.

Another pertinent question: why didn't we get off that hellish roadway? The answer was because it was impossible: we were prisoners until the next slip-road, forty kilometres further on.

The situation was all the more wretched because Corinne, due entirely to greed, had become very ill: she had eaten far too much red bean soup with paprika, and now, doubled up in agony, was weeping silently. We couldn't even stop to let her lie down, and in any case, where could she lie? Not to mention that the horses might move across the roadway, and then an accident really would be inevitable.

Every time I heard the roar of an engine, I shut my eyes, and clung to my horse, terrified that the slipstream would drive us over the edge. From time to time I could hear the drivers yelling at us and though I couldn't understand what they said, or even guess in what language, their tone was definitely unfriendly. You don't have to be a polyglot to understand such furious imprecations, and I certainly couldn't blame them. I didn't even dare stretch my hand out to signal the traffic to give us a little leeway. At one stage a lorry tore the corner of my offside saddle-bag and the string fastening the roll in front of me. They certainly wouldn't hesitate to rip off my arm.

Terrified as I was, Mickey didn't even flick an ear, and in a momentary lull in the traffic I straightened out one shoulder and took a deep breath. I turned round to see Donald behind me, proceeding steadily, and for once sparing us his eternal cavortings. He was too frightened even to twitch the end of his tail and clung to the right, as close as he could to the thin rail, his nose in Mickey's hind quarters. Even Pluto, who normally likes trotting on the yellow line, had become incredibly obedient and taken refuge between Donald's feet.

In spite of this unusually good behaviour, I morally acknowledged my sins: after all, in my capacity as leader of the expedition, I was entirely responsible for this piece of criminal stupidity.

A tunnel appeared, the fifth since that morning, reminding me that the police were supposed to guide us through. Hardly a day had gone by when the police hadn't taken an interest in us, and yet when we needed their help for once they didn't show up.

A placard announced that the tunnel was eighty metres long, but as it had a dog-leg bend we couldn't see the white light at the other end, and had to plunge into a pitch-black interior. It was all the more nerve-racking because all the batteries in our torches were dead so we had no lights to indicate our presence.

I called to Corinne: 'Let's get through quickly, at the trot, before a lorry arrives.'

The horses were nervous of plunging into the darkness and when the enclosing walls changed the tapping of their shoes into a drum roll they became less and less willing.

Mickey had to be urged on. But sometimes horses sense danger and he finally decided to get through quickly. Donald was still close behind, but we hadn't quite got through when I heard the roar of a lorry about to overtake us.

The driver couldn't possibly see us and there was only one thing to be done.

'Holy Mother of God, pray for us . . .'

I closed my eyes—though in any case I couldn't see a thing—and wished I was a tortoise so I could pull my head inside my shell. At the same time I relaxed the grip of my knees and Mickey slowed down to a walk. Whether I left this vale of tears at a trot or a walk, what difference would it make?

I could hear the lorry coming and soon everything would be over. A cadenza of furious tooting played by a virtuoso, head-lights flashing off and on which I could see even through my closed eyelids. Screaming of brakes . . . cries . . . frantic neighs . . . I was very nearly thrown off balance by the displacement of air as the lorry swept past me, and waited for a few seconds before

opening my eyes. I was too afraid of seeing Corinne and Donald
lying in the roadway.

As it transpired I didn't see either of them, or even Pluto until
I emerged from the tunnel. As white as the snows lying on the
neighbouring slopes, Corinne explained what had happened.
Terrified by the roar of the engines, and the glaring headlights,
Donald had swerved violently to the left and bolted, a fraction of
a second before the juggernaut had passed. Leaving Mickey and
me behind, he had galloped at top speed towards daylight, with
Pluto still keeping station between his legs!

We started out again, more terrified than ever, until we found
a sort of flat platform at the edge of the precipice a few kilometres
further on, where we called a halt. We really needed the break,
but also Corinne was suffering more and more from her stomach-
ache. However, she was the first to suggest moving on:

'The sooner it's over, the better. We can't risk being on this
road in the dark. We're too young to die.'

Another tunnel, 270 metres long.

'This time,' I said, 'I'm not venturing in there. We only have
one chance in a thousand of getting out alive.'

We stopped at the entrance to the tunnel, for there at least we
were visible. Motorists and lorry drivers stared at us in surprise:
what on earth were two girls, two horses and a dog doing there?
I would have found it difficult to tell them for what, indeed, were
we waiting for? Probably a flying carpet, but miracle of miracles!
A police car appeared. I waved to it to stop, but it didn't even
slow down: maybe the driver hadn't seen us with the sun in his
eyes? Maybe he was in a hurry?

A second police car appeared. I tried to explain to the astonished
policemen why we were waiting there, but my nervousness didn't
improve my Serbo-Croat and they didn't understand a word.
However, one thing seemed fairly clear, the situation was hardly
suitable for a discussion, so with several imperative '*Heyde!
Heyde!*' ['Come along!'], they waved to us to set off in front of
them, travelling immediately behind us with their headlights on.
This meant that though we were fully visible the horses were
afraid of their elongated shadows sliding over the walls.

Within three minutes, naturally, a traffic jam built up behind us:
dozens of impatient drivers blowing their horns as if that would

solve the problem, and as soon as we cleared the tunnel all the vehicles shot past us at top speed.

Another tunnel, just as long, followed. Same result, same traffic jam. Same mad rush at the exit, but this time the police car accelerated like the others and left us to our fate. But not for long. Two kilometres down the road the police stopped us in a lay-by to ask the eternal questions:

'Passports? *Dokouments?*'

It was just the moment. The light was beginning to go and Corinne groaned as she clung to Donald's neck. The officer who had examined our visas began to understand that she was sick and needed help.

'Would you like me to take her to a doctor?' he offered. 'Maybe she has appendicitis.'

Appendicitis? I found myself back at the beginning of summer and I could hear Paul Winkler warning me: 'You know, a great many expeditions have failed because an appendix blew up at the wrong moment.'

I told the policemen that first we had to find a stable: I couldn't take both horses along that road by myself, unless one of them would take Corinne in the car and the other come with me.

'Impossible. We can only take your sister to hospital. That's the law.'

A long silence finally broken by one of the policemen.

'There's another possibility. After the next bend there is a dirt road which will get you off the motorway. See those lights: it's a village about a kilometre away. Good luck.'

We reached the village eventually, a curious agglomeration that straggled for three kilometres down a single street, and in all that distance only one lamp-post. Not a soul. Finally a man came out of a house. Half-stammering, half-miming, I made him understand that my sister was ill and we wanted to spend the night in the village. He pointed to a tall building, opposite the lamp-post.

'Ask the mayor.'

It was a fine house with whitewashed walls decorated with strings of brightly coloured paprika. I went straight into the kitchen where the entire family was assembled, laid a finger on my chest and got out in a single breath: '*Frantzouski. Kondj stall? Sestere ne dobra.*' ['Do you have a stable? My sister is sick.']

I think they gathered that my sister and I wanted to sleep in the stable, as I hadn't mentioned the horses, and it was only when they came out to inspect the sufferer that they discovered Mickey and Donald. The master of the house made the necessary arrangements immediately. He had a black stallion which he moved out of its stable and into a barn to make room for our two, while the women of the house led Corinne away and undertook to dose her with suitable home-made remedies. By the time I had seen to the horses, I found Corinne feeling a little better.

'I don't want to be operated on in a Yugoslav hospital,' she said. 'Let's wait until tomorrow. Supposing it isn't appendicitis?'

Whereupon there was a knock at the door and a visitor for us. The Cultural Attaché in person, who had planned to meet us at Bela Palanka. This was the town Peter the Hermit's hordes had found deserted, for their reputation was such that the inhabitants had preferred to fly. The pilgrims had profited by their absence to ransack the city and, as it was harvest-time, even the surrounding fields.

The Attaché was all smiles and very proud of himself. Not finding us at the rendezvous, he had still managed to discover our whereabouts in this forgotten spot. I appreciated how clever he had been but was tempted to tell him of the miseries we had been through on his account. However, I hadn't the courage, and besides, I'm convinced he wouldn't have understood a word of my reproaches for he is as ignorant of matters equestrian as he is strong on history. Furthermore, I was too tired and sleepy to lose my temper.

Corinne by now was fast asleep, her breathing calm and regular. No, definitely, it couldn't possibly be appendicitis. The proof was that next morning she joined me happily on the road to Pirot—close to the Bulgarian frontier—as if nothing had happened. What it is to be young.

CHAPTER TWENTY-SIX

Well Guarded through Bulgaria

When we left Paris we knew that crossing Bulgaria would be a piece of cake, for the grand master of Bulgarian Cavalry—I have mentioned him already—had arranged for us to be escorted across his country by four soldiers, two on horseback and two in a lorry. While the riders showed us the roads, the motorists would transport our gear and fodder, and set up the stop-overs.

General Stoytchev meant to spare the two little Red Riding-Hoods from Paris every possible kind of difficulty, in much the same way as the Emperor Alexis of Constantinople had treated the soldiers of Godfrey de Bouillon and Peter the Hermit. With this subtle difference: Alexis's generosity was motivated by the fact that he was afraid of the depredations of the soldiers of Christ. By feeding them adequately, he hoped to stop them stealing and sacking the towns along the line of march, as they had often done since the start of their pilgrimage. Alexis was mistaken, but that's another story, and not at all to the credit of our ancestors, the Crusaders.

I sincerely hope the General didn't have that kind of motivation as far as we were concerned, and if he loaded us with so many kind attentions it was purely because ever since his time at Saumur, France had always held a particular place in his heart. As we were French, and travelling on horseback as well . . .

I should have been delighted, but I was only half-pleased for I don't like attentions which restrict my freedom. In the fable of the dog and the wolf, my sympathies have always been with the wolf. However, we could only hope that our quartet of bodyguards would behave discreetly, flexibly and understandingly, and that the soldiers would make the arrangements they were supposed to organise—choice of route, length of stages, provision for the horses—and see that our co-existence was as peaceful as possible. But perhaps all this military zeal was meant to stop us moving about as we pleased, or seeing anything the Bulgarians didn't want us to see, and most important, to stop all contact between two representatives of the capitalist West and the actual population?

Finally, a vital question: would our escorts be handsome, intelligent and amusing, and would they be able to speak French?

I had to admit the system had considerable advantages. First, we wouldn't have to spend hours looking for food and shelter at the end of each tiring day, for we still had a chain of Balkan mountains to cross. Secondly, the horses could count on regular supplies of hay, which was just as well, for after five weeks of a maize-based diet, Donald was showing disturbing signs of fatigue. Not Mickey, though goodness knows why. Donald's hind legs had begun to swell, and he could only keep pace with Mickey with great difficulty, while the latter remained in dazzling form and even tried to race any horse-drawn carts he met.

Another advantage: the escort's lorry would carry our bags, which would be a great relief for, after some 2,800 kilometres on the road, the horses' coats were beginning to show signs of wear. You could even see the outlines of the saddle-bags on their ribs.

When we presented our papers and General Stoytchev's recommendations at the Bulgarian frontier, they very nearly sounded a fanfare, but the commander had to ask us to wait, for our escort hadn't arrived. He hoped we would accept his apologies, which we did, all the more graciously because we were a week late ourselves and fully appreciated that we weren't exactly expected. Just give him time to call up Sofia, our excisemen assured us, and the escort would be on its way.

Two hours later, the quartet disembarked from a magnificent lorry which had transported both men and horses, and the leader introduced himself: an officer of about twenty-eight, quite nice-looking and wearing his khaki uniform and red epaulettes with a certain air. He introduced his three companions and we set out for Sofia. It was late in the day, but it didn't matter as the capital was quite near. I had time to admire our Bulgarians' mounts:

tall, black, elegant thoroughbreds, making ours look almost like ponies. Not that I was in the least ashamed of them—you are never ashamed of anything you love—but I couldn't help being a little worried. How could Mickey and Donald keep up with such horses that would certainly move much faster? I remembered the recommendations of the Austrian champion Welde: 'Never allow yourself to be influenced by your guide: it's up to you to set your own pace.' I was quite determined to follow his advice, for after all, the quadriga was at our disposal, and not the other way round. In principle.

Sofia provided four days' rest. I nearly wrote 'enforced rest', for our programme, drawn up without consulting us, assumed that we would take a long time to recuperate before tackling the next range of Balkan mountains and the perils of the Near East. However, the arrangements were all the easier to accept when we saw our quarters, which turned out to be quite remarkable from every point of view.

The military camp where we were installed had the most superb riding facilities, and we were immediately surrounded by a crowd of riders, instructors and stable-boys of all colours and ranks. Amidst all the excitement, somebody announced that the General would be arriving at any minute, whereupon everyone scattered like sparrows. In a flash every coat had been picked up and even the straw had been swept away so that the stalls were as clean as if they had only just been built.

Our protector eventually arrived, and in spite of his eighty-two years and Napoleonic figure, his stomach filling out his tunic a trifle too generously, he was a most imposing sight. Besides, you need a fair amount of style to carry off the odd little red cap he wore, the exact colour of his Légion d'honneur button. He complimented us in impeccable French, which we appreciated all the more coming from a great man who had been through several cavalry wars and knew what the crossing of the Balkans on horseback involved.

He invited us to dinner the following evening at his home.

'You know,' he said, 'it'll be New Year's Eve. We'll celebrate your arrival and the New Year at the same time.'

For this special occasion, we decked ourselves out in our best:

clean jeans and embroidered shirts, expecting to dine in a certain intimacy, but the General had invited all the senior officers, a few diplomats and their wives in full evening dress, as well as our four bodyguards. What a meal he gave us, washed down by Bordeaux and champagne because that evening France was being honoured, thanks to the presence of the Coquet sisters.

We found ourselves blushing like two well-brought-up little girls, for our escorts proclaimed what a good impression we had already made on them, because they had seen us looking after our horses before seeing to our own creature comforts.

As for the rest of the conversation, it centred mainly on why two people, apparently in their right minds, had started out on such an adventure? In principle, we always gave the same replies with certain variations, depending on my mood, concerning my age: it varied between sixteen and twenty-six, and Corinne would ask what I was going to say so as not to make a boob. I have to admit that I did get fairly tired of arousing consternation, alarm and pity from one end of Europe to the other. If I said I was sixteen, people seemed to understand more or less: but if I admitted that I had left school some time ago, utter astonishment always set in, and we had the same comments time after time: 'Not really! Not married yet? No children? No home? No job?'

Out of respect for the General, that night I told the truth, and produced the same reactions from the distinguished company as if we had been in the depths of the most inaccessible desert.

The festivities finished gaily in a nightclub, without the General, all the more unexpected because we were in a country where we didn't expect the people to go in much for jollifications. There was one small significant detail: our escort-Commander had had permission to wear civvies, but he kept his revolver hidden under his jacket:

'In case some dancer bothers you,' he explained.

I think he was joking, but can't be absolutely sure. He did eventually use his weapon, for he emptied the magazine when the clock struck twelve. It's true that by then he had been celebrating for several hours.

When I visited the horses I had a very unpleasant start to the New Year, and flew into a terrible rage:

'Who did this? Who ruined my horse?'

The groom who had been told off to look after them, couldn't understand what was wrong.

'*Dobro?*' ['All right?'] he asked timidly.

'*Né dobro!*' I yelled at him, and I had tears in my eyes. I could have grabbed him by the throat and wrung his neck.

My poor Mickey. The groom had cut off the superb mane which I combed so proudly every morning, and worse, he had cut his forelock off short. Mickey looked like a small boy with a crew-cut, and my beloved provençal had lost half his charm. He looked at me as if he were ashamed of himself.

'*Né dobro! Né dobro!*' was all I could say, until I saw the man was still holding the instrument with which he had committed the crime. I grabbed the electric clippers, knocked off his cap, pressed the button and cut a wide swathe right through his coal-black hair. That would teach him! I had only one regret: that he could hide the damage under his cap, unlike poor Mickey.

The poor man was so upset that my anger melted away and I was even rather sorry for what I had done. To make amends I said that Donald had been much improved in appearance since he had had his mane cut straight, and the poor fellow recovered his nerve, smiled and to prove his good intentions offered to clip their feathers.

Certainly not! You must always leave the hair on the pasterns. It acts as a shield for the water, otherwise it may enter the folds in the feet and cause cracks. The mane and forelock, in winter particularly, protect a horse's eyes against the wind and blinding reflections of the sun on snow.

The officer who had come with me intervened:

'Be a good girl! Don't tell the General, or this man will be punished severely. In our country it's a very serious offence.'

What a General! What respect he inspired, and what powers he must have had! His name alone was enough to lift all restrictions, open every door. Even Pluto was allowed into the restaurant where all dogs are normally forbidden. The General's name was enough to make a shop reopen when we wanted to do some shopping after closing time. Once our officer managed to intercept one of the rare taxis in the town though it was already fully loaded. He invited us to get in after the other passengers had turned out without the slightest protest once he had pronounced the famous syllables: 'Stoy-tchev.'

A Bulgarian student we met hesitated for a long time before confiding to us in French:

'I don't know if I should tell you this. You see the General quite often, and you might make trouble for me. My father is an important person in the party, but I'm against Communism myself. Here everyone calls himself doctor or engineer because they've been given titles instead of money, but they're so poor they can't even afford a car. I want to leave the country and go to France. It isn't easy, because we aren't allowed to leave Bulgaria for more than two weeks at a time. Will you give me your address, and if I turn up on your doorstep one of these days, will you help me?'

His opinion didn't exactly coincide with the declaration our officer made to me that very afternoon as he showed me round the Party offices. When I said how surprised I was to find they were neither supervised nor guarded, he replied, 'Why should they be guarded?'

'They might be blown up, or an attempt made on the leaders while they are in conference . . .'

'But the Bulgarian people love the Party. This isn't Paris! The Bulgarian people want Communism!'

To each his own truth.

Eventually the great day of our departure arrived. The General insisted on coming to wave good-bye to us and as a parting gift presented us with a box of studs, some for snow and some for mud, and our escorting quartet were instructed to fix on the relevant sets as and when necessary.

We were already beginning to know our foursome. First, the commanding officer whose name was Ivan. We nicknamed him Ivan Chin-Chin because he seemed even more devoted to raki than his comrades. He tossed it back neat, prefaced each time by a polite '*Nas dravé*' ['Your health'], to which we would reply, equally politely 'Chin-chin'. Another peculiarity of his appeared later: he preferred to travel with the driver in the lorry, leaving the other two to ride with us on horseback. Of course it may only have been that Ivan Chin-Chin was much concerned with choosing our stop-overs and preferred to give his personal attention to our lodging and creature comforts. This meant, of course, that he did the day's journey in an hour, or an hour and a half at most, and the rest of the time he and the driver could spend waiting for us in some convenient café.

The driver was also called Ivan, a tall man of about thirty-five or forty, with a pleasant face and I liked him very much. Ivan the Driver was in civvies, but he wore a revolver in his belt which he never seemed to take off.

Then there was Georges, who played a very special role in the outfit for he was a military jockey, with a jockey's figure and bowed legs. He wore a fur cap perched over one eye, and a tunic and greatcoat that were much too long for him, making him look like Toulouse-Lautrec. As he was very lively, quick-witted and intelligent (he was always the first to understand what we were saying), we nicknamed him 'Le Lutin' (the Goblin).

Finally, there was the eldest, who was about forty-five, called Kiro. He was a taciturn character and scarcely opened his mouth, except to swallow enormous quantities of raki, which probably accounted for his blotchy complexion.

Flanked by our escorts, we managed to ride across Sofia without too much trouble, as their horses protected us from any overtaking lorries. As Mickey and Donald had had hardly any exercise for four days and had been eating like fighting cocks, they were in fine fettle too. Not only did they keep up with their new friends without any difficulty, but they tried to play with their Balkan colleagues, and it was quite hard work keeping the whole escort down to a walk.

Our first disappointment came as soon as we left the town and found ourselves on the detested Trans-European motorway, in spite of my making it quite clear to the General that we only wanted to use country roads. According to our bodyguard there was no alternative, but I didn't believe a word of it, for everywhere we went we had always been able to find minor roads. It may have meant making a few detours, but in my opinion it wasn't too high a price to pay to avoid those appalling juggernauts. I have since learnt that no soldier will ever make the smallest effort if he can possibly avoid it, and high adventure strikes him as completely outside his line of duty.

It was a great pity, for the mountain paths over the Balkans must be very beautiful, and we were also enjoying a spell of fine weather. There was no snow at all in the mountains, whereas just before we arrived, there had been a fall of at least six feet. (While we were in Istanbul, three weeks later, we were told that violent snowstorms had been raging in Bulgaria and the cold had been absolutely unbearable.)

As a result, the daily stages (never more than twenty-five kilometres, never more than five hours in the saddle, we mustn't tire ourselves), proved very uninteresting. The temperature was minus 3°, whereas in Yugoslavia we had experienced minus 15° or 20°, but it was very damp, and as we were bored by all the fuss, we felt it more. I had cold shivers down my back and was absolutely frozen, while Corinne hopped off her horse and walked or ran as often as she could, to get warm. Our escorts, Kiro and the Goblin, copied her example, but like so many cavalrymen, they had forgotten how to walk, and the jockey quickly collected blisters, while Kiro couldn't keep up with the other two.

It was barely five o'clock when we reached Vakarel where the two Ivans were waiting for us in the usual café. Once the horses had been attended to, I made the mistake of telling our male chaperons that it was Corinne's twentieth birthday. So it was entirely my fault that this proved a pretext for bending the elbow even more enthusiastically than usual, with the obvious result that next afternoon we weren't able to start before two o'clock. We were supposed to stop at Kostenec, where Corinne and I wanted to sample the waters, but possibly through a misunderstanding (maybe due to the drunken orgy of the previous night), we missed it. Anyway, Ivan Chin-Chin overtook us on the road and began to swear blue murder at our companions. Some of his bad temper might have been due to the fact that the arrangements he had made for the night were frankly horrific. The hotel where he had booked us in was in the town, but the only stable he had been able to find was in the mountains, six kilometres further back, so our horses would do an extra twelve kilometres for nothing. As for the restaurant where we were supposed to dine, it was two kilometres from the hotel. That night I had serious doubts about Bulgarian logistics but the general bad temper was quickly dissipated by a few glasses of raki.

Surprise, surprise! Next morning, at six o'clock, it was Ivan

Chin-Chin (probably aroused by twinges of conscience) who came to wake me and remind me it was time to feed the horses. It was still dark and we set off on our six-kilometre climb in silence. As I was reasonably fit, I started out at a smart crack, and behind me I could hear Ivan panting, coughing and spitting, for he had the most terrible cold. I certainly wasn't prepared to slow down, so I forged ahead to give him a good lesson. He should have let us sleep in the stable with the horses, but as he was responsible for our safety, he would have had to do the same, so he had forced us to join him in the hotel.

It was high time we got to the stables, for the horses were absolutely parched, and no one had troubled to give them a drink.

Then we had to get back, wake up the others and have our own breakfast. I went faster and faster because the fresh morning air was giving me an appetite, and Ivan followed as best he could, spitting and panting.

The other Bulgarians were startled out of their wits when we burst in. From their red-rimmed eyes and ashen features, it was obvious they were still suffering from the after-effects of the night before, and watched us gobble our breakfast with jaundiced expressions. I might add that breakfast was anything but a relaxing affair, for they gave us soup in the restaurant, coffee in the bar, and the milk had to be fetched from a shop half a mile away. If we wanted bread we would have to get it from the bakery, provided it was open.

Then all we had to do was climb into the saddle and ride down the motorway to Belovo, which our chariot was anxious to reach, for it wasn't just an ordinary Sunday, but the day when the whole of Communist Bulgaria celebrated the Jordanka, a great religious feast. Our escort planned to celebrate with the local garrison in the traditional manner, i.e. by getting drunk. When everyone was completely stoned, according to tradition, a wooden cross would be thrown into the river (here, the Maritza) and the drunkest man present was supposed to dive in and fish it out. By now it was the end of January, so the idea was to get really loaded before taking a header into the icy stream, but long before midnight our valiant knights were in no condition to test the temperature of the water, let alone fish out any crosses.

Half past six next morning and time for the morning feed. But the oats were in the lorry, the lorry was locked, the key was in the pocket of Ivan the Driver, and God knows where Ivan had fetched up after celebrating the Jordanka. At least I knew where to find the other Ivan, so I went off to give him a shake.

'Wake up! The horses are hungry!'

Bleary-eyed and badly hung-over, all he could get out was:

'Ivan tired. Ivan drink too much last night. Ivan sleep.'

I was implacable.

'Give me some oats. You can go back to sleep afterwards.'

Eventually he got to his feet and set off in search of his colleague, but two hours later he returned empty-handed.

'Ivan-driver drunk last night, sleep today, me not know where. No key. Wait here.'

He sat himself down and prepared to attack his breakfast, consisting of a plate of soup washed down with raki, but I wasn't going to let him off so lightly.

'You can eat when the horses have had their breakfast. Off you go!'

And believe me, he went, and didn't come back until ten o'clock, carrying a pail of oats and accompanied by his three colleagues, with faces as long as hosepipes. They stared at me as if asking the good Lord what sins they had committed to earn them the honour of travelling with a shrew of my calibre.

When we halted at Pazardzhik, it was the Goblin who did the honours, for he had friends there, fellow-jockeys who had made all the arrangements. He was delighted with himself and kept kissing the tips of his fingers and saying:

'*Georges dobro, stalles dobro, hotel dobro!*' ['Georges, the stable and the hotel are all fine!']

A grand reception had been organised in our honour, with delicious food, even if we started by drinking orangeade (wine and raki made their appearance later). A folk orchestra played non-stop and everybody danced. In such an atmosphere, how could we not forgive and forget all our past differences?

At five in the morning, only one of the jockeys, a leading rider on the Bulgarian circuit, was still lucid, and we invited him to get in touch with us whenever he came to race in France.

'I'll never get to Paris,' he said sombrely. 'We aren't allowed to travel outside the Socialist countries. I can race in Budapest, Belgrade or Bucharest, but never abroad. We don't have very good horses, and we aren't allowed to be beaten, so we'll come to the capitalist countries later, when we're sure of winning.'

It was just ten o'clock when our military escort came to collect us next morning, though the least that could be said was that they didn't look very wide-awake and even less enthusiastic at the thought of covering twenty-five kilometres on horseback.

'The sky is very overcast,' declared Ivan Chin-Chin. 'If we leave now, in an hour's time we'll be caught in a snowstorm. Better ride in the lorry, it'll be safer.'

What? Do the next stage in a lorry? He had to be joking. What did he take us for? I refused to be convinced.

'We'll leave at once on horseback.'

It snowed, of course, and it was very cold. The clouds were so low that they wrapped horse and rider in damp cottonwool which froze our feet and stiffened our hair, but that day we couldn't use the motorway and I didn't want to miss the opportunity. As a result we discovered a Bulgaria very much off the beaten track, away from the main roads and the traffic. The countryside was really delightful. The small houses, with thatched roofs and bunches of scarlet paprika decorating whitewashed walls had salamis and smoked hams hanging just inside the doors. The women wore long black dresses and flowered aprons: they were huddled up in black shawls and smiled as we passed, their eyes clear and full of kindness. I had noticed that most Bulgarians had beautiful clear eyes set in finely cut features and pitch-black hair. There were exceptions, of course, and as luck would have it, our bodyguard were among the exceptions.

Georges, the Goblin, was delighted to see that the day's trip had pleased us.

'*Romantica!*' he declared enthusiastically. 'In the snow you are as pretty as our own roses.'

I know why he phrased his compliment like that: I needed only to look at Corinne's cheeks and nose, and my own nose and cheeks were obviously the same colour.

It was on the road to Plovdiv that Corinne made an interesting discovery: if she gripped her horse with one leg a little further back than usual, he flattened his ears at once and looked round for someone to kick or bite. We exploited and improved the trick to annoy our escort on days when we weren't feeling pleased with them. As soon as Corinne gripped Donald's back ribs with her left leg and urged him on with her right, he would flatten his ears, bare his long teeth and wait for someone to cry 'Attack! Attack!', whereupon he would hurl himself on the nearest Bulgarian horse, tear off a portion of his backside and turn round to lash out with both hind legs. Then we would pat him to show him how clever he was. Our escort were wild with rage, but what else could we do with such a bunch of slackers? (We were also very glad we had made this discovery before crossing into countries where we might run into brigands or wild beasts.) For instance, at Plovdiv, Ivan Chin-Chin got a woman guide who spoke French to try and persuade us once more to use the lorry over the next section. He explained that the horses in the district were dying like flies from some appalling epidemic, and if we didn't want to lose our own animals, we would have to pile them all on board.

I asked the interpreter to inform Ivan that I didn't believe a word of it.

'Tell him that in my opinion it's a complete invention. If there had been an epidemic I would have been notified. In Sofia I was assured there was nothing new on the health-front, and in any case I'm going to ring up General Stoytchev to see what he advises.'

My reaction struck them all dumb, and after a short confabulation, the Goblin tried another tack.

'There's not another hotel until we get to the frontier post at Kapitan Androvo,' he declared.

'And a good thing too. We'll be able to save money. We can sleep in the stables with the horses.'

A further consultation, and a fresh declaration from the Goblin: 'No stable till Popoviça, and Popoviça is more than seventy kilometres away.'

'Our horses are in excellent shape and quite capable of covering the distance.'

Which was perfectly true, for Mickey and Donald had never been in better form.

The Four-Power Conference was resumed and ended in unconditional surrender.

'Pretty and romantic, snow, isn't it?' said the Goblin, and honourable face was saved all round.

And so we arrived at Popoviça, and then Gorski-Izvor ... riding between gentlemen whose sole satisfaction must have been to know they were coming to the end of their painful mission. They must have been thinking it was high time they returned to more normal conditions, for the mercury had fallen to minus 10° again.

Just before we reached Stoikovo, two stages before the Turkish border, things took a turn for the better. We were jogging along on the snow-covered road when a high-pitched 'toot-toot' made us prick up our ears. It was a long time since we had heard the distinctive sound of a 2-CV's horn. But the one that stopped just ahead of us was anything but ordinary: pale green with yellow stripes, it was manned by two hairy individuals, one of whom got out and rushed back to greet us. It took me a few seconds to recognise my old friend Olivier behind eight days' growth of beard. We had met originally at the University of Nanterre and left together at the time of the troubles in 1968. I had switched to a business school and he had gone off to take a degree in business management, which was a trifle ironic considering he was the kind of lad who strolls through life in a cloud. If you asked him to give you a lift to Paris he would quite likely land you in Boulogne.

In view of the stories he had heard about Turkey, he had become very worried at the prospect of the two of us wandering about without an official protector, and hearing on the radio that we had passed Sofia, he had abandoned his studies and flown to our rescue. He had repainted the car (immediately rechristened the 'Green Mare') and in view of the Turks' reputation had fixed it up as best he could. He had covered the hood, windshield, windows and headlamps with metal grilles which would protect them from stones and knife-thrusts. He had also had the engine wrapped in a sheet of corrugated iron and had the exhaust system installed on the roof, to prevent it being torn off on the bad roads. A spare wheel had been fixed to each door, and he had removed the back seat and replaced it with a comfortable mattress and an elaborate selection of camping equipment, to save him going to a hotel if the locals didn't prove hospitable. Having done all that, armed only with his guitar, he had set out for the savage Orient. Shortly after, he had picked up his companion, Patrick, who was hitch-hiking to Morocco in search of the sunshine and warmth so necessary to his well-being. As the two boys found they got on well, Patrick had agreed that Turkey or the Maghreb would suit him equally well, so they had travelled non-stop for a week to try and meet us before we were swallowed up by the Anatolian Minotaur. All of which explained why, when we met them on the Plovdiv–Istanbul road, on a freezing afternoon, Patrick was wearing sandals and flowered cotton shorts. Apart from that, he had a pullover and a fifty-franc note, but didn't seem in the least worried.

Olivier was slightly better off sartorially, but wasn't much richer than his companion. When he started, he was reasonably well off, but he had changed all his traveller's cheques into Yugoslav dinars, and now found himself with his pockets stuffed with notes that nobody would change.

At our first dinner together the atmosphere was as cold as the weather, for it was clear that between our four crew-cut military friends, and the two hirsute hippies, a current of sympathy was hardly likely to flow.

Once dinner was over, our bodyguard showed the boys the road to Istanbul, for Olivier and Patrick had only been given transit visas for Bulgaria, with a maximum stay of fifteen hours, and were forbidden to stop in towns, hotels or restaurants.

Imagine the surprise of our military escort next morning when we found the Green Mare by the roadside, with Olivier and Patrick calmly cleaning the carburettor. They told us they were in no hurry, and had spent the night in the car. Their fifteen-hour visa had expired. So what?

Whereupon a police car hove into view. The militiamen didn't take the matter quite so lightly, and the Goblin had to intervene. The two Parisians were instructed to get the hell out of there and wait for us on the other side of the frontier. Olivier and Patrick reassembled the carburettor, jumped into the car and departed at full speed. I thought I could see a faint smile on the Goblin's frosty lips, for our jockey friend apparently didn't enjoy sharing us with two boys with whom we had far too much in common, such as funny stories, in French.

We had arranged to meet the Green Mare at Edirne, the first town over the Turkish frontier, and we were more than pleased at the thought of having two friendly compatriots to act as quartermasters in Turkey, and swopping our soldiers for bohemians. I didn't rely too much on their efficiency, for they didn't know a word of Turkish and even less about horses, but I felt sure they were good improvisers. In fact, I knew they were, firstly because they had got as far as they had, and secondly because they had found us by acting on one single piece of information: that we had been through Sofia several days previously. That had taken some doing!

Shall I say that we took leave of our Bulgarian companions with tears in our eyes? I certainly will not. They must have felt exactly as I did, judging by the speed with which they re-embarked (in the lorry) and took the road to Sofia, glad to be relieved of a couple of lunatics. I might make an exception in favour of the Goblin, who I think regarded us with a certain degree of affection.

Talking of speed, I was in such a hurry to leave Bulgaria that I forgot to change our Bulgarian money, or check the lorry, which explains why we embarked on our ride through Turkey without the horses' canvas bucket.

CHAPTER TWENTY-SEVEN

Turkish March

At the Turkish frontier we had to wait for three hours while the Customs men finished their lunch, and suffered patiently, for the sun was pleasantly warm behind the Customs post. An official appeared every five minutes to try and move us on in case the horses soiled the pavement, but we stood firm. I didn't want the horses to catch cold in the freezing north wind. What the Customs officers feared would happen, did happen fortunately . . . plop!

I say 'fortunately' for as soon as the mess had been observed, a little man in uniform rushed out to stamp our passports on the first empty page he could find, ignoring the protests from the motorists and lorry drivers waiting ahead of us. He scribbled a few words about the horses and waved to us to get the hell out of there as fast as we could.

And so the way to the mysterious East lay open, a new world of new sensations. Mickey and Donald immediately showed that they were far from happy. They looked right and left, before and behind, and only moved forward very slowly, distracted by the change of landscape, costumes and faces.

Bulgaria had been very green, but now the steppes unrolled before us, the grass burnt brown by frost and sun, with no sign of greenery on the mountains either. The horses shied at the nightmarish costumes of the veiled women in black, and Mickey snorted and bucked when he saw the dark faces and inky moustaches of the men. Pluto barked at everyone indiscriminately.

'We must make friends with these people, d'you hear? We're going to spend at least two months in this country.'

Like the horses, we were a little on edge ourselves, but delighted
at having got rid of our officer-chaperons. For the first time since
leaving Paris we weren't just setting out on a ride, or a long-
distance trek, but a real expedition. We would have to be ready
to face the worst.

As soon as we could, we left the paved road for the sandy
tracks used by the flocks, feeling ourselves to be already in the
wilderness. We were alone, free and happy, without a village or
house in sight, not even a sheepfold as far as we could see, until
the horizon was closed in by a distant bare hill, covered with a
thin yellowish layer of grass. A little further on, a ditch about two
yards deep barred our way, with a frozen stream about three
yards wide at the bottom. The sides of the ditch, which were
almost vertical, were frozen solid and presented a formidable
obstacle. Donald went first, slid calmly down the slope, walked
across the frozen stream and without making any particular
effort, attempted to climb the opposite bank. Naturally he slipped
and fell on the ice, but got up and tried again. After violent efforts
he managed to scramble up, but I decided I had better look for an
easier passage downstream.

At that point I noticed a shepherd built like an all-in wrestler
who had been watching the entire scene. He began to follow us,
and I didn't like the look of him at all, especially as he was carrying
a shovel on one shoulder. Of course it's perfectly normal for a
peasant to carry a spade, but in the hands of a Turk it looked
somehow different, and could easily become a dangerous weapon.
If he were to attack us, even if we screamed for help, who would
come to our rescue? Other brigands?

There was no question of taking to our heels: as a result of his
acrobatics in the ditch, Donald was limping on one back leg, and
we had had to settle down to a walk, at least for the time being.
I waved to Corinne to press on ahead, but our shepherd stuck
grimly to our side, and I began to feel nervous. When I glanced
round at him, our rural wrestler indicated to us not to go straight
ahead, but move to the left. I was a little reassured, for if he had
meant us any harm, our strange escort would have had plenty of
time to satisfy his basest instincts. We struck off to the left, only
to be brought up short by another stream, even deeper than the
first, but at a place where a kind of ford had been dug out, so that

1 Off at last! Ready to leave from outside Notre-Dame
2 Studying the itinerary with our guide in the Vosges

3 Pluto catching up after a diversion

4 A rest and a snack with our friends from the Alsace riding-school
5 Good-bye to France, leaving our friends at the West German frontier

6 Evelyne plays her harmonica while leading Mickey in the Black Forest
7 A rather unusual bridge; Pluto bravely goes first

8 A rest and a snack on the banks of the Danube, Austria

9 It can be quite hazardous riding through long grass

10 Serenity in Austria
11 You can lead a horse to water, but it isn't easy to make him cross

12 An unexpected hitch in Hungary—our soldier escort bridge an
   irrigation ditch
13 Our Hungarian escort with his big black horse

14 Pluto has a drink of snow in Hungary
15 Going to the fair, on the road to Šid, Yugoslavia

16 Crossing the Balkans, not too much snow here
17 A cautious welcome to Turkey

18 Turkish hospitality

19 Pluto sports his protective spikes
20 Turkish schoolchildren pose for a class photograph

21 We stop for a drink at an Anatolian village well
22 A village in the Anatolian mountains with the usual reception
from the menfolk

23 A meeting with camels in the Taurus Mountains
24 Dining in style, Turkish fashion—the best meal we had eaten for days

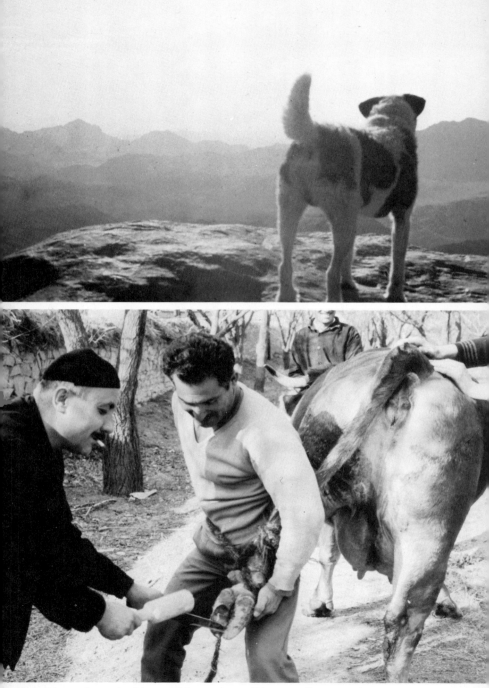

25 Pluto views the Taurus Mountains—did we really cross these?
26 Trimming a cow's hoof in Adana, Turkey

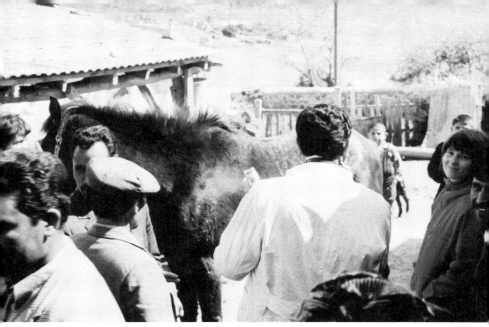

27 The Turkish vet about to give Donald his injection
28 Donald is sick, so we have to walk

29 Ready to cross
into Syria

30 The orange-seller
at Dam Sharko

31 Adnan's house, Jeble, Syria
32 Leaving Payas Castle

33 Riding through the gateway of Baniyas Castle

34 The lettuce-buyer

35 Grinding coffee at Jebel ed Druz

36 Dressed *à la mode* in Ramtha, Jordan

37 Carrying problems solved in Jordan; the young woman on the right shows her fashionable tattoo

38 Trading for cucumbers

39 Signs of the times; barbed wire divides Lebanon and Israel

40 Pluto passes an abandoned tank by the roadside

41 After seven months on the road we cross Allenby Bridge into
Israel on 17 April 1974
42 The Jericho to Jerusalem road

43 Mickey and Donald are reluctant to greet a camel
44 We have arrived: Jerusalem at last!

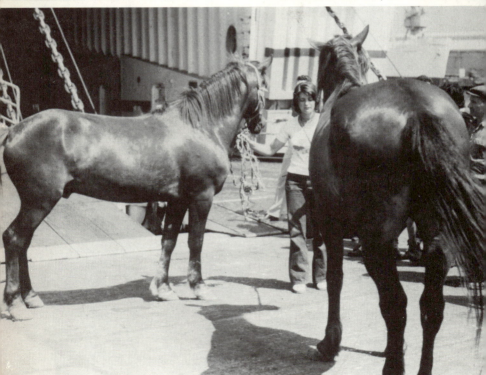

45 We give a press conference in Jerusalem
46 Homeward-bound, ready to load the horses onto the *Iris*

we were able to cross without giving an imitation of a three-day event. Our cut-throat was in fact merely a friend in need, and it taught me one lesson: I had been over-conditioned as to the bad habits of the Turks, though of course we had been in their country only for a few hours, and before we left, we would have to cover something like 1,400 kilometres.

We reached Edirne just as the sun was reddening the sky with its last rays. Minarets soared upwards from cupolas and pierced a sky striped with vermilion, mauve and burnished copper. The very twilight seemed to bring a promise of riches! The East began precisely at that point, so striking was the contrast with the monotony of the Bulgarian greyness. The silhouette of the mosques against that burning sky gave us the impression that we were on the threshold of an infinitely more luxurious world than the one we had left behind.

While we pushed our way towards the centre of the town (a veritable anthill) through narrow streets lined with small shops, I noticed that they were filled with consumer goods—what a change from Bulgaria, the country I had nicknamed '*Nema*', the Bulgarian word for 'there isn't any', a word we came up against every time we went shopping. Carts were driven at top speed down the narrow alleys: sellers of tea and kebabs were busy with charcoal pans (proof that it was possible to eat and drink) and shoeshine boys by the dozen (proof that the natives didn't necessarily run about barefoot). The animation was extraordinary —after the austerity and monotony of the past weeks it was heartening to listen to shouts, laughter and song.

We were reunited with our hippies in the square outside the principal mosque. They had faithfully carried out their role of scouting party for they had discovered a stable, an English professor who would act as our guide-interpreter and lodgings for the night. If the stable cost a bomb and forage was even dearer, the interpreter was charming and helpful, and our host Mehmet was too honoured to accept a penny-piece in payment. He wasn't exactly a nobody himself, for he had been to Munich with the team of wrestlers who had done so well in the Olympic games. In between bouts, he made leather coats and with such a bodyguard we had nothing to fear, except perhaps from him.

He invited us to sleep in the annexe to his workroom, which was cosy enough, for there was a charcoal fire among the racks of garments, not entirely for our benefit but to maintain a constant temperature for his collection of goldfish, his passion in life. The aquarium had an electric immersion heater with a thermostat, but there had been a breakdown in the electrical supply.

The boys slept in the same room, but on the floor, though having spent four nights in the 2-CV in temperatures of minus 10°, they considered this the height of luxury. We were given a very special bed, for Mehmet installed us on a pile of goatskins with more goatskins to use as coverings. As far as he was concerned, he asked permission to sleep in one of our sleeping-bags, for he had never come across one before and was keen to see what it was like.

CHAPTER TWENTY-EIGHT

The Paradise of Unliberated Women

First stop on the road to Istanbul: Neçatiye. To the delight of the inhabitants we rode in at the same time as the shepherds with their flocks. This was a typical Turkish village, with no particular centre: the mosque here, the café there, the school at the other end, and the low houses, most of them wattle and daub, scattered all over the place. As for the few shops, they were square earthen boxes stuck side by side, with unglazed arrow-slits instead of windows.

A group of men with bristling moustaches waved at us to keep to the right, as we were clearly expected. We found our attendant cavaliers waiting at the end of an alley with a young Turk of about twenty-two or twenty-three, named Fathi, who spoke a little English. With much mystery, Olivier and Patrick announced they had a surprise for us, which was obviously going to be a pleasant one, judging by their grins of satisfaction.

As a start, Mickey and Donald were comfortably installed in a sheepfold, together with Pluto, for in Muhammadan countries dogs are considered to be impure. Having seen to their comfort, we went off to a house that was definitely finer and richer than the others, for it belonged to Fathi's father, the *mukhtar*, or mayor of the village.

The entrance was very welcoming, the walls hung with coloured embroideries, with a thick woollen carpet on the floor. At the back an enormous oven was steaming and giving off a delicious smell of new bread. A second room was even more beautiful, its walls draped in fine white lace scattered with roses embroidered in *petit point*. There was also a very big Syrian tapestry showing life in the harem in the old days, before the Ataturk revolution, while the floor was covered with Persian carpets, furs and huge cushions.

The mayor squatted on his heels and Fathi sat down cross-legged, while we lowered ourselves on to the cushions as best we could, considering our stiff knees and general weariness. A woman veiled in white appeared and disappeared almost at once—apparently she had no right to stay while there were two strange men in the room, so Fathi had the job of 'laying the table'; he spread a cloth on the carpet and then brought in a heavy pierced silver tray at least a yard across and began to fill it with good things. A huge bowl of milk appeared, then hard-boiled eggs, cream cheese, brioches, black olives, a tureen of onion soup crowned with toasted bread, a dish of red and green pimentos, several bowls of rice, white, pink and yellow, and even honey-comb covered with thick fresh cream. (I discovered later that this was reserved for especially honoured guests.) Each of us was handed a slab of flat bread and a spoon. We four infidels were so impressed by the ceremony that none of us dared attack the meal.

'There aren't any plates or forks,' said Corinne in amazement. 'What do we do?'

'I don't know. Wait and copy the others.'

In the meantime Fathi had poured the tea into tiny waisted cups, like miniature hour-glasses, and the *mukhtar* motioned to us to eat. Fathi understood our difficulty and showed us how to cope: the milk and soup were meant to be eaten with the spoon, while everything else was scooped up with pieces of bread.

While Olivier brought out his guitar to provide an after-dinner entertainment, a little girl whispered to the *mukhtar* that the women of the household would very much like to meet Corinne and me, so we followed her into the area reserved for women.

I really thought I must be dreaming, or that we had been transported into another century. The sight that met our eyes was fairy-like, all the more because it was lit by half a dozen oil-lamps that flickered over a group of women with welcoming smiles, each more beautiful than the last, to say nothing of their clothes: baggy pants of multicoloured floral materials, short embroidered velvet waistcoats. Each of them wore a white veil, edged with pearls, but drawn aside now that they were among females. Their features were delicate and finely cut, with milky, transparent, perfect complexions. Most of them squatted on their heels, or sat with one knee on the ground and the other leg bent in a yoga position. The eldest, whose hair showed a few white streaks, was spinning thread, while another was playing with a little girl of about three, combing her startlingly auburn curls. A teenager was embroidering a tapestry while her sister plaited her long hair. I hardly dared move for fear of seeing the entire Thousand and One Nights scene disappear.

Two of the women came towards us, moving so gracefully that I felt like a clumsy puppet. Our astronaut-type anoraks impressed them tremendously and through Fathi who had rejoined us, they asked if the jackets filled with air. I took mine off, squeezed the sleeve just below the armhole and blew into the cuff. The sleeve puffed out like a sausage and ripples of laughter greeted my demonstration. I explained that the anorak was stuffed with goosefeathers, which kept us beautifully warm in winter, where-upon the woman who had been playing with her little girl showed me how the Turkish women keep out the cold. She unhooked her top bodice, then under a velvet waistcoat embroidered with gold, she showed me another made of sheepskin, another in some woollen material, then a third knitted in fine wool and finally a silk blouse. She had the fine white skin of the true redhead which was confirmed when she untied her headscarf and shook out her thick Titian-red mane.

Some of the women came up carrying a pile of garments and started to undress us. In three seconds we were down to the minimum and they were amazed by our short hair, because they had already been spying on Olivier and Patrick. Both boys in fact sported Samsonesque hair-styles that could have been the envy of most women.

When they found I was wearing a bra, the general excitement redoubled, not that there was anything remarkable about it, apart from the fact that I had reinforced the shoulder-straps to make it stand up to months and months on horseback. They passed it from hand to hand and examined every stitch minutely, without in the least understanding what it was supposed to do. I explained as best I could, miming the mamillary shake-up a woman has to

undergo on horseback, and tried to make them understand that
without some support, hard apples quickly become flabby melons.
I don't know if they got the message, but the beautiful redhead,
anxious to push the comparison as far as possible, unhooked her
final bodice and revealed a pair of round, firm and beautifully
shaped breasts a good many women would envy.

Two of the girls appeared with jars full of hot and cold water,
and my redhead pulled me along to the bathroom, a sort of
alcove curtained off from the rest of the room. She motioned for
me to crouch down, as that's the accepted bathing position in
those parts, and showered me first with boiling water, following
this with the contents of the cold jar: a sort of Turkish sauna, in
fact. She soaped me thoroughly from head to foot, amusing herself by making as much lather as possible, and then blowing on the
bubbles, laughing like a child. To round off my toilet she gave
me a rubdown with eau-de-Cologne and made me climb into
baggy pyjamas patterned with tiny flowers, a cotton waistcoat and
a turban.

Then it was Corinne's turn.

I have never felt so comfortable, relaxed and free as within
those four walls where life is lived under the aegis of beauty and
harmony. I couldn't help remembering with a certain smile the
various accounts I had been given of Turkish barbarism, but after
all, we had only been under the shadow of the Crescent for twenty-
four hours, and there was still plenty of time.

From Edirne to Istanbul is not far short of 250 kilometres, and I
had worked out that in principle we should reach the Bosporus
in five or six days: our horses were in very good shape, and we
could easily ask them to do up to forty or fifty kilometres a day,
and complete the Paris–Istanbul journey in four months. Godfrey
de Bouillon and Peter the Hermit had only taken three and a
half, but our breakdown at Osijek explained our delay and our
Bulgarians had organised very short stages for us. I was beginning
to wonder if we would be able to reach Jerusalem by Easter, but
it didn't matter very much: the important thing was to get to the
City of David.

Our Christmas present—the mild weather—seemed to have
been used up, and the thermometer had dropped below zero

again, while snow fell day and night. Our anoraks were warm but
not waterproof, so we were soon soaked to the skin and looked
like a couple of bedraggled birds. The snow prevented our using
the country roads, and we had to go back to the main highway
where snow-ploughs and lorries assumed they had priority.

It took us anything between ten and twelve hours to reach our
planned destinations for we had to stop many times to chip out
the frozen snow that balled dangerously under the horses' feet.
As a result of tramping along the macadam, the horses began to
show disturbing signs of fatigue. Donald lost the energy he had
displayed in Bulgaria, and Mickey became very peevish as the
result of a swelling on his ribs. As for me, I became exhausted: my
cold had returned and so had my temperature. Corinne was
definitely the toughest of us all. One day, after struggling to stop
falling asleep on horseback, I dismounted, hoping that walking
might keep me awake. I slept on my feet until I was nearly knocked
down by a heavy lorry, and got away with nothing more serious
than a long tear in the sleeve of my anorak.

On top of everything, we had some difficulties which might be
described as topographical, firstly because the Turkish maps
would often have a village where there wasn't even a rabbit
hutch, and if we asked the locals for directions, they were usually
miles off the mark. One morning the boys came back to meet us:
they had scoured the entire district without finding a large village
called Ballalanli, clearly marked on the map. Eventually a shepherd
told us it was in a diametrically opposite direction, and not on the
road to Istanbul, so we settled on a rendezvous at the next marked
village, Büyük Çekmece, about forty-five kilometres further on.
The prospect wasn't at all attractive, as it was already midday and
we would only arrive very late at night.

At sunset, we found a landscape like a tourist poster: a village
beside the sea, divided by a canal spanned by a stone bridge. The
village seemed to be floating on the water, and didn't appear on
the map, though it was big enough in all conscience. Corinne
asked a passer-by its name and he pointed to our stables. We had
arrived at Büyük Çekmece four hours ahead of time. It wasn't
at all where it was supposed to be.

A new kind of nuisance: dogs. We were constantly being
attacked by packs of huge, half-savage animals who harassed

even the horses. Donald had had a chunk taken out of one leg during one of the fights.

However, we did have our little extras. For instance, it was very pleasant to pile our gear into the Green Mare. It was a great relief for Mickey and Donald and it saved an hour every morning because we didn't have to strap everything onto the saddles. It was also very pleasant to link up with Olivier and Patrick twice a day and warm ourselves with instant coffee brewed up on their spirit stove. Above all, we had no worries about our night's lodging, for armed with my letter from the Turkish Tourist Office in Paris explaining what we needed, our two gallants would go straight to the mayor or to the chief of police, who always bent over backwards to give us an appropriate welcome.

At the little town of Silivri, for instance, our noble colleagues deserved ten out of ten for the preparations they had made. Two large loose boxes awaited us, individual lodgings for the horses, with no draughts, clean and well provided with straw, a bale of lucerne (the best kind of fodder) in the racks, three kilos of oats in the mangers and two buckets of water at exactly the right temperature.

As for us, the mayor's secretary had installed us in a tourist bungalow on the beach, and as we were the only occupants, we were spoiled and waited on like nobody's business, or rather just as we had often been treated since we reached the land of the Crescent. I don't know how many times in restaurants, after stuffing ourselves with lamb cooked in the most delectable way and at very moderate cost, the patron refused to give us the bill because another client, without introducing himself, had already paid it. Sometimes one of these generous benefactors, considering that we hadn't had enough, would order salads and desserts for us that we hadn't intended to eat.

Everywhere, too, the police showed themselves incredibly helpful. When they stopped us it was never to ask for our papers, but to wish us good luck and offer help. Invariably their chief would pick out one of his men to stand guard all night over the comfort and security of the horses, and there was usually someone who stood guard over us too: usually the *mukhtar*'s wife. To give one example: at Silivri, about sixty kilometres before we reached Istanbul, the *mukhtar*'s wife installed us in a comfortable bed, with a mattress and eiderdown edged with the finest lace, and unrolled a mat on the floor where she spent the night herself. Every time I coughed or moved, she got up and came to see if I needed anything. Never do I remember such kindness, but apparently it was the local custom. We were guests (whose guests?), so we had to be looked after, and apparently it was something to do with religious custom. In Muslim countries, unmarried girls never sleep alone, there is always another woman, a sister or grandmother, with them. Obviously they never installed us in the same room as the boys.

At six o'clock our protectress pulled aside the curtains as we had asked her to do, pointing to the deep snow outside and indicating that it would be better to stay in bed and wait for the snow-plough. She was sure we wouldn't be able to leave until after breakfast, but it was a luxury we had to refuse: we were already so far behind schedule as it was.

When we took the road again, painfully, plunging through the snow, we admired the village women trotting along with pails of water slung on a yoke over their shoulders, but I wondered how on earth they managed to walk so gracefully with a thirty-kilo load.

CHAPTER TWENTY-NINE

Man's Best Friend

I have already mentioned the Turkish dogs: we had been warned over and over again about the brutal and licentious local males, but our friends should have talked about the real hazard, I mean the dogs. In no time at all we made the acquaintance of these half-savage creatures, thin and yellow, with mangy coats and bodies covered in festering sores, scavenging among the refuse dumps for scraps. Only the sheepdogs were more or less properly fed, well protected against their ferocious colleagues or even the odd wolf, by wide steel collars barbed with sharp spikes seven or eight centimetres long. The trouble was that although they were well fed and well looked after, these privileged animals were even more of a threat to strangers.

Our Pluto, who came up only to my knee, looked smart enough with his protective collar from Hermès (a present from Olivier). We bought him a local model in a village bazaar, only as it was designed for the local monsters it was too big and heavy for him to wear. However, we did manage to find some leather collars studded with small spikes and protected his throat with several of these 'ornaments'.

Every time we passed a pile of rubbish, the dogs rushed out, hackles up, snarling ferociously, determined to drive us away from their stinking El Dorado. Pluto usually got the message and wisely stayed between the horses' feet. We avoided the villages as far as we could, but it wasn't always possible, and of course, at night we did have to stop somewhere.

Even before we reached the first houses, our arrival would be announced by a chorus of menacing barks. Dogs would rush up from all sides, and settle into a well-organised pack surrounding our group. The Turkish dogs had never seen such tall horses, and this enraged them even more, but it was always Pluto, perhaps because he was bold enough to growl back at them, that the huge beasts were determined to tear down first, and they did their best to drive him out from the protection of the horses.

We helped our little dog as best we could, and quickly learned some effective manoeuvres. I would push Mickey forward into the midst of the pack, lashing out at sensitive muzzles with my long reins as hard as I could, trying to break up the group, and push Pluto in front of me. But Pluto didn't always make things easy: as pugnacious as a fighting-cock, even though he had been bitten several times already, he would turn back again and again to face the threatening fangs.

Then Corinne would take a hand with Donald, who you will remember had learnt a trick when urged of rushing at his aggressors and biting them with great enthusiasm. Stunned by the blows across their noses, the dogs in front would break away, but others always pressed forward and attacked Pluto from behind. One day I saw three of the brutes grab him under the collar and wrangle over him: then the biggest carried him off in his mouth exactly as I had seen Pluto carrying a mole, and he would obviously have been finished if Donald, driven on by Corinne, hadn't attacked with teeth and hind legs. Caught fairly and squarely by a set of studs, the Turkish dog dropped his prey and fled, yelping blue murder.

We took to our heels ourselves under the terrified gaze of some peasant women, and a little further on I examined Pluto who was wet with saliva, but seemed to have suffered only a few superficial bites. After a dusting with antiseptic healing powder, there was no sign of his wounds a few days later, except for the glorious scars.

On another occasion we nearly got into trouble ourselves. The dogs surprised us as I was reading the map and Corinne was playing her flute. We had dropped the reins and the horses' violent reactions nearly unseated us both. I would certainly have found myself in trouble if I hadn't clung to Mickey's neck and the pommel of the saddle. I still have cold shivers when I think I might have landed up like Jezebel. Out hunting, I have been in at the death many times, but never imagined I might one day find myself at the centre of the pack. Once again we owed our safety to flight—at top speed, horizontal on our saddles.

As this kind of misadventure seemed likely to be repeated we decided that the best way to keep Pluto safe was to hand him over to Olivier and Patrick, but our little dog hated the Green Mare, and looked so miserable we were forced to let him come back to us. A touching mark of fidelity, but it made us run terrible risks.

The most memorable battle we had took place in the loveliest setting imaginable, about fifty kilometres from Istanbul. We were walking along peacefully, on a sandy path at the edge of some steep cliffs. To our left, snow-topped mountains sparkled in brilliant sunshine, and to the right, at the foot of the cliffs, the sea curled lazily onto a narrow strip of sand, where a solitary figure, probably a shepherd, was playing a pipe and occasionally uttering piercing incantations. The peace of Allah reigned over all, until the shepherd's dogs—I might more accurately call them ravening beasts—appeared, fangs bared and snarling horribly. We were in an extremely tight corner and Pluto, who had been exploring along the beach, took refuge between my legs. His tail, which had been wagging happily a moment before went rigid and he moved forward very slowly, his ears drooping. I had never seen him look so cowed.

There were six of the dogs, and they surrounded us scientifically while we continued as if nothing were the matter, though Corinne and I were both in a cold sweat. There was no question of re-mounting, for we knew that if we tried we might give the animals the signal to attack. There was nothing for it but to walk on without hurrying, and keep our cool.

I'm not usually afraid of dogs, but that lot were really terrifying. Then they began to grow bolder. One of them made a snatch at Donald's tail, and pulled out a handful of hairs. Growing bolder still, he snapped at Mickey's hocks, and war was declared. Mickey and Donald turned on the aggressors behind them, and bit the ones attacking from the side. I snatched up a stick and struck with all my strength at a dog that was about to demolish Pluto. He sank his teeth into my elbow, releasing a cloud of feathers from my anorak, but Mickey saved me by taking a bite out of my aggressor's side.

The shepherd, who could hear what was going on, stopped his solo act and whistled, but the dogs were too excited to obey. A few well-placed kicks held them off until we could climb down the cliff, but once on the beach, the pack worried us unceasingly while a reinforcement of local dogs, hearing the commotion, came pouring down from the hills. Panic stricken, I could think of nothing better to do than to plunge into the sea. Corinne, the horses and Pluto followed me to a man, but not the Turkish dogs who stayed on the beach, barking furiously, obviously not at all keen o n the icy water.

We were saved, but they were still there, growling and making their murderous intentions only too clear. My arm was getting stiff and we wondered how long we would have to stay in the freezing water. When, oh miracle!—standing at the top of the cliff, what did I see? Patrick, hair and beard streaming in the breeze, preparing to act as our saviour. What could have brought him there, in the nick of time, if not the finger of God?

The odd thing was that he was smiling. He stooped, picked up some stones and let fly at the dogs, scoring a bull's-eye every time. And we saw our terrible monsters turn tail and scamper away as fast as they could. And that's how we discovered that Turkish dogs don't like being stoned, and all we had to do was bend down as if to pick something up and they all turned into lambs.

I washed my wound in sea-water; the salt burned and blood ran down my arm. I counted four teeth-marks round the joint, and Pluto came and licked me sympathetically. I used the same technique as I had on him and sprayed healing powder according to the vet's prescription. Of course it stung, but I smiled heroically, thinking that the result could have been infinitely worse.

CHAPTER THIRTY

The Bosporus and Beyond

23 January: Byzantium at last! Or, if you prefer, Constantinople
or Istanbul. We came to the first city of the Orient along a road
lined with prefabs while lorries and cars of all shapes and sizes
shot past, hooting their way through the carts and horses. How
far were we from the centre of the town? According to various
reports, two kilometres, twelve or twenty kilometres. Snow fell
intermittently, and I wondered if there was another road, but the
Turks didn't understand my questions. We were on a tarred road
cleared of snow, what more did we want? Besides, they weren't
at all worried themselves: horse-drawn vehicles travelled calmly
along the motorway, stopping or making U-turns whenever they
pleased, and bare-backed riders galloped along the shoulders.

Corinne and I were speechless: fortunately by now the horses
had acquired a certain philosophy, but we ourselves had become
much more sensitive to noise and exhaust fumes. When we tried
to escape from that hellish road and ventured down a side turning,
we were soon lost in a suburb which I was never able to identify on
any map. A man driving a cart appreciated our difficulty and
waved to us to follow him. He led us straight back to the motorway: so we had to put up with it, and perhaps it was just as well,
for we were soon hailed by the manager of a big service station
doubling as a tourist information bureau. Olivier and Patrick had
been there that morning and left a message to say everything was
ready for us. We were to meet them at the hippodrome, ten kilometres further on.

At the hippodrome we had a marvellous surprise. Having been

contacted by M. Montheillet, President of the Riding Club of France, and General Stoytchev, our Bulgarian protector, the local Jockey Club, the cream of Turkish horsemanship, had decided to take charge of us during the next five days. Mickey and Donald would stay at the hippodrome itself, in loose boxes as big as cathedrals, separated from the other horses for fear of contagion, fed by a special stable-boy assigned to their service and guarded day and night by two policemen, while we and our faithful escorts would be put up at the Çinar Hotel, a luxury palace.

Sightseeing in Istanbul for me meant not only the splendours of the Golden Horn, or the Princes Islands, the picturesque crowds in the bazaars, the treasures of St Sophia or Topkapi, but also a pilgrimage to the places where Godfrey and Peter the Hermit had left somewhat distressing souvenirs. Our soldier-pilgrims had sacked the outskirts of Constantinople and even attempted to take the town by storm, until they were given a sharp lesson by the troops of the Emperor Alexis.

I have to admit that we too had a few disappointments, for there wasn't a single letter for us, and not a penny at the bank. When we asked for our visas at the Syrian Consulate, we were given a categoric refusal—understandably enough, for fighting was still going on against Israel on the Golan Heights. However, we had one consolation: lunch with the French Consul provided a welcome change from our daily fare: in particular, a marvellous Camembert as well as delicious fresh Normandy butter.

The Jockey Club had organised a series of interviews, press conferences and photographic sessions which we couldn't possibly avoid, and as it was the least we could do for them, we went off to the hippodrome in a body, because the cameramen wanted to film our horses as well as ourselves. They were given a successful display, for Mickey and Donald were as skittish as kittens. They had never seen a racecourse before, and the green grass, and their colleagues masked from head to heel in bright colours with gold trimmings, amused them enormously.

We were made to pose beside some petrol pumps, to stress the contrast between two civilisations, and next day the *Hurriyet*, a big daily, headlined its article with: 'Two French girls find the answer to the petrol crisis'.

The journalistic bonanza continued with an official banquet

where we were the guests of honour, ending up at the nightclub of the Çinar. The representatives of the Fourth Estate insisted that we went up on the stage to join a famous belly-dancer, wearing a filmy transparent costume emphasising her not inconsiderable charms. Corinne and I were wearing our official costume, i.e. jeans and Mickey Mouse tee-shirts, and did our best to follow the rhythms of the local music. Our mixture of rock, cha-cha-cha and samba convulsed the audience, as well as the champion abdominal manipulator, and my only consolation was the good laugh I would have got out of seeing her on horseback, gauzy pants and all.

We had two surprises on the last day of our stay in Istanbul. The first was very unpleasant: the blacksmith at the hippodrome had given both our horses a complete set of new shoes. It was a real calamity because as they had been re-shod in Sofia barely eighteen days before, the horn hadn't had time to grow again. To make it worse, he had used racing plates, too thin and narrow to last even three days on the road. You might just as well expect a mountaineer to climb Everest in ballet shoes, so we would have to replace them as soon as we could, and it would be impossible to set the next lot of nails correctly.

The next surprise was better. When we returned to our hotel, we found all our clothes and underwear washed, ironed and mended. They smelt delicious, so we were able to pull on our blue jeans without blushing, and Corinne climbed back into her long Damart flannel underwear, which from being greeny-yellow was once more white as snow.

On the ferry across the Bosporus I watched Istanbul and its mosques melting into the fog. Our last sight of Europe. Ahead lay Asia. Our companions were unanimous: Anatolia was already under snow and in some villages it was only possible to go in or out of the houses through tunnels! Entire families, they declared, were dying of cold and hunger: wolves, driven mad by hunger, had been attacking the men.

Conclusion: unless we wanted to commit suicide, we'd much better retrace our steps and wait quietly in Istanbul for winter to be over.

I knew all that before I left Paris, and what I also knew was that Godfrey de Bouillon, having reached the Golden Horn at Christmas, only resumed his journey to Anatolia the following

May, and the drought and heat of the Turkish plateau ravaged his army. Of the two evils, cold and heat, Corinne and I had chosen the first. There was no question of turning back.

In view of our determination, we were advised to stick to the coast road: we would find it less cold, it was less frequented by bandits and more popular with tourists. I replied, 'Yes, of course' to everyone, and yet I was determined to avoid that particular route. Why? Because it was the one taken by Louis VII during the Second Crusade. Tired of being attacked by brigands, the French king and his men had taken ship at Antalya. By the most optimistic reckoning, this crossing represented an additional 800 kilometres, so I decided to remain faithful to Godfrey and cross Anatolia diagonally.

In one respect at least the warnings were correct: it was definitely much colder on the Eastern shore of the Bosporus, but we still left the main road at Izmit, and struck off into the mountains. We had barely left the suburbs of Istanbul when we ran into a couple of hunters who spoke good English:

'Excuse me. What nationality are you? Where are you going? It would be much wiser to stick to the road. You might be attacked...'

'Thank you, gentlemen...'

We pretended to return to the main road, but left it again as soon as possible, taking a dirt road to our next objective, Samandira.

It was a day of brilliant sunshine, the landscape patched with immense squares of greenery: little trickles of water gurgling in every fold in the ground. Three hours previously we had been warned that if we ventured into that region, we would find snow well above our horses' heads. Both of them were in their seventh heaven: Mickey in particular amusing himself by clearing every rivulet as if it were the water-jump at Longchamp.

At Samandira we were given fresh warnings, this time by two compatriots, professors of French in Istanbul, who had driven out to spend the day in this desolate spot.

'And you dare speak to these people?' they marvelled. 'But it's very dangerous. Weren't you told what you might be letting yourselves in for?'

But of course! And yet 'these people' greeted us warmly everywhere with touching kindness. To begin with, the horses were lodged in an enormous chicken-house, with the ground specially covered with hay, and given vast quantities of oats. The *mukhtar*'s wife had laid on a positive feast for us, her eyes filling with tears when she discovered that Corinne was suffering from a tummy upset and couldn't eat. Immediately she was bundled into a warm bed and our hostess sat up with her all night, periodically dosing her with cups of hot cabbage juice, though unfortunately her remedy was fairly ineffectual.

Next morning I was able to register two reassuring facts: nobody had slit my throat, and the Turkish money I had hidden in my boots and in the pocket of my anorak inside the front door was still there.

Next morning, off we went, still following the mountain paths. We were virtually alone—virtually that is, because every ten or fifteen kilometres we would stop for coffee provided by the Green Mare: Olivier and Patrick considering that in such weather we should be given regular hot drinks.

We were late at our rendezvous at Mollafeneri once again thanks to the usual attacks by those dreadful Turkish dogs. To avoid a general skirmish I had thought it wiser to cut away down an unmarked road, with the result that the day's thirty kilometres became fifty. When we finally arrived, our two hippies informed us that we would lodge with a local teacher, who was supposed to be instructing his pupils in the language of Racine. In fact, he couldn't speak a word of French, so Olivier and Patrick had volunteered to spend a few hours next morning in the local school. It would give them something to do, for once they had made our coffee and found lodgings and a stable, they had nothing to do but play the guitar or the Turkish shepherd's pipe. A little school-mastering would be a welcome distraction.

Once more we took the road, bound for Izmit, and this time we couldn't dawdle: we had nearly sixty kilometres to cover, more than usual, but next day we would be able to rest. The sun struck sparks from the snow, and the glare was so intense that we had to keep our eyes lowered. On this side of the mountain black goats, with long silky hair, scratched at the snow looking for grass, and the shepherds, with long goatskin capes with squared shoulders, looked like prehistoric men. We even saw a few tractors.

At about four o'clock, a peasant informed us that we still had forty kilometres to cover before reaching Izmit. We couldn't believe it, but at least it had been a glorious day. As darkness fell, we were walking beside the horses, and a car drove past and stopped just ahead of us. We scrambled back into the saddle nervously but it was only the chief of police from Izmit who had driven out to see if we needed anything.

'You shouldn't travel in the dark,' he told us. (Now where had we heard that before?) 'We can escort you into Izmit if you're afraid. Have you arranged where you'll spend the night? No? You don't want an escort? Sure? Very well. We'll see you later at the Grand Hotel. They're expecting you.'

Gradually the road dropped down and we came out of the clouds to see the lights of Izmit sparkling in the distance. Another car with blinding headlights screeched to a halt in front of us, and then another and another: the local correspondent of the *Hurriyet*, anxious to catch us on the hoof.

It was nearly ten o'clock when we reached Izmit, and the police showed us an excellent stable, with grooms who seemed to know what they were about.

What else could we wish for? A comfortable, quiet hotel, where we needn't move for at least forty-eight hours. Alas, the Coquet sisters might propose but the *mukhtar* disposed, for he had arranged an official banquet for all of us. There was no way of getting out of it, as we were the guests of the municipality.

Filled to the eyeballs with mint-flavoured yogurt, tomatoes, peppers and stuffed vine-leaves, rice with pine nuts, kebabs, baklavas, Turkish delight and other delicacies swimming in cream and honey, we staggered back to the hotel, our stomachs distinctly queasy, thinking of nothing but the blessed relief of sleep. Not a bit of it: a journalist was waiting for us and demanded an immediate interview. At midnight. I begged for a little charity.

'Very well. Tomorrow morning,' he compromised.

'Fine, fine. . . .'

What had I said? At seven o'clock the telephone rang: this time it wasn't one journalist but a whole horde. We refused to budge until eleven, but then the gentlemen of the press banged on the door so insistently that we had to surrender.

When they had finished we went back to sleep, but not for long.

First we had a visit from the police, then the two boys wanted to tell us about their day. Afterwards, there was a small fire. The journalists swarmed back into the hotel, and who do you think they wanted to interview first?

When it was time to start again we were anything but rested and in particular the first evening's banquet was still very much with us. I don't know who was sicker, Corinne or I.

CHAPTER THIRTY-ONE

Apotheosis at Eskisehir

I couldn't stand up straight and I didn't know if it was a hangover or an infection. For several days I had been feeling tired and now the top of my head was threatening to come off completely. For once I would have given anything for Corinne to go and feed the horses, but there was no way of making her open even one eye until the muezzin had given his final call to prayer—and his invitations to the faithful were loud enough in all conscience. Just to show how ill I felt, I would willingly have exchanged our blessed horses for a small car which wouldn't have had to be fed at the crack of dawn.

Outside, the icy wind made my head spin and tears stung my eyes, but I carried out my functions dutifully, without complaining. Once Mickey and Donald had had their breakfast I could go back to bed and sleep a little longer with a quiet conscience. If we didn't start on time, it couldn't matter less, or rather, it might even be a good thing, for the horses made better progress when they had had time to digest their meal.

That morning it was the police, not the military, who escorted us in a huge, black American car, stopping at every roadside hut to explain who we were.

We needed their protection mainly because of the children, who were a real nuisance, curious and fingering everything, as un-inhibited as flies buzzing round a pot of honey.

The boys demanded French cigarettes (in a country world-famous for its tobacco) while the girls had more feminine ambitions. One of them admired a big gold St Christopher hanging round my neck, a present from my mother the day we left, and wanted to swop it for an aluminium medal of Ataturk which she brandished under my nose crying:

'*Tamam?* Agreed? It's pretty!'

'No, not "tamam" at all.'

So she swooped down on Corinne and demanded her necklace of sky-blue beads.

'*Güzel,*' she repeated. '*França?*'

I started to laugh, surprised that she hadn't recognised the necklace, costing only a few pennies, worn by every Turkish horse, with the star and crescent engraved on the beads. One of the stableboys at the Istanbul hippodrome had given it to us, and when I explained this to the little girl she changed her mind at once.

'*Anorak güzel! Trousers güzel!*'

She wanted to swop with me and I don't know which would have been funnier, the little Turkish girl in a pair of washed-out, patched Levis, or me in mauve-flowered baggy trousers.

As we couldn't satisfy her on the ornamental or sartorial fronts, I offered her a handful of small change, whereupon she planted a sticky kiss on my cheek and departed, waving happily.

Back in the country, instead of the big American car and its policemen, we had a jeep with five soldiers armed with revolvers, machine-guns and a few assorted daggers.

As the sun set, the wind turned colder, whipping up small clouds of snow which stung our faces. We were so cold we dismounted and tried to get warm by walking, but with the wind in our teeth we were quickly exhausted. There were only ten kilometres to go before Gunduzbey, but in those conditions it seemed interminable. At last we heard some dogs barking, and though God knows we weren't very fond of Turkish dogs, the sound was a relief, for it meant we were nearly there.

At 5.30 next morning, even before the piercing '*Allah hou akbar*' from the muezzin, the jeep was at the door, with a double escort, for Olivier and Patrick had rejoined us. After a brief international conference, it was agreed that our French protectors would go first in the Green Mare and the jeep would bring up the rear. After that, we had precious little chance of getting involved in an adventure.

When they saw us about to walk—we had to try and get rid

of our morning stiffness, not to say rheumatics—the soldiers explained that we should ride and let Pluto go in one of the cars. As it was so cold—the mountains were covered in snow—there was every chance that wolves might be on the prowl.

We refused for we hadn't believed in the big bad wolf bit for a long time. And besides, what else were our bodyguard and all those weapons for? I may say there were people who would have been delighted to hear that the Coquet sisters had been attacked by Turkish wolves: the local journalists. They'd been publicising our overland trek at such length that really exciting news items were becoming rather thin on the ground.

Suddenly, the weather turned warmer and the wind dropped. Everyone had drummed into us that Eskisehir was buried under snow and the temperature was down to minus 30°. Now the thermometer had climbed to 2° above freezing and the village streets were so wet that the horses' hooves went 'plop ... plop ...' at every stop. The soldiers couldn't get over it.

'You're incredibly lucky,' they told us. 'This warm weather is absolutely unheard of. You must have brought it with you from France.'

Maybe we had, but the warm spell didn't last long, for two days later the entire region was completely frozen over again.

While we trotted along the sandy track that would eventually become the Paris–Jerusalem highway, I gazed at the rocky landscape with passionate curiosity, for I knew that here one of the greatest battles of the First Crusade had taken place. A little further north, the victorious Christians under Godfrey had decided to split up into two groups on their way to Dorylea (now Eskisehir). The second section was to follow twenty-four hours later. The first, under Bohémond de Tarente, consisted of Normans from Bohémond's own command, soldiers under the Count of Flanders and the Comte de Blois, and a Byzantine battalion which was supposed to act as guides. The second army, handed over to Raymond de Toulouse, was made up of the Comte de Vermandois's troops and soldiers from the south of France and Lorraine.

The sultan Kilij Arslan, who had been beaten at Nicea, was waiting near by to take his revenge on the Christians and, shouting their warcry, his archers fell on the first part of the Crusaders' forces at dawn on 1 July 1097. But Bohémond, who had been expecting an ambush, organised his defence with great efficiency and dispatched messengers to Raymond de Toulouse to hurry to his rescue. Bohémond's troops, although encircled and out-numbered, fought with the courage of despair, knowing that any survivors would end their days in the slave-galleys and much preferring to perish as martyrs on the field of honour.

They were about to be overwhelmed when, at midday on the crest of the hill they saw the standards of Godfrey and Raymond, and the Turks, who had believed they held the full force of their adversaries at their mercy, began to give way. At the same time they had yet another surprise, for a third Christian army appeared from between two hills, displaying the colours of Adhémar de Monteil, bishop of Le Puy. Whereupon the ranks of True Believers wavered and broke and the valiant soldiers of the sultan fled to the east, allowing the treasures of Kilij Arslan and his vassals to fall into the Crusaders' hands.

What always struck me in the account of this battle was that the victors (who had suffered very heavy losses) were loud in their praise of the military prowess of their adversaries, and the anonymous Norman chronicler of that particular Crusade declared that the Turks would be the finest race in the world, if only they were Christians. He also created the legend that Franks and Turks were cousins, and descended from the heroes of Troy.

I was jerked back from my historical musings by a black R-12 which stopped beside us. Four men in dark raincoats emerged and one of them, who sported a fine moustache, presented me with a bouquet.

'Welcome to Eskisehir,' he announced in French. 'Will you do us the honour of accepting this bunch of roses?'

If only Godfrey and his companions could have seen me!

The flower-bearer continued:

'Allow me to introduce myself. I am professor of French at the University of Eskisehir, this gentleman is the mayor, this is the chief of police and this is the correspondent of the *Hurriyet*.'

The last-named had already snapped at us at least a dozen times.

'We have organised a lunch at the next village, and I hope you will agree to join us.'

'With pleasure. But it's very cold and we can't leave the horses out in the open.'

'Don't worry. We'll find a stable for them. *Tamam?*'

'In that case, *tamam*.'

For the first time in my life I jogged along on horseback hugging a bunch of roses.

It goes without saying that at Eskisehir itself, our new friends had done things in style, and we were treated as if we were the ambassadors from the Most Christian King to the Sultan of the Sublime Porte. One detail gave us a slight giggle. The article in the *Hurriyet* was headed: 'Around the world with two young French riders'. Around the world! Was that all? Obviously the journalist considered that Jerusalem was practically next-door, and preferred to add something rather more spectacular.

As soon as we reached the houses people lined up to cheer us. Outside the town hall, the crowd was even thicker and the cheers more enthusiastic. If we hadn't been protected by soldiers and policemen, I doubt if we would have come through that apotheosis alive.

The banquet was very special for the *Hurriyet* had carried an interview with us a few days previously asking 'Which particular Turkish dishes do you prefer?' and we had replied with a long list of goodies. Our kind hosts had arranged for every one of them to figure on the menu.

Once again I realised that on a long-distance expedition like ours, it wasn't the back, the legs or thighs which were put to the severest test, but the digestion.

CHAPTER THIRTY-TWO

Olivier Throws in the Towel

We left Eskisehir preceded by the Green Mare and followed by the R-12 with the French professor and three policemen in civvies on board.

The horses were practically breathing fire as they pawed the riding-track, their splendid form being due entirely to the professor. As he escorted us round the National Stud at Eskisehir he had explained how they raised (he said 'cultivated') horses, on a mixture of barley, oats and molasses, a by-product of the local sugar industry, and we had tried out the mixture on Mickey and Donald.

The policemen did their duty nobly. Every time a driver stopped or slowed down to chat us up, they bawled him out and sent him smartly about his business, while three soldiers took it in turn to escort us—on foot. They strode after us with great determination, puffing like grampuses, even though we allowed ourselves to trot as often as possible. Our foot-sloggers were soon outdistanced, but as they had a keen sense of duty they caught up with us again—by hitch-hiking.

Mahmudiye in the mountains is one of the most important names in the international riding world. Three hundred stallions and brood mares are maintained there, and more than 100 foals are born every year. Magnificent pure-bred Arabs, with rounded hind-quarters, arched necks, very delicate heads, silky manes, short alert ears, shining coats, sure-footed and straight-legged, they break into an extended trot quite naturally as soon as they are taken into the ring, knowing how lovely they are and how much everyone admires them.

Officers and vets spoke very good French, for they had all spent a certain amount of time in France, and many French vets go to Mahmudiye for months at a time, fascinated by the beauty and qualities of the true Arabians.

Three mares, having been artificially inseminated, had foaled that morning, the first colt still resting after his exhausting ordeal. The second was already on his feet, his coat rumpled and damp, but full of curiosity for this brave new world. The third was trying to suckle but was having the greatest difficulty in balancing on his rubbery legs. I would have been very happy to choose between those three little wonders, but alas, the half-million that such masterpieces of nature cost was way out of my range.

For Olivier the end of the journey was in sight, for he had decided to leave us at Belpinar, about thirty kilometres further on, throwing in the towel after three weeks of gallivanting. He had always dreamed of travelling for at least a year between university and military service, but there it was. Man cannot live on air alone, and he had to write a thesis before the end of May; there were documents to be completed in connection with his military service. Perhaps he had also grown a little tired of the limited charms of Anatolia.

There was nothing for it but to bid him a fond farewell, hoping that the Green Mare wouldn't fall to pieces before the end of his trip. 'Good-bye, good-bye, you've been a living doll, you know . . .'

Olivier's departure threw the team into a certain amount of confusion. First there was our gear, which had increased considerably since we left Bulgaria, not surprisingly, for as it was usually on board the 2-CV we didn't have to keep whittling away a gramme here and a gramme there. Now we would have to go through everything again with a fine-toothcomb. As for Patrick, he was all in favour of sticking with us, or going on ahead, but he had no means of transport.

'But of course,' cried Corinne, 'Patrick can ride in the jeep and we can put our baggage on board as well.'

Well argued, of course, provided our military friends agreed, but when they said '*Tamam*', the problem was solved, at least for the time being.

Although Mickey had refused to eat his oats and damp straw because I couldn't find him any hay, he was still in fine form and sprang into action as soon as wheels were turning. The jeep followed soberly at walking speed, with its load of soldiers, sub-machine-guns at the ready, and its civilian passenger, Patrick, with his shepherd's pipe between his teeth. Twenty kilometres later, halt. The soldiers explained that they had reached the limit of their own zone and their mission was accomplished. Without another word they prepared to dump Patrick and all our gear into the middle of the snowy waste.

'From here on,' they said, 'you come under the gendarmerie of Emirdağ.'

On a high plateau swept by icy winds Patrick was uneasy and we were hardly delighted: trying to sort our possessions in this minor Greenland didn't seem very practical, and Patrick tried to talk the soldiers round without success. I had to join in with a charming smile, and eventually they agreed to transport our bundles and our companion as far as Emirdağ.

Two hours later we met the jeep that decanted two soldiers and then pressed on to its own destination. I can't say much for their physical fitness for even when we were walking they thought we were going too fast, and tried to make us slow down. Bored by their grumbling, we suggested they should climb into a farm cart loaded with manure which happened to pass at the psychological moment, and they certainly didn't need a second invitation.

I don't know what they said to their superiors when they arrived at the next halt, but the military authority decided that we must be escorted properly, by a jeep at least. In spite of this decision, next morning we were alone again, free and happy, on a track leading to Bolvadin. We had managed it by the simple expedient of getting up earlier than arranged and departing before our escort was even awake.

The weather was almost mild, no wind, rain or snow, and we were completely happy.

'Do you realise', I said to Corinne, 'we haven't seen a car, or horse or a shepherd all morning. Isn't it wonderful!'

As if to give me the lie, a blast from a horn made us jump and a

bus swept past us and stopped. It was typical of the local transport, the engine coughing and boiling, the bodywork tied
together with string, overloaded with passengers, some crouching
on the running-boards, others standing on the bumpers, clinging
to the roof-rack and even stretched out on the wings! The doors
opened and sixty or seventy men poured out and surrounded us
excitedly, leaving only a few veiled women sitting demurely
inside.

What did they want? My heart began to thump and I didn't
feel too happy, but once again, their intentions were strictly
honourable. They had seen us on television, read about us in the
papers and were obviously delighted to see the Coquet sisters in
flesh and blood, fulfilling their equestrian duties. They offered us
cigarettes and oranges and inquired if we were enjoying our stay
in Turkey.

The driver sounded his horn, the interlude was over, and our
fans squeezed back into the bus which went on its way coughing
like La Dame aux Camélias.

Alone at last—but not for long. This time it was 'our' jeep that
caught up with us, the officer in command absolutely furious
while he told us exactly what he thought of us. What a fuss about
a small escapade! Apparently they don't have much sense of
humour in Turkey.

Bolvadin: there was almost a riot round the stable where we
had parked the horses and the entire town seemed to have turned
out to see us. Our escort had a hard time forcing a way for us
through the crowd until a police car drove up with reinforcements. In the midst of the general excitement questions were
fired at us from all sides, in an English that was only relatively
grammatical but was at least comprehensible. Many of the men
wanted to know if we could help them find jobs in France, and
could they have our address just in case?

As a result of the previous day's escapade our protectors
decided not to leave anything to chance. When we left the
enthusiasm of Bolvadin behind, a military Land-Rover preceded
us, a police car followed close behind and we were flanked to right
and left by soldiers, each carrying a sub-machine-gun slung over
one shoulder and a cutlass hanging from his belt. It was only at
the end of the day, when we reached Degirmenkoy, that the

procession broke up, but even so the *mukhtar* took up station alongside.

I know that the Turks are paved with good intentions, but all the same it was very tiring to be so closely supervised. Whether we went to the stables to water our horses, or wanted to sample the local sanitation (which wasn't always all that close to the house) an armed man dogged our footsteps. They explained that it was to stop us being attacked by brigands (what brigands?), to protect us from the local dogs (we knew all about them), and also to prevent our being worried by over-curious children or men. In that suffocating atmosphere the women were the only people I could bear: they were so calm and gracious, always smiling and friendly. Besides, unlike the men, they never shouted—they whispered, so much more restful.

The horses, too, were on edge, particularly Mickey who gave an unusual display of temperament when he met horses, donkeys or even oxen on the road. I thought he was showing signs of a certain perversity, and took far too much interest in everything on four legs. He whinnied at the slightest provocation, and shied whenever he heard a scream of brakes, however faintly it reminded him of a colleague. As the weather was very fine, I thought his amorous transports might be due to an early spring, but then I discovered the real reason. When our host, the *mukhtar*, carried a bucket of hay to the stables, Mickey fell on it enthusiastically. The hay smelt to high heaven of curry, or some other spice, and there was no need to look for any biometeorological explanation as to why Mickey had been stirred to the depths of his soul.

Arğithani . . . Ilgin . . . Tossunoglu . . . an enchanting landscape in the heart of Anatolia. Snow-capped peaks sprang into the blue sky, and little lakes of sapphire sparkled, edged with tall reeds and golden willows. For several days the sun had been shining with all its might, and the ground had dried out beautifully. According to our guards, no one had ever known such a thing in mid-February. All would have been for the best if every time we went through a village we hadn't been submerged by waves of men and children, particularly children. At Kadinham, for instance, a largish town two days from Konya, there must have been a thousand of them, aged between five and thirteen, who ran round us like Apaches surrounding a column of American pioneers, screaming, waving their arms and whistling. As they grew bolder they slipped under the horses' bellies, clinging to the saddles, hanging on to the stirrups, grabbing at the baggage. Some even got kicked and fell, but nobody seemed to care, they were trampled underfoot and the war-dance went on.

They pulled Pluto's tail and threw stones at him. He growled, barked and snapped, or took to his heels, but the children still chased him.

The two soldiers who were supposed to protect us could do nothing with the swarming urchins until happily a lorry appeared with a reinforcement of gendarmes. Blows rained, truncheons were wielded to good purpose, and we needed every bit of their help to pull us clear of the yelling crowd, only to fall in with another gang, who followed us for another six or seven kilometres. Tough road-merchants, those Turkish children, and I began to understand why the Turkish infantry is said to be among the best in the world.

Calm was eventually restored, and the silence was broken only by the murmur of a stream, or the prayers of one of the guards telling his beads.

CHAPTER THIRTY-THREE

Dolce Far Niente

I had had high hopes of an extended stop at Konya. The soldiers of Godfrey de Bouillon and Raymond de Toulouse had rested in that same Anatolian city (then called Iconium) after an exhausting journey across the desert. Of course, our ancestors had launched their offensive at a time when we would more normally be taking our holidays, i.e. July and August. When they got wind of the approach of the terrible soldiers of Christ, the Turks had abandoned the city, taking with them everything they could carry: an extremely early example of the scorched earth policy, though they had had no time to fire the fields and orchards. Raymond de Toulouse who had been so desperately ill that he had received the last rites, recovered his health as if by a miracle, and so indeed did Godfrey, who had been mauled by a bear while out hunting.

We hoped that Konya would have the same effect on us and the welcome we were given was quite up to the inflated reputation we had been given by the Turkish mass media.

Everything seemed set fair. We were still more than a day's ride from Konya when a motorcade met us, bringing the welcome committee organised by the Provincial capital, consisting of four soldiers, three police officers, five journalists and an interpreter, easily the most impressive personality of the lot, though personality may be rather a high-flown way of describing a fifteen-year-old, even if he was as bright as a button. His name was Assam, and he began by announcing that in Konya we were to be the guests of one of the richest industrialists in the town, the owner of a group of flour-mills, whose passion in life was the improvement of his bloodstock lines. Not only would Corinne and I be given the red carpet treatment, but so would Mickey and Donald, not to mention Pluto.

The reality certainly came up to expectations, apart from Konya itself, which in spite of its 200,000 inhabitants wasn't a large town at all, but an overblown village, a mixture of wooden houses and mud huts inhabited by gentlemen of the old school, deeply attached to the traditions Ataturk had done his best to sweep away.

The house where we were to stay was not only very fine, but had been Europeanised in the sense that we weren't invited to squat, but were given chairs and a table, while other Western innovations included a telephone, an intercom and a record player, with an assortment of mainly American discs.

Assam opened his huge black eyes very wide and said, 'You're very lucky to be here, you know. It isn't as modern as this at home, we don't even have electricity . . . My family doesn't live like this at all.'

His tailor father was a very strict practising Muhammadan, who took the teachings of the Koran very seriously, so our interpreter enjoyed the privileges of an eldest son whenever his father went away. This meant that he became the head of the family, and all the women, including his mother, had to obey him. He could ask their advice if he liked, but wasn't obliged to follow it. His sister was sixteen and only left the house to go to school, but she came home directly lessons were over.

'If a man tried to speak to her, still less touch her,' continued this precocious adolescent, 'my father or I would kill him and if she ever showed any interest in a man, my father or I would kill *her*.' And he didn't seem to be joking. A woman's place is in the home, where she should look after the males of the family, beautify the house with embroideries or lace, which the girls make during the long winter evenings, bent over their oil lamps. As far as marriage goes, they don't have any say at all, it's all left to the father. As for education, only the most emancipated go to university.

'What about the others?'

'They embroider.'

We met Ibrahim's daughter, Usnier, a very pretty eighteen-year-old brunette, who was obviously one of the lucky ones, for she was attending the local university, and was even allowed to wear a mini-skirt at home, though not in the street. We wondered if this meant that Ibrahim's Westernisation had gone beyond his furniture, but apparently not, for when I spoke to him of our own social customs, he threw up his hands.

Usnier was allowed just five minutes to get home from her classes, and she had never danced 'in Western fashion' with any man except her father. As for contacts with the opposite sex, her father raised his eyes and pointed a finger to heaven, repeating almost word for word what Assam had said. 'If my daughter noticed a man, I would kill her.'

I was quite sure he would, for the night before, as we came out of a cinema, a young man had brushed my shoulder. I hadn't noticed particularly, and he might not even have done it on purpose, but when we got home Ibrahim took us into his bedroom and brought out a small pistol and a huge revolver, both fully loaded.

'I will protect you as if you were my own children. Today I have three daughters, Evelyne, Corinne and Usnier. Coming out of the cinema, a young man jostled you, didn't he, Evelyne? Well, you needn't worry, I'll have him punished.'

'I sincerely hope he won't be killed for anything so trivial.'

One morning Ibrahim piled us all into his red Chevrolet and after dropping his wife and Usnier off at the hairdresser (they had to be beautiful, if only for his benefit), took us to meet one of his business colleagues. This friend, Sinan, who spoke French perfectly (he had studied in Paris) had a private stud about four kilometres from Konya where he had bred several champions.

Shorter than the average Turk, his hair a little longer than our own fashions, wearing a well-cut business suit, relaxed but dynamic, Sinan looked every inch the 'young executive' and took us in his car—the regulation Mercedes—to visit his establishment.

The buildings were sensational, with huge loose boxes filled with plenty of straw. Even in Ibrahim's stables the horses had to lie on the bare ground, covered with soft earth which the stable-boys swept up in the morning and spread out again at night. Here the mares and foals roamed about freely in open fields, separated by rows of apple trees, and here Sinan had a second home, its only point in common with the normal Turkish houses being that it was built of wattle and daub: apart from that, it reminded me of a Normandy manorhouse, with all the mod cons that a Turkish millionaire could think of.

'How would you like to come out here and stay for a few days?' he asked. 'You'll be much more comfortable than in town, and you needn't worry about anything: the house is empty for the moment and I shan't even be able to come out for the week-end as I have to fly to Paris on business . . .'

An offer like that couldn't be refused.

'O.K?' asked Sinan. 'Bravo. I'll just have a word with my people.'

I asked if it would be possible for one of our friends (I meant Patrick, of course) to come too.

'But of course,' he replied immediately, and then added, 'I would just ask one thing: don't bring your dog into the house. He'll be perfectly all right in one of the outbuildings.'

How odd to find this touch of tradition in the midst of such sophistication.

Ibrahim was very sad to see us go but realised that we would much prefer the pure country air to the very doubtful attractions of the centre of Konya, so in due course Sinan sent an estate car to fetch Patrick and our gear. We trotted comfortably behind and reached the stud in record time. The chauffeur handed us over to the caretaker, an enormous man, six feet tall, with colossal shoulders and a yellow complexion. With three days' growth of beard, moist unfocused eyes, his brows clouded, he looked as cross as a bear that had been roused from hibernation.

'Opium,' hissed the chauffeur, winking at me conspiratorially.

The bear closed the iron gates, a grille strong enough to keep out a tank, and as a twelve-foot wall ran round the whole property, there we were, locked up for several days.

Not that our prison was all that bad. There were European divans and deep armchairs in an enormous living-room, with a pile of logs glowing red in the fireplace. In one corner was the latest stereo with dozens of French records and a sortie to the kitchen revealed a fridge bursting at the seams. Obviously Sinan had thought of everything.

I spread a pile of sheepskins beside the fire and stretched out, and was just about to doze off when a series of Red Indian war-whoops woke me up. Corinne and Patrick had been carrying out a thorough inspection of the kitchens and come upon treasure trove: Nescafé which we much preferred to the thick Turkish coffee, fresh Normandy butter, French sausages and potatoes. All we had to do was roast them in the warm ashes on the hearth, making a nice change from dolmades and kebabs.

Pleasantly full, relaxing in the scented warmth, rocked by an Albinoni record, I fell fast asleep on my pile of sheepskins.

CHAPTER THIRTY-FOUR

The Camels are Coming

Our week's break at Konya had given us all a chance to recuperate and brace ourselves for the crossing of the desert. According to the calendar, it was still mid-winter, but the dry season had already begun, dust clogged our throats and the water-bottle was quickly emptied. We had to be extremely careful, for wells were few and far between and very often dry, even as early as this. We could pick out the river-beds easily enough, but they were dry channels with only a thin trickle of water glinting in the sunlight. Not an insect, not a bird. Nothing and no one, not even our two military friends carrying our baggage, who had long ago given up trying to keep up with us, for Corinne and I gave way to the temptation of a good canter whenever we came to a suitable piece of ground.

More and more I realised that my decision to cross the region in February and March wasn't as crazy as it seemed, for in a few weeks' time we wouldn't have been able to find enough water for our own needs, let alone the horses', who between them got through between sixty and eighty litres a day.

Above us rose the chain of the Taurus mountains, an impressive rocky barrier patched and broken by old eruptions of lava, forming waves and bands of strange colours and shapes. I rubbed my eyes, for what I saw at the foot of a slope was a lake, of dark, almost black water. At first I thought it must be a mirage, but it was real: the fact that it wasn't marked on our map didn't matter in the least, for there it was and we would have a chance to refresh ourselves.

As we drew nearer, the ground turned grey and so soft that our feet sank in up to the ankles, and the horses were obviously afraid, refusing to go any closer, though they must both have been very thirsty.

Suddenly piercing cries broke out, barbaric yells and shoutings, and I saw that a caravan of camels had halted by the roadside, and a group of camel-drivers were running down the slope towards us, yelling. Two alarming-looking individuals grabbed me by the elbows, two others seized Corinne, while the rest took the horses by the bridle and forced us to climb back up the slope. It would be an understatement to say I was terrified, for obviously everything we had been warned against was about to happen. The Turkish Government wouldn't have given us an armed guard unless they had had good reason.

I looked at our abductors more closely. Obviously we could expect no mercy from these little yellow men, with their sunken eyes half-hidden under their caps. I remembered that these were the descendants of the Tartars and Huns, the savage tribes that had spread terror from faraway Mongolia right into the heart of Europe.

I even found I was no longer afraid: I was resigned. After all, it was entirely my own fault, and I merely hoped that our sufferings wouldn't be too prolonged. Moments passed—an interminable period of suspense. Why were these children of Attila waiting to live up to their reputation? One of them began to harangue us volubly, but what was he saying? Our death sentence? Not at all. Finally, waving his arms towards the lake he embarked on an elaborate pantomime and repeated with enormous conviction several times:

'Yok . . . Yok . . . Yok . . .'

Which probably meant: 'No, no, don't drink the water, it's dangerous.'

That evening, when we stopped at Eregli, we were told all about the poisonous stagnant water, the quicksands round it, as well as horrible stories of men and beasts perishing there miserably. I was even assured that a terrible monster lurked in the depths and swallowed up everything that came within reach. Every country has its Loch Ness.

In the meantime our saviours refilled our water-bottle from

their own supplies and gave the horses a drink. I explained to one
of them that I had never seen a camel, except in a zoo, and would
like to get a closer look. But of course. What struck me most was
that they were smaller than I expected, and the soles of their feet
were hard enough for them not to need shoes—one complication
less. Their knees too were as horny as their feet.

Seeing the loads they were carrying—apart from the water-
bottles, an incredible amount of fruit and vegetables, hay and
straw—an idea came into my mind: wouldn't this be the ideal
pack animal to transport our baggage—and Patrick during the
rest of our journey? Our hippy-courier could even gallop ahead
to set up our stop-overs. I asked Corinne what she thought.
'Brilliant' was her opinion.

I asked our caravaner what he wanted for his camel, and after
counting on his fingers he named a figure which would have been
the equivalent of about 1,000 francs. Not very much. I was really
tempted, and the only thing that made me hesitate was that I
knew absolutely nothing about camels, and if we took on one of
those beasts we might have real problems. I went up to the smallest camel and patted his neck. Immediately I discovered why a
disagreeable customer in France is called a camel, for he spat at
me, broke wind and stared malevolently, while at the same time
displaying a double row of threatening yellow teeth.

The camel-driver roared: 'RRRrrr! Grrr!' The hideous beast
knelt down, his master climbed astride the humps and motioned
to us to mount, as he planned to lead us to the outskirts of Ereğli.
Behind each camel walked his driver, urging the animal on by
hurling stones from a sling at their ridiculously small hind-
quarters. Completely indifferent, the camels moved along, rolling
and pitching like rowing-boats in a choppy sea: even watching
made me feel seasick. No, very definitely, I preferred my horse.

Ereğli . . . Gakmak . . . Porsuk. *Mukhtar* followed *mukhtar*, and
so did their wives, each one cosseting us as best she could, and
then came Pozanti which deserves a special mention because it
was absolutely hideous, with a tarred road and a tourist snack-
bar, while Porsuk was a ravishing village clinging to the
mountainside, almost invisible and reached by virtually unscalable
paths. But those tiny houses, set in the living rock, revealed
treasures the like of which I had never seen: embroideries, jewels

and carpets: nor did we ever meet women more anxious to please strange Amazons who seemed to have dropped from another planet.

And then we reached Camalan, a village Corinne and I have good reason to remember, where we stopped only because our way was blocked by a landslide. All the houses, made of pinewood, followed the same pattern: a ground floor where all the pack animals were installed—donkeys, oxen and a few rickety horses—and an upper storey divided into a kitchen and a single large room where the entire family lived and slept.

I combed the village in search of oats, but all I could find were a few grains of barley mixed with the scrapings of a sack of flour, some corn cobs and a small sack of chopped straw. I couldn't find any bread, potatoes, carrots or sugar, so poor Mickey and Donald would have to tighten their belts.

When I returned, empty-handed and out of humour, I found the stable surrounded by a crowd of agitated peasants. When they saw me, the villagers parted to let me through, turning worried faces on me.

'Madam! Madam!' one of them cried. '*Accidentt! Accidentt!*'

And then I saw Corinne, flat on her face just outside the stable, lying on one of our saddle-cloths, white as a sheet and groaning.

Patrick, who had been in the courtyard at the time of the accident, said he had seen her coming out of the stable, doubled up and screaming, holding her backside with both hands. Fearing she had hurt her spine, he had made her lie down at once. The fact that she had been screaming and could walk reassured me a little, for it didn't seem as though she had fractured her spine.

Corinne opened her eyes and tried to speak. I waved the spectators back as I wanted to see where she was hurt, and when they didn't move, the *mukhtar*, a solidly built person, with biceps like footballs, threw a volley of stones at his fellow administrators. They beat a hasty retreat and regrouped a little further off while they waited.

I could find no actual wound or bone injury, but just below her coccyx there was an angry red mark. The *mukhtar* picked her up as if she were a feather, and carried her up to the first floor, laid her down on a bed and she explained what had happened. She had been brushing Donald when he started to fight with Mickey, something that often happened. They would begin by rubbing noses, and nibbling each other, then they would bite each other's necks and what had started as a game degenerated into a serious fight. As they were wearing studs, the results were often bloody and though the answer would have been to keep them apart at night, it wasn't always possible.

Corinne had been caught between them, a kick had sent her flying and she had landed on her bottom on a water-jar. The jar hadn't even broken, but she had had a severe jolt. It wasn't a total catastrophe, but to put it mildly, it was inconvenient.

Next morning Corinne could neither stand nor walk, let alone ride, and we couldn't possibly stay where we were until she was better. It might take some time, and we couldn't stay in a village where the people may have been kind, but food for the horses was non-existent. We had to get her to some reasonably large town where she could be properly looked after. Adana wasn't too far away, and I would have to manage as best I could with the two horses.

I contacted the president of the Racecourse Society at Adana, who had been told about us by the Riding Club of Istanbul. I was able to ring him up, for the phone at the local police station actually worked, and as an additional stroke of luck (there are days like that) the president's wife answered and spoke excellent French. Immediately she promised to send a car to pick up Corinne.

When I left Camalan with the two horses and a minimum load, I wasn't too worried. Corinne was looking forward to a few days' rest, for she had discovered an entrancing occupation: the women of the household had shown her how to string wide collars of beads.

CHAPTER THIRTY-FIVE

Over the Taurus Alone

So there was I, all alone, facing an enormous rocky barrier with 10,000-foot peaks soaring upwards. It was odd how history had repeated itself—or very nearly. Nine hundred years ago, Godfrey de Bouillon had parted company with his brother Baudouin because they couldn't agree on which route to take. Acting on the advice of his Byzantine guides, Godfrey had chosen to bypass the mountains to the north-east in order to avoid what were described as impossible roads, but the route he used was almost as difficult. Baudouin had preferred to scale the mountains, even at the risk of having to swarm up dangerous precipices, and the two brothers met again, after terrible losses, at Marras, about 300 kilometres south-east of Ereğli. As I was due to pick Corinne up at Adana, Baudouin's route had more or less been chosen for me, and I can't truthfully say I was upset. In fact, the prospect of meeting such a challenge lifted my spirits considerably.

If I was to believe the map I consulted at the police station at Camalan, there wasn't a single attractive way to the top, only the main highway, not at all my idea of heaven. But I could see a track running from Karaisali down towards Adana, though I would have to travel due east for fifteen kilometres through the wildest mountain scenery, in a landscape so deserted that it would satisfy the austerity of an anchorite.

From the start I pushed Mickey on because I wanted to get out of sight of my gendarmes as quickly as possible, before they could try and persuade me to go back to the main road again.

The ground was very broken, stones rolled beneath the horses' feet, they slipped, twisted their hocks, jumped down on to rocky plateaux and landed with a jolt, all four feet together, so that it hurt me to see them. Donald followed us leisurely, stopping to graze among unidentifiable bushes, quite happy to catch us up from time to time.

At the foot of a ravine that we had scrambled down by taking enormous risks, ran a little stream, clear, sparkling and refreshing; general halt for a quick drink. A cluster of red tulips struck a gay note among that abomination of desolation, and then we had to climb up the other side.

A rough path seemed to lead through the rock, but almost immediately we found ourselves paddling in thick mud, for the snow was melting fast and if the horses didn't lose their shoes it was because the last blacksmith at Konya had been a genius. The slope was almost perpendicular and I was out of breath, pulses hammering, my head throbbing. Five kilometres of climb, five kilometres of torture, but from the top of the crest, knees buckling, I could see the whole fantastic panorama of the range.

Could I be dreaming? Two paces away was a kind of pathway leading in exactly the right direction, and everything looked easy for we would be going downhill all the way. But man proposes, and my poor horses had to suffer, for what I had taken for a path was merely the dry bed of a stream, and neither Mickey nor Donald enjoyed the slipping stones and sharp flints, which cut them to the bone. The extraordinary part was that the region wasn't entirely uninhabited: here and there little grey donkeys basked in the sun while their masters sowed goodness knows what over those barren pastures. To hope to harvest anything they must have been confirmed optimists.

At one point Mickey stopped short, his ears pricked, and I wondered what he could have seen or heard. I could see nothing but the desert, not a sign of life, and then I could feel someone watching me and realised a man was squatting on his heels almost at my feet. What on earth was he doing there? He was probably wondering exactly the same thing about me. I couldn't understand why I hadn't seen him before, but he watched me pass without batting an eyelid. A little further on a camel and his master stared at me, one disdainfully, the other amazedly, though neither of them moved as I rode by.

At last I came to a well-travelled dirt road, though it couldn't have been the one I had seen on the map, for to reach it I would have had to cross a railway and I hadn't seen so much as a sleeper. However, it didn't matter, for the road must lead somewhere, and all I had to find out was where. Of course I could have asked one of the human statues I passed every now and then, but I knew they would all automatically answer 'Yes' whether I pointed to the left or the right. The Turks may not mean any harm, but I had noticed that they never disagreed with anyone either.

However, I did ask some of the goatherds in my best Turkish if they knew where the road went, and they merely waved me on, so on I went. The road surface was very good, and I remounted, for I had been walking since early morning and was really exhausted. Two hours later what was due to happen, happened! A flourishing oasis appeared, a hamlet surrounded by green fields and I was welcomed with loud cries of joy (I couldn't have been more surprised) as a blessed soul escaped from the rocky Gehenna of the mountains.

I was shown to a café and given a chair, the only female among a crowd of heavily moustachioed unshaven men, who each insisted on buying me a cup of tea, but as I was more hungry than thirsty, I tried the small grocery store opposite, but only managed to buy some peanuts. My bewhiskered cavaliers vied with each other in shelling them for me, so I could eat without tiring myself. They waited for me to explain who I was and where I was going, and listened as if I had been a messenger from Allah.

I asked for something for the horses, and one of them produced ten litres of barley, enough to satisfy Mickey and Donald's hunger until the evening, so once the horses had been fed and rested, I decided to carry on. There was only one snag: while I had been having my 'lunch', pitch-black clouds had covered the sky.

One of the men offered to guide me, and I accepted gratefully, but hardly had we set out than the storm broke. And what a storm! Enormous flashes of lightning lit up the landscape, and thunder rolled among the mountains, while torrents of water descended on our heads and my anorak was soon dripping like a sponge.

My guide struck off the road to take short cuts, and I followed him until suddenly we came on the expected railway. The track ran north–south, whereas I wanted to go east. My man shook his head, and by drawing his hand across his throat, explained that if I did, I would be risking our lives. As it was nearly dark when he left me to go back to his village, I went on alone in a southerly direction, without really knowing where I was going.

With my hood pulled down over my eyes against the rain I couldn't see a thing, but I could still hear and what I heard wasn't very reassuring. Put yourself in my place: what would you think, alone in the Taurus mountains, during a storm at night, if you heard the sound of shots? I pulled back my hood and turned round to see three dark figures running towards me. My heart was in my mouth, until I saw that two of them were carrying guns and the third had long hair.

'Evelyne . . . Evelyne . . .'

It was Patrick and our two gendarmes. My blood-pressure returned to normal, and I listened calmly to the furious reproaches of the escort for having once more given them the slip. But I was far more interested in what Patrick had to say about Corinne for he had seen her in the hospital at Adana where she was being treated like a princess.

The gendarmes cut short our effusions by inviting me to follow them and this time I had no reason to refuse. To my surprise we arrived, not at Karaisali, as I had thought, but at Kelebec, twenty kilometres further south, a totally pardonable mistake in the circumstances.

The *mukhtar* was hospitable, but his means seemed somewhat limited: on an evening when I was famished I was given one hard-boiled egg, three black olives and some dry unleavened bread. I thought nostalgically of the fragrant soups we would have been eating at home. The *mukhtar*, who had eaten no more than I, lit a stove to dry my clothes and brought me something to change into, but I couldn't tell if the trousers were meant for a man or a woman; not that it mattered, for the Turks long ago invented unisex trousers and all I had to do was tighten the string round the waist.

When I wanted to sleep I was shown to a room where the floor was covered with carpets the like of which I have rarely seen, and a bed hung with beautiful embroidery. The disparity between the luxury of the homes and the quality of the food never ceased to amaze me, and as for the generosity of the locals, it was quite staggering. Next morning, with dazzling smiles, the villagers presented me with charming parting gifts: a gold (well, almost) ring, ropes of beads, an embroidered wedding veil, a silver charm, a glass vase . . . Good heavens, where was I to put it all? Fortunately Patrick was with me.

However, Patrick had decided to make an experiment, and even though he had never ridden before, wanted to spend an entire day on horseback. He was heavier than I, so I let him have Mickey and rode Donald myself, as I was very tired after the previous day's march.

As we travelled down towards the plain, the vegetation changed, and the aloes and cactus gave way to rows of palm-trees, precursors of the Mediterranean warmth. Our horses snatched lettuces from the fields beside the road, and we picked enormous juicy oranges which had been overlooked in the last harvest. Suddenly, round a corner, a green valley lay below us, with Adana in the middle distance, dazzlingly white, under a blue sky spanned by a brilliant rainbow. But it went on raining all the same.

It was eleven o'clock when we reached the town centre, and the traffic was tremendous and very noisy; neon signs adding their multi-coloured advertisements to the traffic-lights, but we barely had time to ask our way before a light van pulled up alongside. The driver was a stable-boy from the hippodrome out for a ride, and he had recognised me from my photograph in the daily paper (the Turkish press was definitely giving us the full treatment). When I asked him about Corinne he told me she had left hospital and gone to stay with friends, which seemed a very good sign.

I was less pleased when he told me that the hippodrome where the horses were to be lodged was ten kilometres further back, on the road to Mersin, a detail that our guardians-of-the-law friends should have known about. As a result we clocked up a record day's journey of seventy kilometres, though we hadn't stopped once, and our teams of escorts had kept up extremely well. (I use the plural because the army, wary of our endurance, had organised relays of infantrymen who changed every twenty or twenty-five kilometres.)

Patrick had even more reason than I to be furious. The fact of setting up a record, even at some personal inconvenience, tickles my ego, but the poor fellow could only think of one thing, that it was inhuman to inflict such a marathon on a novice. He had never regretted the Green Mare more, and if he didn't express his rage more forcibly, it was simply because he hadn't the force. When I congratulated him on his courage—I could see him gritting his teeth—he merely threw me a glance full of rage and distress.

When we reached the hippodrome, I telephoned the president to find out where Corinne was.

'She spent the afternoon with one of my friends,' he said, and gave me directions as to how to find her.

Off we went, and found her relaxing on a pile of feather-beds, surrounded by flowers, a box of chocolates on her bedside table and a glass of champagne in her hand, being photographed by newspapermen. She who normally fights shy of publicity, was all smiles. Obviously it suited her to sit down hard on water-jars!

The master of the house and his wife, naturally, refused to let us depart, seeing it was nearly midnight, and were indignant when they discovered that Patrick and I hadn't had any dinner.

'You ought to be ashamed of yourselves. Couldn't you have told us sooner?'

In two ticks the table was spread with those delicious little dishes which are the glory of Turkish gastronomy, and I had a good gorge, but poor Patrick was on the verge of collapse and had to be put to bed at once. He was rubbed raw and bleeding from thigh to heel. Musihe, our hostess, already busy with Corinne, found herself saddled with another invalid.

In the salon, surrounded by a friendly group, including the president of the Racecourse Society, I was having the time of my life. Forgetting the day's excitements, I was so happy among those kind people who all spoke French or English, that I held the floor unashamedly. My audience was tremendously appreciative, and every anecdote was greeted with loud outbursts of laughter. How pleasant it all was. I began to hope that Corinne wouldn't recover too quickly, for after all, Jerusalem was less than a month away.

CHAPTER THIRTY-SIX

The Little Horse is Sick

As soon as Corinne could walk (though not sit) we started again. Our departure from Adana was reasonably spectacular, for in the middle of the crowded bazaar at the edge of the town, Mickey kicked over a bicycle. He would have trampled the cyclist under-foot if he hadn't leapt acrobatically on top of a pile of oranges, while our little horse got more and more worked up as he tried to kick free of the pedals. As a demonstration of solidarity, Donald tried to climb up on to the empty trailer of a stationary articulated lorry, whereupon Pluto, completely terrified, ran under a car and came out the other side, with his tail stiff, and his ears flattened, yelping at the top of his voice. What a performance!

But traffic and houses were soon left behind and we found ourselves in open country. Once again we had taken French leave, slipping away from our gendarmes whose usefulness had become less and less apparent. They drove us mad because they didn't like going fast, and their favourite road song—a kind of nasal chant which they entoned while they told their beads—wasn't at all inspiring. As guides they were utterly useless: indeed, their incompetence was frightening. The men of the first Crusade had had arguments with their guides as they crossed Anatolia. Accusing the Turks of having deliberately led them into a particularly arid region, the Crusaders had stoned them, but we hadn't quite reached that point yet.

The only times we regretted their absence was when we were confronted by our two hereditary enemies: dogs and children, the latter particularly, because our technique for getting rid of the former was fairly effective, but what could we do with small boys who greeted us with stones, when they weren't peppering us with a hail of pebbles from their slings? They were true descendants of David, and when we were caught in their stinging volleys, the horses bucked and reared, so the children would begin all over again, laughing, just for the fun of enjoying a free rodeo.

I would have laughed myself if we weren't quite liable to lose an eye in the skirmish, and I lost count of the numbers of one-eyed children I saw in the villages, victims of this time-honoured sport. Corinne and I realised that, as we couldn't possibly win such battles, there was only one course to adopt, and following the example of Napoleon in love, beat a hasty retreat. One morning Corinne made a mistake, for finding herself cornered, she tried to retaliate and threw a large stone at her assailants. The children scattered and hid behind some rocks, but then regrouped and returned to the attack. Fortunately I was able to stage a one-woman re-make of the Charge of the Light Brigade and rode into the mass of children again and again until Corinne was able to escape.

One evening, at six o'clock it was already dark, but we could see lights on the slopes of the mountains. We asked some shepherds if this was Yonikoy Nazimbey, the village we were aiming for, but apparently that was twelve kilometres further on. There was no question of our reaching it in the dark, for we would have to cross a positively lunar waste without the shadow of a path. So why not spend the night in the village ahead which was called Kisildere?

It was the first time since we had been in Turkey that we had found ourselves absolutely alone. Up until then we had always been helped by Olivier or Patrick, our police-chaperons, or even by locals to whom we had been directed. In Kisildere, a village of troglodytes with houses melting into the rock, cut off from everything, no electricity, no telephones, not even a television aerial, no one had ever heard of us.

As I didn't want to beg for food and shelter (I had lost the knack), I attacked the problem obliquely by asking the few ragamuffins who had rushed up to stare at us: 'Which is the road to Yonikoy?'

Their reaction was precisely what I had hoped for: 'You can't get to Yonikoy at this time of night. You'll have to sleep here.'

Even before I could ask: 'Yes, but where?' one of the lads invited us to come home with him. Child's play! All the same, we thought we had better decline his offer and trust ourselves to the *mukhtar*, for if anything were to happen to us, he'd be the one to deal with the authorities. Our would-be host directed us to the mayor's house, but as he had gone to the café, a child darted off to fetch him, while his wife, a solid matron with no false modesty, came out to examine us, flanked by her sons, two upstanding stalwarts aged about eighteen or twenty.

'You tourists,' she demanded. 'Girls or boys?' She didn't wait for an answer but began to feel Corinne's chest. As my sister usually carried a passport, a card case and other items in the pockets of her anorak, doubt continued to reign, whereupon she began to examine me too. She went about it so vigorously (and I don't like being pinched) that I protested loudly.

The boys intervened: 'Maman, stop, that's enough.' But the she-wolf wouldn't listen and continued her investigations, whereupon I yelled even louder. It was ironic that people had always warned us against the Turks but never against their wives.

The eldest son grabbed our tigress and sent her about her business. 'Mother, go back indoors.' She obeyed, but as she departed, the mad creature yelled to her sons: '*Güzel! Choch güzel! Heyde!*'

My bad Turkish was quite fluent enough for me to understand that she was encouraging them: 'Pretty girls, go on my sons, what are you waiting for?'

Fortunately the *mukhtar* arrived, not a moment too soon. We held out our letter of introduction from the Turkish tourist office in Paris, which he didn't even glance at (perhaps he couldn't read), and without a word, beckoned to us to follow him. He led us to his stable and installed our horses, then ordered his sons to take us to one of their cousins, which meant we were spared further assaults from their hysterical mother.

Afterwards the two boys led us to another house where we were given a cold meal. While we were busy tucking in, who should appear but Patrick. How on earth did he always manage to find us when we didn't even know where we would be stopping for the night? He must have had a sixth sense.

For some time I had been saying to Corinne every time I examined the horses: 'Donald's hind legs are all right.'

This was by way of reassuring myself, for his forelegs worried me a good deal. Ever since we left Paris, every specialist had noticed that he hadn't got good legs: some had even predicted that he wouldn't last more than 100 kilometres, but to date he had covered more than 4,000 and hadn't done too badly. Now I was forced to admit that his right foreleg was over-heating slightly and wondered if perhaps we shouldn't have been more careful. But after all, our two friends had seemed to be in fine fettle, and as they were given plentiful rations of oats, we had pressed on, even allowing ourselves short spells of trotting when the ground was suitable so that we could reach our stopping places a little earlier than planned. Besides, I had an additional personal reason for wanting to trot: the hotel maid who had patched my jeans in Istanbul, knowing nothing of the particular needs of riders, had used a piece of very stiff material and some nylon thread, so that my jeans chafed horribly, and I was only too glad to give my bottom a rest by trotting, standing up in my stirrups.

As soon as I appreciated Donald's difficulties, I didn't hesitate to sacrifice my own comfort. First of all, I decided, no more trotting. Next, Corinne and I would change horses. As Donald had swollen and painful legs, and I had problems with my backside, I would walk as much as possible, leading Donald, while Corinne (the episode of her coccyx being a thing of the past) could ride Mickey. Donald and I would be more or less playing the part of the halt leading the halt.

We could console ourselves by thinking that most of the crossing of Anatolia had been carried out by the Crusaders in similar or even worse conditions, the knights having to go on foot because their horses had died of thirst. A few rare privileged souls found a way of being transported—by oxen.

We wondered what had become of the freezing temperatures which only a few days before had reminded us of Siberia. At Sarimazi, on the way to Iskenderun (the old Alexandretta), we were driven from our beds by the heat at four o'clock in the morning.

Next morning, when we opened the stable, it looked as if it had been struck by a typhoon, with everything tossed about in wild disorder. The horses must have been fighting half the night, and they had broken down the partition I had put up between them. Mickey stood with his feet in the debris and Donald lay full-length, his head under the manger, and didn't move, not even when we held a bowl of oats under his nose.

'Come along, little one, up you get.'

Noise, daylight, fresh air, oats, caresses, slaps on the rump, nothing could move Donald, who gazed at us sadly, raised his head a little and let it fall back on the soiled bedding with a profound sigh.

I was afraid he was seriously hurt, for his left foreleg was stretched out in front of him, completely limp, in an unnatural position. I untied him, pulled his head and tail to help him get out from under the manger and stand up. The leg wouldn't bend, and I wondered if it was broken. My throat went dry, tears not far away. Would we have to put him down because he had broken a leg fighting in a Turkish stable? It would be too unfair, but as he continued to moan and his eyes expressed all the suffering in the world, I could well believe that he was trying to say he had come to his journey's end and was imploring us to let him die in peace. All the same I made him stand up, which was the only way of finding out if the leg was broken or not. He managed to scramble up eventually and stood swaying, not knowing which leg to stand on.

No, I didn't think the leg was broken, but he had obviously had a bad kick on his left thigh and had hurt himself on the shoulder joint, probably by bumping into the stone manger. I imagined that he was suffering from lumbago and arthritis as well and the previous day's four hours on the rocky bed of a dry mountain stream, plus four hours of scrambling about in the mountains under a blinding sun, hadn't done him any good at all. In short, Donald was in such bad shape that we couldn't possibly leave that morning, and I asked if we could send for a vet.

'There's one at Ceyhan: about eighteen kilometres away and he'll have to be fetched in a tractor, but he works for the Ministry of Agriculture and you'll have to get permission first from the sub-prefect.'

I was given the green light quickly enough, that's to say after five visits to five different civil servants working in five different offices and after drinking the five obligatory cups of coffee.

At Ceyhan the vet didn't wait to see his patient before writing out a prescription for a few basic medicines, including a healing lotion for his feet, which couldn't possibly do him any harm. He recommended a day's rest, though I would have expected him to be more generous, but in any event we couldn't stay where we were. Our host, the *mukhtar*, had had to leave his cows out in the sun while our horses occupied his stable, and as that situation couldn't possibly continue, the vet advised us to walk the horses as far as Turunglu, a small village by the sea, about five kilometres away. The *mukhtar* was quite happy to transport our saddles and gear in his tractor while we took the horses down a gently sloping sandy path.

As we went on, Donald seemed to perk up little by little, only very slightly of course, but unfortunately the heat didn't help his swollen legs. Every time we stopped, he wouldn't stand on his right foreleg, but merely touched the ground gingerly with the tip of his hoof. Obviously it hurt him a good deal.

We had to turn a donkey out before we could install our horses in his stable, and I took care to build up a very solid partition, firmly fixed with a heavy beam, and tied Mickey up very short so that he couldn't interfere with Donald.

No sooner had he reached the stable than Donald lay down and stretched his head out in the dust. I was so upset I nearly cried.

Then I decided to reduce his rations by half, for perhaps he was suffering from over-eating. We had been giving him twelve litres of barley a day which was rather a lot. I had noticed that the Turks always mixed their barley with chopped straw to stimulate digestion, but our horses had refused the mixture and Mickey had already gone on hunger strike (for a week) until I had given in and omitted the straw before he collapsed from malnutrition.

Corinne reconnoitred the beach to find a place where we could take Donald to bathe, but it was pitch-dark before she returned: the sea was much further away than we had imagined, so Donald's sea-water cure would have to be put off until next day.

In the morning I had an inexplicable presentiment and let Corinne go round to the stables alone. A moment later she

reappeared, white as a sheet and out of breath, her eyes staring:
'Come quickly, he's dead!'

I flew to the stable and found Donald lying on his right side,
all four legs rigid, his head in the sawdust, his eyes turned up and
the muscles of his back as hard as iron. In spite of the noise I had
made, he hadn't moved an eyelid, but when I touched his head I
discovered he wasn't dead, at least not quite, for he was still
breathing, his sides lifting and falling gently. His eyelids closed
and then reopened, but the look he gave me was completely
desperate. I raised his head gently to let him breathe some fresh
air instead of dust, and then I started to talk to him, as if he were a
dear friend, which of course he was.

'Honey-child, my dear little horse, please don't die . . . You've
done such wonders already . . . nearly 5,000 kilometres in five
months, that's a wonderful achievement . . . I know you're tired,
but I can't leave you here, you know how the peasants treat their
horses . . . Please get up and come with us . . . it's only another
1,000 kilometres to Jerusalem and that's not so very much. We'll
go very slowly and we'll stick to the beach all the time, so you
can go for a swim every day, and after that, we'll take you home
to France. You'll spend the rest of your days in green fields with
fresh grass and lucerne as high as your heart . . .'

Donald tried to get up, using his knees to prevent straining the
painful tendons and managed to get to his feet with a groan of
pain. When he was finally up, he rested his forelegs by putting
all his weight on his back legs and arching his back, for his
muscles had lost all their elasticity. He kept resting one forefoot
on top of the other as he tried to get comfortable. I gave him a
drink and settled him outside on the grass, while Corinne and I
rubbed him from head to foot with vinegar and water. I was just
about to give him another injection when the headman of the
village grabbed my hand.

'Wretched woman! You can't give him all that—you'll kill
him.'

And apparently he knew what he was talking about, for he was
a qualified male nurse. Yet the vet, as far as I had been able to
understand, had told me to use the rest of the bottle for a second
injection. The nurse showed me the prescription, but as it was
written in Turkish . . . however, he took the syringe, squirted out

twenty-five per cent of the remaining liquid, gave Donald the injection and swore it was quite sufficient to make my little invalid canter all the way to Jerusalem. I could only pray that Allah had heard his disciple.

In any case, my mind was made up. To pamper Donald and let him do nothing was the surest way of condemning him to death. We had to get him on the move again, taking things very gently, only five or six kilometres a day, obviously without any kind of load. Corinne and I could ride Mickey turn and turn about, and Patrick could be safely entrusted with Donald's saddle and the rest of our stuff. He was perfectly capable of organising that kind of staff work, and there were any number of carts and tractors travelling in our direction.

Even though it was only the beginning of March, the sun was hot enough to give us both headaches, and the horses suffered from the heat even more than we did, particularly our little sick friend. It took us much longer than we had expected to get back to the seashore once we had rounded the bay and crossed a road through orchards and vegetable plots. The labourers were incredibly kind, offering us fruit or water for the horses, and pieces of bread for Pluto. The nearer we got to the Syrian frontier the more we had to resign ourselves to the fact that we never would see the famous Turkish bandits.

Finally we reached the beach, and Mickey and Donald were able to have their first bathe. Mickey was afraid of the waves and didn't seem to like the salt water much, so I didn't try and force him, but Donald stood quite calmly in water up to his belly, for a good half-hour, as if he understood that this was his only chance of recovery. We splashed him with water and afterwards, of his own accord, he waded into deeper water until he was swimming, and then returned to the beach, where we let him dry in the sun. Later he went off exploring (the sea air had obviously given him an appetite) and showed a marked preference for the flowering thistles that grew everywhere. I thought he looked slightly better.

Until we reached Alexandretta, there were no new developments. Thanks to his injections and daily swims, Donald managed to cope more or less, but after Alexandretta it was a different story. We had to leave the coast in order to cross the main plateau of the Amanus and climb down again towards Antioch. The ascent was tough on everyone: for Mickey who had to carry one or other of us, for Corinne and me who had to climb on foot, gritting our teeth because we both had blisters and were terribly stiff, and for Donald whose laboured breathing didn't sound at all good.

Every morning when I woke up, my stomach turned over for fear I might find he had died in the night, and I would wait as long as I could before going into the stable on tiptoe, as if it were a sickroom.

One morning, at dawn at Gopbogasi, Corinne got up first and was so nervous that she broke the rusty key in the lock, and the door had to be smashed in with a pickaxe. I heard the horses getting to their feet and the whinny from Donald which meant 'Get a move on, I'm hungry.' He may have been ill, but he was still the greediest horse I have ever known, so once more I could feel a little optimistic.

Donald looked at me sideways, obviously pleased with himself, and I knew that he must have something on his conscience. To see him up to his tricks again was an absolute joy, and on this occasion his mane and forelock were stuck full of little pieces of white fluff: his halter was hanging free at the end of the picket, so I knew what must have happened. After we had left them the previous night he had spied a better place than his stall, so he had pulled up the stake and gone off to roll in a pile of freshly picked cotton. The trampled mess showed that Donald had spent the night on that ultra-soft mattress rather than on the ground, unlike that great fool of a Mickey.

CHAPTER THIRTY-SEVEN

Two Nights in Gaol

Antioch: the Turks welcomed us as if our forefathers hadn't massacred · their ancestors, and our horses were lodged in a caravanserai that specialised in housing mules, camels and other beasts of burden. Godfrey, who hadn't been able to join in the capture of the town because he was ill, had made up for lost time by sending 150 Muslim warriors to their eternal rest with the help of a mere dozen Christians. Even the children didn't seem to bear malice and offered handfuls of clover to the horses, and bars of chocolate to us. We couldn't make out why we were being given this treatment, unless it was because of certain remarks we had made on television concerning the behaviour of Turkish children.

An inspector of police had been sent to look after us and see that we were properly installed at a hotel. He turned up next morning to escort us to the caravanserai where we found poor Donald in a very pitiable state.

Lying on the soiled bedding, panting slightly, he opened one eye when we arrived, lifted his head, tried to stand up and fell back, groaning. I asked for a vet and the inspector did his best to find one. Once again it wasn't so simple: it took five or six documents issued by five or six different authorities before the expert in question arrived and began by putting on a white coat and gloves. He then examined his patient with a grimace of disgust, for Donald's odour was really overpowering. Finally he delivered his opinion: 'Your horse is very tired, he has walked a long way and needs five days' rest.' It really must have taken years of study to reach such a brilliant conclusion. I asked if he couldn't suggest something to relieve Donald's pain.

'The only remedy is rest,' he said, but as I insisted, he prescribed a lotion. 'Rub him with this if you like, once a day. It will help relax his tendons.'

One thing we could do while we waited was to bring the horses out of the stuffy, underlit stables and give them exercise and fresh air. While Mickey pulled at the spring grass, we led Donald down to bathe at the mouth of the Orontes.

Getting out of the town was a problem in itself: we had to thread our way through the bazaar down a narrow alley lined with small booths where porcelain, hardware, spices, carpets, jewels, fruit and various bric-à-brac were piled high. All went well until Mickey, his nostrils tickled by the enticing smells, snatched at a bunch of pimentos. The effect was electric: he shied so violently that he backed into a display of oranges and sent them flying in all directions. The fruitseller began to shout, but fortunately the inspector who was with us managed to calm him down. At last we reached open country, and while we led Donald down to have his daily soaking, Mickey stuffed himself in an adjoining meadow.

Back we went to the caravanserai and the hotel, with the usual quota of excitements as we went through the souks. A herd of goats took on Pluto and tried to butt him, whereupon our mongrel, who had no desire to become an expert at this kind of corrida, lost his habitual aggression and took refuge between my legs. But that was nothing compared to another attack mounted against Corinne and me by a pugnacious cock. I don't mean an ordinary dunghill bird, but a real fighter that pecked at our calves with frightening intensity. It wasn't easy to get rid of him, and our well-aimed kicks only seemed to spur him on. Even when we emptied our water-bottles over his head, he returned to the charge. Finally, his owner had to grab him and hold him firmly under one arm before we could be left in peace.

Next we had to go through the necessary formalities for crossing into Syria, and have ourselves vaccinated against cholera. The dispensary where this operation was carried out hardly came up to the highest standards of hygiene, but to make up for it, the young doctor was the most handsome Turk we met. Corinne submitted to the injection without a word of protest, in spite of her personal horror of vaccinations, and was only sorry she wasn't given an anaesthetic. She would have enjoyed swooning into the arms of that magnificent specimen with turquoise eyes— a word derived originally from 'Turk' and at last I understood why.

I decided to climb to the church of St Peter, on top of the hill above Antioch, for it was there that the first Apostles brought the Church of Christ to Asia Minor. It was there, too, that during Godfrey's Crusade a fragment of the lance that pierced Christ's side as he hung on the cross was discovered in a grotto. At least, this was the story related by a curious Provençal pilgrim, who said St Andrew had appeared to him in a vision and revealed the hiding-place of the relic—and at the same time renewed the fighting ardour of the Crusaders.

Although I had become a thorough unbeliever, I wanted to put up a prayer from that very special place: 'O God, who art all-powerful and Whose compassion is infinite, please restore our little horse to health. The local vets are so bloody incompetent.'

When I came down again I felt happier and somehow comforted, and indeed I wouldn't have been at all surprised to find Donald as good as new, frisky and full of beans, raring to go. We wouldn't have to wait for five days, and we'd be able to get back on the road the very next morning. However, I was rather presumptuous when I imagined that my prayers would be answered, and when we did start again, Donald could hardly stand, but after filling his lungs with oxygen, his step grew firmer. He walked slowly, but he wasn't limping and after six kilometres we stopped for an hour to let him bathe in a little stream. Take your time, my darling, we don't have to meet any deadline. After his bath he seemed to have lost most of his energy and it took tremendous patience to coax him up a short hill to the dream village where we were supposed to spend the night.

Herbiye was one of those leftovers of the Earthly Paradise that we came upon from time to time. A cluster of houses in a valley surrounded by rose-pink mountains: at one end a rushing stream spraying out into a delicate waterfall surrounded by flowering trees, where according to legend, Daphne was turned into a laurel bush to escape the amorous clutches of Apollo. I could well imagine it to be true, for I never remember a more poetic land-scape. We needed only to put out a hand to pick wild bitter oranges, and the gardens were full of enormous lemons that Donald bit into but dropped because they were still too green.

In the middle of an orchard a delicious smell told us that some women were baking bread in a vertical oven, and one of them invited me to come and try my hand. Even though I kneaded the ball of dough and flattened it as I saw everyone else doing, I couldn't get the hang of slapping it on the floor of the oven with-out breaking it. My 'teacher' consoled me with a beautifully brown one of hers, which I ate while it was still hot—delicious.

A little further on, some shepherds let us taste their ewes' milk and we played with the young kids and newborn lambs who ran about unsteadily on their matchstick legs. Their fleece was clean, soft to the touch and curling already.

In that idyllic atmosphere on a beautiful spring afternoon I felt much more optimistic, though Donald didn't seem any better and the lotion we used to massage him regularly didn't appear to have any effect. He seemed to perk up a little only when he had his daily injection of a preparation I had had made up for me by a vet at home. It seemed to revitalise him for a couple of hours, long enough for us to cover about ten kilometres, but anything over that, and disaster would strike.

Kislac. I have a particularly vivid memory of this little town. We were greeted by a young officer aged about twenty and a civilian, apparently a professor, a sort of playboy straight out of a fashion magazine. The bottles of raki covering their table showed how they had passed the time while they waited, and they embarked on fresh libations to our health during a sensational dinner whose crowning point was a chicken cooked with almonds—pure poetry. Unfortunately, our officer got fairly high, and suddenly decided to make his orderly drink some raki, though as a practising Muslim, he was forbidden to touch alcohol on pain of mortal sin.

Unhappy and embarrassed, the soldier lifted the glass to his lips and put it down again untouched, but the officer made him take a mouthful, whereupon he spat it out at once. The officer stormed at him until the poor devil had to swallow the raki, and to celebrate his victory the young idiot knocked back several doubles and pulled out his revolver. The joke threatened to turn very sour, but luckily we had noticed a small lock-up in the corner of the room which was none other than the local gaol, and Corinne and I quickly took refuge there before a stray bullet could do any damage. The straw mattress was a trifle narrow for two people—plus Pluto—but we had managed to grab the key and lock ourselves in. Where could two girls be safer than inside a prison?

Next day we clocked up another fifteen kilometres, as far as Yayladagi, stopping practically every half-hour to socialise with officers, police, Customs officials or journalists. As this was our last leg in Turkish territory we were a trifle over-escorted, but I was quite happy to swop civilities because every stop gave Donald time to catch his breath and steal enough fresh grass to carry him on for another three or four kilometres. While he was busy feeding, Mickey and Pluto played games with the tortoises that lived beside the road.

At police headquarters at Yayladagi, a farewell banquet had been laid on, and all the commanders of the units that had looked after us from Antioch onwards sat round a table that must have been at least forty feet long. The menu matched this gigantic party from shish-kebabs or doner-kebabs, spiced with onions and aromatic herbs, tomatoes and onions, to imam bayaldi (a kind of mixed salad with a base of aubergine), eggs scrambled in olive oil, and fish from the Mediterranean or the Orontes; it was enough to tickle the most jaded appetite. As the raki and white wine flowed like water, our escorts very quickly became a little more than merry and burst into song. When it was our turn, we excused ourselves, Corinne on the pretext that she was too shy and I (truthfully enough) that I sing so out of tune that nobody could stand it, but we couldn't in all decency refuse to dance with our hosts. They had in fact enlisted the services of a trumpeter who attacked his instrument with such enthusiasm that Pluto began to bark his head off, whereupon a junior officer, as round as a butterball, flung himself down on all fours and began to bark too. Pluto, whose sense of humour isn't always up to this kind of behaviour, hurled himself on the playful military gent and sank his teeth in his cheek, whereupon, terrified of what the outraged animal-impersonator might do, Corinne, Pluto and I took refuge—

in the lock-up. I can't really say that our last nights in Turkey were spent among the beautiful embroideries we met during our first hours in that marvellous country. We had been assured we would meet a fate worse than death, whereas we had found that everyone was kindness itself, and everything in the garden was literally lovely.

CHAPTER THIRTY-EIGHT

The Runaways

A delightful road bordered with olive trees and cactus brought us to the frontier. The scent of pines, fresh moss and heather: the frogs croaking as they splashed in the little pools: the birds singing their hearts out; everything proclaimed that spring had come. At last we arrived at the little hut where our companions of the previous evening had grouped to bid us a fond farewell, a few hours' sleep having put them all into fine fettle again. This was the last of Turkey: 300 yards further on, another little hut: the beginning of Syria.

Corinne and I were a little worried, for we still hadn't got our Syrian visas: the different consuls or vice-consuls representing the Damascus government having always replied: 'When you get to the frontier, we'll see.' Our nervousness was increased by the fact that the press and Turkish television had created a certain amount of furore around us, and had proclaimed pretty well everywhere that we were going to Jerusalem, capital of the state of Israel. Considering the relationship of Syria with the Israelis, we wouldn't have been at all surprised to find ourselves beating against a locked door.

Half an hour later, all obstacles had been removed. It had taken about ten minutes for the officers to stamp the pages of our passports together with remarks in beautiful Arabic script: the other twenty minutes were spent exchanging courtesies and sipping cups of bitter Turkish coffee.

The pretty Turkish road we had been following continued on the Syrian side. The village where we hoped to spend the night was fifteen kilometres further on, but we had barely covered three when Donald began to fail. That morning he had seemed so well that I hadn't considered it necessary to give him his usual injection, and now his legs were obviously paining him a good deal. Because of the heat, his circulation was very bad and he panted and could move only very slowly, so I let him stop as often as he liked and tried to encourage him by stroking his neck. Would he be able to reach the next village? I had serious doubts, in which case what should we do? Sleep in the open under the pines? I would willingly have given him another injection, but as my last syringe was broken there was nothing for it but to press on. With Corinne leading the way on Mickey, Donald limping on three legs, Pluto with his tongue dragging on the ground and me climbing the hill with my back bent double, our caravan really can't have looked very smart.

If the countryside had remained the same, there were some noticeable differences in our surroundings. The houses were mostly grey cubes of reinforced concrete with a single narrow window and a low doorway. The metal framework stuck out on all sides so none of the buildings looked finished, though they were all occupied. The people too were dressed differently. The woollen bonnet of the Turkish shepherds was replaced by a turban that everyone wound in his own personal style. I thought the shepherds had a certain chic with their jellabas worn over trousers, but I found it completely incongruous when Western-type suits were topped by the same kind of turban. Between their headgear and the rest of their bodies there was a certain dichotomy.

As Donald could barely lift his feet and the slightest unevenness made him stumble and fall, we moved over on to the asphalt. With eight kilometres to go, Donald was nearly at the end of his strength. He looked at me sadly, and I was ashamed at having to force him to go through this agony, and yet it was only at the village that I might with luck find the life-giving syringe. Tears were stinging my eyes, and Corinne too was finding it hard not to cry. Would Donald, the greedy and clever little horse who had kept us amused and won our hearts over the last months have to end up like the Turkish and Arabian donkeys whose carcasses had been strewn along our route, miserable little beasts whose masters had abandoned them after literally working them to death?

Donald of his own accord began to move again, and as I followed behind I kept saying he could never do more than five kilometres a day, and at that rate (provided he could keep it up) God alone knew when we would get to Jerusalem. Only if he reached our journey's end would we have the smallest chance of taking him home, and as far as we were concerned, that was absolutely essential.

We started on a long, painful descent, with Donald falling at almost every step. Each time I tried to help him, each time I heard him moan as he struggled to get up, I had the feeling my own heart was being pierced by red-hot needles, and then suddenly, there was our village. A hamlet, rather, which seemed completely deserted, but we found the police station, although there too, doors and shutters were closed. I nearly gave up in despair, for it was only in the policemen's first-aid kit that I could hope to find a syringe.

The weather was so beautiful that I allowed the horses to crop the grass, without hitching them up. It could do Donald only good, and in the state he was in, he couldn't possibly run away. As for Mickey, all I had to do was watch him out of the corner of my eye: there was plenty of fresh grass around, and he wouldn't be tempted to wander off to find what was literally under his feet.

I had noticed that Donald didn't look quite so miserable when he had his nose buried in green grass, and his companion was eating with every sign of satisfaction. Alas, not for long. Suddenly I saw Mickey rear and as I knew what was likely to happen, I rushed forward to catch him, but too late. He had already taken off at full speed, galloping up the slope. Then he turned sharply left, jumped a ditch at least three yards wide, landed with all four feet on the tarred surface and tore off at top speed, straight back towards Turkey.

And then what happened? Our little dying horse, probably feeling lonely, matching his own speed to his colleague's, striking sparks from his hoofs, galloped off to join his companion.

Corinne and I set off after them as best we could, not that we had the slightest chance of catching them, unless they were prepared to wait for us, and for a time we could hear the frantic drumming of their feet on the winding mountain road, and then silence. We questioned the peasants travelling in the opposite direction and yes, they had seen two horses galloping along, whereupon our motorcyclist escort reappeared with a syringe.

'Get up behind!' he ordered.

With both Coquet sisters on the pillion, the scooter didn't climb the hills too well, but after ten kilometres I saw the horses trotting along the roadside with their tails streaming. I let out a rude word, for never since our departure from Notre-Dame, had they covered such a distance in such a short time, and they seemed perfectly prepared to continue at that pace all night.

I was absolutely shattered by the way our dying animal had behaved, and when I remembered that I had been crying with despair . . . Unless my prayers to the Virgin had been answered and Donald had recovered the use of his legs by a miracle!

When they heard the scooter, the horses pricked up their ears and turned round to look in our direction. As soon as he recognised us, Mickey indulged in a whole new series of cavortings and set off at a gallop again with Donald at his heels. The mad chase continued: the more we pressed them, the faster they galloped. I feared the worst for the little horse: his heart would give out: his legs wouldn't stand the jarring on the asphalt and next morning would be as stiff as telegraph poles.

I saw them swerve round a bend to the left by cutting across it diagonally and, at the same time, a bus rounded the same bend. Terrified and unable to stop, the driver stood on his horn. Mickey, after a perfectly executed double capriole, flung himself into the ditch, followed rather less gracefully by Donald, but both managed to avoid crashing into the bus.

The cantering began again. As the popping of the engine seemed to excite the horses, the policeman decided that we should try and follow them on foot, which meant that almost immediately they were out of sight.

'Very well,' said the policeman, 'let's get back on the scooter and go very slowly.'

No sooner said than done. Even though we were travelling no faster than some stroller lost in a reverie, I had cold shivers at every bend because it isn't easy to keep your balance when three of you are perched on such a machine. Eventually we managed to sight our fugitives. They had left the main road and were using a mountain path, not very far from the Turkish border. They had dropped to a walk and let us come quite close to them on foot. But not too close, for Mickey uttered his war-cry and set off again at top speed. Donald hesitated—he must have been exhausted—and then followed manfully.

We were in the depths of a pine forest and night was falling. The frogs struck up the overture to their nocturnal concert and the birds fell silent one by one. A fork in the road: the path split three ways. Which should we follow? The ground was too rocky to show any trace of the horses, so there was nothing for it but for each of us to take a path, agreeing to meet again at the same place later.

We all returned with nothing to report. The new moon lit the sky reasonably well, but down in the forest, you couldn't see a thing at three paces. I had no real hope of finding the horses that night, and we would just have to wait for daylight and hope we could find hoofmarks, or question the shepherds and peasants from the surrounding villages. I told myself that the weather was mild and the situation might have been worse: I said that I would rather know that Donald was free on a mountainside than lying dead on an asphalt road.

All three of us were sitting on a rock without really knowing what to do next, our eyes beginning to get used to the darkness so that we could even see the shape of the surrounding trees. From time to time the long cry of some night bird would break the silence, and then we heard a new sound: something like a stone rolling down the hill.

'Corinne, did you hear?'

'Yes . . . d'you think it's them?'

'It came from this side, don't you think? Let's go and see.'

We pushed our way through thorns and branches as silent as Red Indians. The runaways must certainly be further on, for unless they are incredibly clever, horses never stay among trees but go somewhere where they can find some grass. The silence was complete but we pressed on all the same until we reached a small clearing. Again the sound of a falling stone.

'There they are,' whispered Corinne, who has eyes like a lynx, and in fact, two silhouettes could be seen against the grey darkness of the clearing. Mickey and Donald lifted their heads and looked at us—without moving. Not even when we slipped the halters round their necks. They probably considered they had had enough fun and it was time to end their escapade. We absolutely agreed, and we might even have taken the whole adventure in good part if we hadn't had to do the whole journey again, having spent the major part of the day with a dying horse on our hands. The only difference was that now the same horse was able to step out at quite a lively pace.

CHAPTER THIRTY-NINE

Home Thoughts from Abroad

That night Mickey and Donald had to sleep in a barn with a concrete floor, which was entirely their own fault, for by the time we got back to the village it was too late to go out and cut branches for their bedding. Neither of them appeared to be the worse for their mad gallop, at least Mickey's legs showed no sign of fatigue, and even Donald's were less swollen: in any case, unbelievable as it may seem, the tendons didn't even seem to be hot. Those dreadful animals had tired us out so completely that we were past caring about their creature comforts. As Donald was obviously capable of galloping down a main road when it suited him, he could perfectly well walk as far as Jerusalem.

Two things, however, surprised and disturbed us, the first being that Syria, at least in that particular province, seemed even poorer than Turkey in hay, barley, oats and straw. The previous night we had found nothing in a grocer's shop but a little wheat and some granulated sugar. The peasants obviously had a small amount of barley, but refused categorically to part with a grain of it. Secondly, the Syrian highway police weren't anywhere near as keen to look after us as the Turks had been, even the policeman who had so kindly helped us retrieve our runaways abandoned us in the middle of the forest at midnight, merely saying: 'Good-night. My wife must be getting anxious about me.' No Turk would have behaved like that, and while I know that at that time they were at war, the front was a good 350 kilometres away.

On the other hand, we weren't too unhappy at being left to our own devices. Even Patrick had said good-bye, for when we reached El Ladhiqiya, he had decided to leave us, feeling that we wouldn't need him all that much from then on: besides which he had just remembered that he had some chums somewhere in India, and he was off to join them by way of Iraq, Iran and Pakistan. He reeled off the stages to this latter-day Nirvana as casually as stations on the Métro.

We would miss him sadly, our hippy with the Christ-like appearance, and while I didn't know just what he might have been able to do for us in Syria, I certainly won't ever forget the many occasions in Turkey when he seemed to appear in the nick of time to rescue us from awkward situations.

Lately he had made himself responsible for transporting our little sick horse's saddle and our excess baggage from village to village by tractor. However, this latter problem had now virtually disappeared for we had sent our winter gear home, keeping only two tee-shirts, a sweater and a macintosh each, plus one spare pair of jeans between us, an aerosol tin of aluminium powder, a few shoe-nails, a brush, a camera and some toilet articles. In other words, the absolute minimum that Mickey could carry without noticing. I wondered if Patrick made his great decision merely because he had been deprived of some of his responsibilities. After all, even a hippy has his dignity, though at the time I always thought he was perfectly content to play his flute under a flowering orange-tree. I told him we would miss him very much, and that having come so far, he ought to stay the course and carry on, but he shook his head.

'Paris–Jerusalem on horseback is your affair. I'd stick out like a sore thumb if I turned up there with you. No, I don't feel at all involved in your adventure and I'm off to do my own thing. I'm a big boy now. Good luck.'

We'll meet again in Paris.

After the twenty-five kilometres we had covered the previous day, Donald once more seemed to be distressed and began to pant. The four intramuscular injections I had given him during the past fortnight weren't being absorbed properly: big lumps were coming out on his neck and I didn't dare try and give him another. Besides, I'm afraid of injections and I'm not very good at giving them anyway. Once a lump as big as a football came out on a horse after an anti-flu injection given by a clumsy amateur and it was five months before the swelling disappeared.

I did take some special lessons with a nurse who taught me how to give injections, using a sponge. But the trouble was that the sponge kept still and let me take as long as I liked to clean it, disinfect it, choose the right place, jab in the needle, adjust the syringe and inject the serum slowly. I never had the slightest difficulty with the sponge.

'Slap the neck or chest and at the same time plunge your needle in at right angles to the skin up to a depth of two centimetres. The horse won't move if you have correctly synchronised the two actions.' That's what the first-aid manual said, and I quite believe it. But with Donald I didn't have time to slap any part of him. He would stand straight up on his hind legs and try to climb into the manger as soon as I produced the syringe, and even if I hid it behind my back and pretended to be bringing him a lump of sugar, he still saw, or perhaps scented it. If by any luck I managed to get the needle into the right spot, it took a good twenty minutes of caresses alternating with physical struggle to fix the syringe to the needle, which by this time had usually come out, so I had to start again from the beginning.

When I finally got to the point of making the injection, I was always afraid Donald would jump another foot in the air and send all the sterilised material flying, with me into the bargain, so I had to get the stuff into him as quickly as I could, in spite of the very clear instructions: 'To be given intravenously, preferably by a veterinary surgeon. If not, inject the liquid slowly and at several intramuscular points.' If I managed to give him the dose in two separate amounts, this was already a triumph. Undoubtedly I still have great progress to make before I can consider myself a professional for whom giving a horse an injection is child's play. It was still a major undertaking as far as I was concerned, and the result for the horse, his rider and her assistant, was extremely doubtful. As so many experts thought (and said) before we started, if anyone was to be chosen for this long-distance adventure, Corinne and I would have been the very last to be picked. And I've always agreed with them.

The trip taught me one thing at least: if ever I have to choose someone to carry out a mission, I wouldn't pick the one with the highest qualifications, but the most enthusiasm—and luck.

In Dam-Sharko, a village set among orange groves, fifteen kilometres from El Ladhiqiya, a boy scout doing his good deed for the day found us a stable attached to a house. The proprietor, a middle-aged, squat individual, with beady eyes and a mouth like a gash in his wrinkled face, was sitting on a stone bench occupied in what his compatriots seemed to spend most of their time doing, i.e. sipping a cup of coffee. He wore a long white jellaba with narrow blue stripes, and the keffiyeh—a kind of muslin veil worn by all the oil sheikhs, held in place by a blue silk cord, plaited with gold thread.

He invited us into his house which consisted, in reality, of a single room, though it was divided (technically) into two parts. On one side, an elderly woman, about to complete her journey through this vale of tears, was lying on a plank on the ground, and on the other a cow chewed away at some yellowish hay. In order to bring our horses under cover, the Arab turned out the cow, but left the grandmother where she was. Once these arrangements had been made, the boy scout took us home with him, assuring us that his parents would be delighted to house two French girls, and indeed they were both charming. They seemed to harbour a certain nostalgia for the heroic past when our compatriots were the lords of their land, and though we were dropping with exhaustion the scout insisted that we should give his family a few samples of our native folk-lore, songs and popular dances.

'There's one song', he said, 'that my parents are very fond of,' and turning to them he commanded: 'Show them . . .' Whereupon our hosts burst into '*Savez-vous planter les choux, à la mode, à la mode* . . .' And we could hardly do less than join in.

Next morning a bus took us to El Ladhiqiya where we were to spend forty-eight hours while the horses had a brief rest. Our hotel was the perfect example of the anti-luxury school, with the worst smell we ever encountered: you had to remember to wear rubber boots every time you went to the lavatory. On the other hand, you couldn't be too choosy about an establishment that only charged three francs a night.

Wandering through the centre of the town, we found the pavements crowded with chairs and tables, where turbaned men

lolled about drinking coffee, smoking narghiles or playing back-
gammon. I often wondered how they lived; they couldn't all be
oil millionaires?

One of the coffee-drinkers waved to us, and turned out to be
our peasant-friend from Dam-Sharko. We sat down and chatted
about this and that, soon getting used to his bad French, and
finding his conversation most instructive. He showed us how a
head-band if well handled can become a very effective weapon, for
the woven cord is heavy enough to be used as a whip or even a
truncheon.

'But I've got something better than that,' he added, and rising,
went over to his scooter. From the saddle-bag he produced a
dismantled sub-machine-gun and several ammunition belts.

'I'm a commando leader,' he told me.

A commando of what? I didn't dare inquire, as everyone in
the area was extremely nervous of spies. Suddenly, through an
association of ideas, I remembered that we had left our tee-
shirts drying on the hotel veranda, the very tee-shirts that were
emblazoned with the inscription 'Paris–Jerusalem on horseback'.
It was essential that I should retrieve the incriminating evidence
forthwith, for in a country where everyone damns Israel to
perdition and fanatics are trigger-happy, it would be wiser not
to run unnecessary risks. The previous night our host had been
asking which way we were going, and we had told him Beirut.
And then? To Damascus. And then? To Amman. And then?
Because no one in their senses would ride 6,000 kilometres merely
to stop at Amman we had said we hadn't made up our minds, and
he hadn't insisted. But the boy scout's parents had scented something not quite right in the wind:

'Are you by any chance going to Israel? Don't tell us you are
Israelis . . .' And immediately the atmosphere became electric.

Eventually we were able to get back to the hotel and retrieve
our washing before anything untoward happened. The passers-by
either hadn't seen the inscription or as they couldn't read the
roman letters they didn't realise what they meant: quite apart from
the fact that in Arabic Jerusalem is called 'Al Qouda'.

CHAPTER FORTY

An Unfriendly Village

In order to avoid an infernal jungle of concrete buildings, pipe-lines, storage tanks and such-like installations on the outskirts of El Ladhiqiya, we had to strike off through the fields, and then follow the coastal plain which in principle stretched unbroken as far as Tripoli in the Lebanon.

Once more we left the main highway and set out happily down a country road, but a peasant stopped us: 'Don't go that way—there's water as high as this,' and he measured it against his shoulder.

'That's all right,' I said. 'We can ride across.'

If we had listened to all the Serbs, Turks and Syrians who had advised us to change our direction for one reason or another . . . They saw deadly marshes where there were only a few puddles, rushing torrents where a tiny stream rippled, blinding snow-storms when there had only been three snowflakes: all of which meant that once again we refused to give up a pleasant ride through olives, fig-trees and almond groves.

It had indeed rained a good deal the previous night, but at no point did the water rise above our horses' hocks. Our main obstacle that morning proved to be a military patrol that very politely requested us to turn back. I saw their point, for actually we were in the middle of an army training-ground where tanks, guns and weapon-carriers were manoeuvring, each one of them a good reason why we had become undesirables.

So once more we returned to the beach, and very pleasant it was to trot along beside the waves: the horses found the wet sand easier going, though with one slight difficulty: we had to cross dozens of streams, small or large, which flowed into the Mediterranean. We had to be very cautious, for sometimes the channels were very deep. Generally we would go upstream a little because there the current was less strong.

Once when I drove a six-foot stick into the water and couldn't touch bottom, Corinne suggested a way across:

'Over there, there's a kind of half-moon of calm water. There must be a sandbank, a causeway just under the surface. We can cross there. I'll show you.' And she set out along the crest of the sandbank, reaching the other side without the water coming above her knees.

'Now I'll come and fetch Donald,' she cried and crossed the water again without incident, then went back again, leading Donald, who walked along quietly.

All I had to do was follow with Mickey, only he is too much of an individualist to stick to a straight line, through water or anywhere else. He did begin by taking two or three steps in the right direction, then suddenly changed his mind, plunged off to one side and let himself be carried away by the current, with the result that both of us were in the water up to our ears. The waves took us back to the bank where Mickey climbed out and shook himself vigorously. He had been afraid, and so had I, but our enforced swim had refreshed us both. I was soaked to the skin, of course, but it couldn't have mattered less under that hot sun.

Everything would have been fine if the same pantomime hadn't been repeated every time we met anything like a real body of water. When it was too wide to jump, Mickey would spring in the air and land with all four feet together, sinking into the sand, whereas Donald would proceed cautiously without any fuss.

Eight kilometres from Jeble, we found another military base and once more had to move inland. Presuming that we had finished with the waves for the day, I changed out of my tee-shirt and filthy jeans into a sweater and our spare pair of breeches which luckily had been kept dry in Donald's saddle-bag, and felt distinctly more comfortable, though my feet continued to squelch inside my boots. But alas, my optimism was premature. A little further on, another river barred our way, thick and opaque, for there was a cement factory upstream. I sent the best swimmer of the group, Pluto, off to reconnoitre, then Corinne rode across on Mickey, sinking in up to his hocks. Donald crossed alone, without any trouble, the water barely coming above his fetlocks, after which it was my turn. The water filled my boots, I over-balanced, stumbled into a hole, and the current drove me against a concrete pillar round which the water swirled and gurgled.

I managed to climb out safely, but the camera I carried round my neck in a plastic bag was soaking wet, and the water had got into the case where I carried maps, passports, cash and traveller's cheques, etc., all of which were in a pretty appalling state. I wasn't much better off myself, sticky, smelly and dripping, and I had nothing to change into.

When we stopped in the middle of Jeble, we were immediately surrounded by a crowd of children. As Corinne and I hesitated whether we should ask one of the horrible little urchins if there was somewhere to stay, or try our luck somewhere quieter, a pretty dark girl in her mid-twenties, wearing a well-cut shirt and a mini-skirt, came to our rescue.

'Hallo,' she said with a charming smile, 'can I do anything for you?'

Luckily she spoke very good English, and I was able to explain our needs.

'Fine,' she said, still smiling. 'You're in luck. Here's my cousin Adnan who will look after you, won't you, Adnan?'

The young man beside her was reasonably good-looking. He spoke English as well as our new friend, and declared he would be delighted to help. He had a farm not far off where we could install Mickey and Donald; all we had to do was follow him, and he climbed into his sports car, a powerful-looking open job.

'I'll just nip round to my place,' he called, 'to pick up a revolver. You never know what you may meet on these country roads.'

His house was beside the water, a fine building, almost a castle, where he lived with his mother, and as long as we stayed in Jeble, we would be his guests.

Off we went to the farm. The road was so bad that Adnan could only travel at walking speed and as it was already pitch-dark, he turned on his headlights to make sure no marauders would spring out of the shadows to attack us. He seemed so nervous that we ended up by being equally on edge ourselves.

Once we reached the farm, where he raised several thousand chickens, he showed us two spirited stallions, who were as much his pride and joy as his sports car. The stabling was perfect, except for a water-purifier that was so noisy Mickey and Donald were both terrified and refused to eat their supper. Adnan had to turn off the machine before our horses condescended to fall to.

When we got back to Jeble, I noticed that Adnan took the precaution of locking all the doors and laying his revolver down on a bench beside him. I told him I found it difficult to imagine we were in quite so much danger.

'More than you think,' was his reply. He explained that his family used to be enormously rich, but since the socialists had seized power, they had lost practically everything: the new regime had left them only their house and the farm, which according to some, was still too much.

'Some terrorists came to the farm yesterday to requisition chickens, or so they said. Our dog barked at them, and they killed him with a burst of machine-gun fire. I know that one day they'll try and do the same to me, which is why I always go armed. Wherever I go, to the cinema, the university or the village, or even more when I go to the farm, I always carry a weapon. The robbers, or the terrorists who saw us going, know that we'll come back down that road—it's the only one—and they'll have all the time in the world to prepare an ambush. No, I definitely don't like taking that road at night.'

I thought it sounded very odd coming from a young man who seemed to be the most gentle creature in the world.

When we returned to Adnan's house, our room was ready and a meal prepared: green olives, scrambled eggs in olive oil, cottage cheese flavoured with olive oil and black olives. Personally I like olives, so I found the dinner excellent, but for someone who hates them as much as Corinne, it was the perfect non-fattening diet. The menu was pretty well the same every night until we reached Israel.

Next morning we took the road to Baniyas, still following the sea, with the elegant Adnan on one of his stallions. I had never ridden an Arab and Adnan agreed to swop horses. I was surprised because the little horse covered the ground so easily that in a moment I was several hundred yards ahead of the others and had to slow down. Instead of a saddle, I had a comfortable linen-covered embroidered cushion, stuffed with straw. The reins were plaited wool, and very strong, attached to a chain bit. Behind the saddle Adnan had fastened a box containing an iron chain and a picket for attaching the horse wherever we stopped so that we wouldn't have to watch him, and the inevitable revolver.

When I found myself alongside Mickey again, I asked Adnan if people were allowed to carry firearms, but he said no, you needed a permit.

'Then why do so many people have them?'

'Because the permit is given automatically to every soldier, who is responsible for his rifle, sub-machine-gun or pistols. You realise that there are a great many soldiers, either on active service or on the reserve, and military service here lasts for three years. Obviously just now, when we are in a permanent state of war, the young men spend most of their time with the colours.'

'You haven't done your military service yet, have you?'

'No. My whole family has been excused since the installation of the new regime.'

'So you won't fight against Israel?'

'If the government needs men, I shall be called up—unfortunately.'

I glanced at him. He really looked like an angel who wouldn't hurt a fly.

'If anyone attacked us now, you would fire? You'd risk killing somebody?'

'But of course! Only everyone knows I carry a gun, so they'd think twice before they attacked me . . . I hope . . .'

'Who are you afraid of? The Israelis?'

'Certainly not: they'd never come as far as this. No, it's terrorists I'm afraid of: they complain we don't help them enough. You'll always find men who under pretext of defending an ideal do a little robbery on their own account. In any case, I always take my precautions.'

I understood perfectly, for as we rode through a village, I had seen a soldier outside a café twirling his revolver on his forefinger with all the brio of a Hollywood gunman and none of the customers was even bothering to watch.

We made a detour with Adnan to visit the fantastic fortress of

Tel Qulaat, near Baniyas, built by Richard Cœur de Lion at the end of the second Crusade, and then our aristocratic escort rode back to his farm, having arranged to meet us in three days' time in Tripoli, where he had a flat.

By now, Donald was much better. We spared him as much as possible, but Corinne did ride him now and then, a little more each day, and he was soon able to stand up to a daily journey of twenty-five to thirty kilometres.

Hamidiya was the last village we reached before the Lebanese frontier. The weather was very mild and we were dressed accordingly. We got the impression the entire village had turned out to inspect us, and far too closely for my peace of mind. We tried to force our way through the crowd which consisted largely of children and teenagers.

A young man invited us to his home, but we were so anxious to get out of there that we didn't even answer him and pressed forward as best we could, followed, preceded and surrounded by a yelling mob. As we reached the edge of the village, a light of hope dawned, for there was the police-station and we decided to ask the cops to help us out of trouble.

Intrigued by the crowd swarming round their gates, several representatives of law and order appeared, and we gave them a pithy account of the situation. Apparently it was going to take more than that to shift them.

'You can't stay here,' said one officer. 'There isn't a hotel, restaurant, stable or any fodder in Hamidiya. Carry on to the Lebanon. It's quite near.'

Quite near? It would take at least two hours.

I pointed out that as darkness was coming on, when we eventually got to the Lebanese border all the offices would be closed, so we really had no choice and would have to stay where we were.

He had to agree.

'Very well, if you insist, you can stop where you like, in the open. But I warn you, you won't be at all safe. You've seen these people: they'll torment you all night.'

I wouldn't take no for an answer. I asked him to appreciate that we had covered 5,000 kilometres through almost a dozen countries and always found suitable accommodation: that we were perfectly willing to pay our way, that we weren't asking for charity.

Replied our policeman: 'There isn't a family in Hamidiya that will take you in. Please don't insist. Good-bye.'

I was outraged, and told him exactly what I thought of him. What good, I demanded, were he and his colleagues if they were incapable of protecting two females in distress? He turned his back and slammed the door.

There was nothing for it but to move on, under a hail of stones and curses. The inhabitants of the village were obviously furious that we should have complained of their welcome and I was beginning to wonder if they might not turn really nasty when who should appear—and it wasn't the first time since our adventure began—but a *deus ex machina* in a car. He was a French business-man of about fifty, who offered to help. He had lived in Beirut for about twenty years, and knew the whole coast like the back of his hand: better still, everyone in the area knew him equally well, for the moment he spoke to us, the stone-throwing stopped immediately.

He thought we had been very stupid to go to the police.

'In the Near East, when the police don't make trouble for you, you take good care not to go to them. Do you need something? You should have appealed to the locals, but these people are very touchy: you must have annoyed them and we'll have to try and put things right.'

He called up a peasant and exchanged a few words in Arabic.

'Here's a piece of luck,' he said. 'This man has a stable he'll put at your disposal, only unfortunately there's no lock. You'll have to leave your saddles and baggage somewhere. Just a moment.'

He went into a grocer's shop and returned to announce that we could leave our gear there. The proprietor nodded, showed us a key and mimed turning it.

'You see,' said our *deus ex machina*, 'he's closing up in a few minutes: but I promise there's nothing to worry about. In any case, you can't refuse now, you'd be casting aspersions on his honesty and he'd be very annoyed.'

'God forbid.'

We had to agree, but there was still our own accommodation to settle.

'No problem,' said our saviour. 'I'll take you to Tartus, where I have a bachelor flat. You'll be perfectly comfortable.'

The idea of spending the night in a bachelor flat with a fifty-year-old compatriot, fifty kilometres from our horses, didn't fill me with any kind of enthusiasm. I preferred not to make a direct reply, for if he had acquired the mentality of the locals, he might have been mortally offended too. I merely said I would first take the horses to the stable and see to their night's lodging and food.

'A waste of time,' he objected. 'Leave your horses with this man [the stable owner], he'll see to everything.'

'I'm afraid that's impossible.'

I felt I had no right to hand our companions over to a complete stranger, more particularly because the good man, Muslim or no, seemed to me to have been knocking back the raki rather too enthusiastically. Seeing my hesitation, the Arab said something, laying his hand on his heart.

'He swears on his honour that you can trust him,' translated our Frenchman. 'Do as he says, I beg you, as I can feel he's beginning to take offence.'

I wouldn't budge. I didn't give a damn if I was hurting this peasant's feelings. I couldn't possibly allow anyone else to bed down Mickey and Donald, particularly Donald, who needed very special attention.

'Come,' said our Frenchman, 'he has pledged his honour.'

'It is I who would be dishonoured if we went off without knowing exactly how our horses will be lodged and fed.'

The *deus ex machina* began to lose patience, and so did the Arab. The first drew the second a little apart and I saw the argument continue with many gestures.

During this passage of arms, Corinne had remained outside the circle, surrounded by a group of teenagers. When they started to vie with each other in pinching the curves nature has endowed her with, she lost her temper, kicked, bit and scratched, and I admired her performance tremendously. I prayed the little fiends wouldn't come near me, for I felt quite capable of wringing their necks, or giving a few of them a smart cut with my whip in places where it would hurt them most.

After half an hour our compatriot returned with the peasant, who seemed to have calmed down. He was quite prepared to take us to his stable, and better still, invited us to sleep at his house.

'Tell him yes,' whispered the Frenchman, 'but you certainly mustn't stay with him. He's as tight as a tick, and as soon as your horses have eaten, we'll give him the slip and go off to my flat in Tartus.'

I was less and less happy about the arrangements. Supposing the Arab should be annoyed at our disappearance and vent his spite on the horses? But there was only one thing to be done: go to the stable and then trust to the mercy of Allah. Fortunately the stable was quite near, and indeed very well equipped. Unfortunately the cupboard was completely bare. Laying his hand on his heart, the Arab embarked again on his oath-taking: he would go and fetch something for the horses later and I had to keep insisting that he should settle the matter at once. If not, I was quite certain that the moment our backs were turned, he would disappear to sleep off his alcohol.

The commotion outside the stable was getting on my nerves. The gaggle of ragamuffins had followed us all the way, and while I argued inside, Corinne protected the entrance, standing with her arms folded and giving an excellent imitation of Horatius at the bridge. Whereupon our compatriot had an excellent idea: perhaps the grocer had some oats? It took him only a few minutes to go and come back, triumphant, and we should have thought of it sooner. I would have liked some hay as well, but it wasn't the moment to be difficult.

As he carried his load into the stable, a few of the villagers slipped in after him and I tried to drive them out.

'Only the children,' our friend advised. 'Not the adults. If you upset them, I won't answer for the consequences.' Whereupon he went out with the drunk, taking the oil lamp and leaving me to deal with the horses and villagers in pitch-dark. I was surrounded: hands touched . . . pinched . . . squeezed . . . kneaded me. I blew my top and grabbed a shirt collar. Inside the collar there had to be a neck and on top of that a head. The owner struggled but I held on like grim death, pulling and shaking. I heard the head bang against a stone manger, and shook again . . . and again . . . until I felt the body go limp in my hands.

The gentleman from Beirut reappeared with the lamp, throwing fantastic shadows on the walls and revealing a curious silhouette: a pair of trousers topped by a headless cotton shirt. The sleeves began to move: they tucked the shirt-tail inside the trousers and a head emerged. My victim said never a word, nor did anyone else, and the silence was heavy with menace. We three left the stable in single file, but no one laid a finger on us.

Outside, we found the drunk who kept insisting we should go home with him, while our French rescuer was urging us to get into his car. How on earth were we to escape? We needed another *deus ex machina*, but it was far too much to ask. And yet, suddenly, there he was. A man-mountain, who addressed the mob in a voice like a foghorn and scattered them in the twinkling of an eye.

'I saw you were in a bad way,' he said in English. 'And I don't care for that sort of thing. Come and spend the night with me, I'll be glad to put you up.'

'But who are you, sir? Do you live alone or are you married?'

'Don't worry. You'll be as welcome in my home as if you were my own children.'

We didn't hesitate for a moment and chose to go with the man-mountain.

'When you arrived at Hamidiya this afternoon,' said the second rescuer, 'my son invited you to come home with him. It was a pity you didn't listen, you'd have saved yourself a lot of trouble. But I understand your scruples. Come and see my house: if you think it's what you want, *ahlan wa sahlan* [you will be welcome], if not, you can go elsewhere.'

I explained to the man from Beirut that we preferred to sleep fifty yards from the stable rather than fifty kilometres away, and he admitted it was a valid point. He took his leave, dragging the Arab, who was less and less steady on his legs, and understood less and less what was happening.

In the man-mountain's house the family was centred on an old grandmother, and waited on her hand, foot and finger. While the women set to work to look after us, the grandmother told fairy stories to the open-mouthed children. Calm after storm. Everything would have been perfect except that when we were seated on the rush-mats in the big common room, Corinne and I could see the faces of the village delinquents, pressing their noses against the windows.

The man-mountain guessed what we were thinking.

'Don't pay any attention,' he said. 'They'll soon get bored. Would you like to clean up a little before dinner?'

CHAPTER FORTY-ONE

Grass and Lettuce

Our departure from Hamidiya was less exciting than our arrival, for to begin with, we found our horses, saddles and baggage safe and sound, and the demonstrators of the previous evening had calmed down. Only a score of children escorted us and when a young man met us coming from the opposite direction and the hooligans didn't disperse quickly enough to please him, he threatened them with a dagger and they melted into thin air.

Hoping to avoid any more interference, we left the main road and continued along the beach, until a fairly wide river barred our way. In two ticks (there wasn't a soul in sight), Corinne and I stripped off and all five of us swam across.

As far as the eye could see, there was nothing but sea and sand, and as a light breeze cooled the air pleasantly, everyone was in fine form, including Donald who even broke into a trot without urging.

Suddenly, from behind a sand-dune, a car appeared: a flying squad of Customs officers, who demanded our papers.

'Excellent,' said their leader, 'everything is in order,' and he signed to one of his men to bring out the inevitable cups of coffee. Even when the office is on wheels, the time-honoured courtesies are never omitted.

At the frontier post there were no complications. A '*mâ'al salâma*' ['good-bye'], marked our departure from Syrian territory. Fifty yards further on, the Lebanese officer in charge declared that in his ten years of service he had never known anyone on horseback ride across the frontier, and barely glanced at our passports.

'Can I see the the papers for the dog and horses?'

I hunted through the case, but nowhere could I find the permits issued by the Lebanese Embassy in Paris. Could I have left them at home? Or lost them during the journey? It was all the more annoying for of all the countries we had had to cross, Lebanon required the greatest number of visas, vaccinations and certificates.

The officer was very helpful. 'The central office in Beirut must have copies of your papers. I'll try and ring them up. Wait here—this may take some time.'

Corinne took advantage of the hold-up to go for a swim with Donald (the Customs post literally had its feet in the sea), while I waited for the head man to finish his wrestling-match with the telephone. To pass the time I amused myself by playing with Mickey who I thought was looking very handsome. The neighbouring field-workers, passing through the Customs post, all thought so too, and formed a circle round him, loud in admiration. In splendid condition, his coat shining, he went into his act enthusiastically, arching his neck, dancing up and down, stamping his forefoot and neighing at the top of his lungs. To tease him, I tapped him (very gently) on the nose with my fist and he pretended to bite me, but when I stopped, he nudged me with his head to make me go on. The Arab peasants were utterly enchanted.

A good hour went by before the officer announced he had had no luck. 'The telephone isn't working, and by now all the offices are closed. You'll have to spend the night here.'

Mickey's and Donald's lodging presented no problem: one of the farm labourers had a stable near by. As for Corinne and me, we could use the cots of the Customs men who were off duty, and would we like a hot bath?

'Five minutes away there's a natural spring that comes out of the ground at forty-five degrees. If you fancy the experience, some of my men can go with you.'

An opportunity not to be missed, and our Customs men proved kindness itself. Unfortunately, one of them insisted on initiating us into the joys of the artificial paradise, as he had a supply of hashish confiscated from a smuggler, who had been arrested. Another cache of forty-five kilos had been found under the seats of a car driven by a young German girl, who was also currently in the cooler, and I wasn't at all anxious to make the experiment. The legitimate and earthly joys to hand were quite enough for me, and Corinne agreed.

Back at the Customs post, we found the chief waiting to take us out to dinner—in Tartus, the very place where we had refused to go with our saviour in Hamidiya. This time we accepted, and in any case I was anxious to see the town that nine centuries ago had fallen to Raymond de Toulouse. The noble knight of Occitania had carried the stronghold without shedding a drop of blood, merely by lighting hundreds of camp fires outside the walls, whereupon the governor had been convinced that the Crusaders had an enormous army and considered it wiser to surrender forthwith.

Our host was delightful, gay and amusing, but once again, the evening was spoilt by the Customs officer with the Indian hemp who tagged on to us and became frankly boring.

'Why won't you try it?' he kept asking. 'I don't understand. You don't know what you're missing.'

We certainly weren't going to find out.

Back at the Customs post, the commander presented us with some minute briefs and bras in pink lace. He had a whole pile of pretties that he had brought back from Germany for his girlfriend, but while he had been away, she had shacked up with someone else. As our own smalls were pretty far gone, we accepted gratefully—without any strings, of course.

By nine o'clock next morning, a Saturday, lorries loaded with fruit and spring vegetables were queuing up at the Customs post but it was still impossible to get through to Beirut. In any case, the man who could help us would probably have gone off for the week-end. What with Friday being a day of rest for the Muslims and Sunday for the Christians, we couldn't really hope to make contact with anyone until Monday. We decided to fill in the time with a little sight-seeing, as Krak of the Knights, the most imposing monument left by the Crusaders, was quite near.

We expected to find a fort, but it was much more than that, a whole complex built at a time when instruments of war were also masterpieces of architectural and religious art. A Turkish fortress had existed on the same site, but when the troops of Raymond de Toulouse attacked it, the defenders preferred to abandon it rather than resist an enemy already famous for its cruelty. The armies of the Cross were surprised to find that the Infidels in their flight had forgotten to destroy their food supplies, so the conquerors were able to remain there for three weeks and recoup their strength before proceeding to Jersualem. It was only later that the Franks constructed the formidable fortress which could house 2,000 men. The Krak stood for several generations, resisting countless assaults, including one by the famous Saladin in 1187–8, and yet a century later, due to the unrest in France, following the death of St Louis, as no reinforcements were sent, the fortress, by now only defended by a few hundred men, was carried by the sultan Beybars. Today it is still virtually intact, and I would have loved to have spent a few days there—there was certainly plenty of room, including stabling for something like 300 horses, even the rings for tying them up, set in the stone, were still there.

By Monday morning we began to get restless. Still no news from Beirut, and, warned that the Syrians wouldn't let us embark on a shuttle-service between frontier posts, there was nothing for it but to sit tight and chew our finger-nails down to the knuckles.

For lack of anything more amusing to do, I watched the Customs men dismantle a minibus in the hope of finding drugs. The owner was a slightly eccentric American woman who had been trundling round the world for the past eight months—not that I mean any criticism, for after all, I'm something of a trundler myself.

She watched impatiently while her seats, carpets, toilet articles, hot-water bottle and various other belongings were laid out on the ground, then philosophically took advantage of the situation to give the minibus a thorough clean. She told me she was mad about pure foods, and was a pioneer of ecology.

'I never smoke, not even tobacco: and I never touch tinned goods or anything made up, so just imagine me with hashish or any such rubbish. I've never had so much trouble at a frontier, and I've been through eighteen countries so far. I shan't forget these Lebanese in a hurry.'

The Customs man decided to call off his search, and as a peace-offering suggested a cup of coffee.

'No coffee, thanks. Bad for the health.'

'Some fruit juice, perhaps?'

'Fruit juice? Yes, delighted.'

The Customs man brought her some cartons of orangeade, but the devotee of macrobiotics pouted: 'Sorry, but I only drink natural juices. How on earth can you stomach *that*,' pointing to the cartons, 'when you've got such wonderful orange groves all round you?'

The Customs man gave up.

The American lady had only just gone when another sports car pulled up that we recognised at once: our friend Adnan. He had expected to meet us in Tripoli, if we ever managed to get into the Lebanon.

Finally, the commander of the Customs post managed to get through to Beirut. Better still, he spoke to someone who gave us the green light. I don't really understand what happened; we were supposed to fill in a mass of papers for the horses and Pluto: we did nothing of the sort and no one ever seemed to worry.

A few kilometres on Lebanese soil were enough to show us we had entered a new world. Of course, it was still the same sea, sparkling under the sun, the same palms and fruit trees, but there the likeness stopped. No sign of the elderly jalopies, tied up with string, which seemed to be the rule on the Syrian side of the border. Nothing but the most imposing cars, and never in the world have I met such a mustering of Mercedes.

Along the beach a succession of luxury villas proved rather a bore, for we were constantly forced to ride round their garden walls. The inhabitants were mostly in European dress, and very few wore the keffiyeh or the jellaba.

Another thing pleased us very much: in Syria we only ever saw mules or donkeys: here there were fine horses cropping the grass, tethered by a long cord knotted round a hind leg, just above the hock. The system is bad in that it irritates the leg at a sensitive point, but the horses hardly ever seemed to get their feet entangled, whereas our system can lead to nasty accidents. To give the horses even greater freedom, and still stop them running away, they are sometimes hobbled by having two legs tied together, either both hind legs, or both front ones, or sometimes a forefoot and hind foot diagonally. The colts are always left completely free and several of them galloped up, tails in the air, nostrils quivering, to get a closer look at the strange caravan plodding past their fields.

A young colt fell so much in love with Donald that he would have followed us to Jerusalem! He firmly refused to go away, no matter how much we shouted or waved our arms. He even ignored his mother's calls, so I threw a rope round his neck and tied him to a picket, after which we went on our way with a clear conscience.

In order to avoid the motorway and because the beach had become too rocky, we struck off into the interior before turning due south again. The landscape became wilder and we realised that life for the 'mountain folk' is as remote as the antipodes compared to that of the 'shore folk'.

Not far from Arqua we stopped to consult the map, and an Arab sitting in the shade of a hut cobbled together out of plastic bags, rose when he saw us. He was wearing a red and white checked keffiyeh and a chiroual, the baggy trousers of the local mountain people. His skin was copper-coloured, shiny with sweat, his eyes as black as coals and his moustache blacker still.

'I'm not mad about his looks,' whispered Corinne. 'He frightens me.'

I was less anxious, as I consider that it isn't only blondes who can be friendly.

All the man wanted was a little water: the first time we had been able to help a native since we arrived in the East. We held out our water-bottle, and he swallowed several mouthfuls with obvious satisfaction, but pulled a face afterwards. I smiled, for he couldn't be expected to know that we always disinfected our water with chlorate of sodium and he must have wondered what sort of spring it could have come from.

He thanked us very warmly and asked if he could do anything for us in return. I replied, 'Yes, find a stable for the horses, and beds for the night for my sister and me.'

'You need only come to my village up there.' It was as simple as that. 'Only I must ask you to wait a little, as I want to sell my produce.'

All this expressed in gestures, of course, for our Arabic was less than rudimentary. Under his improved shelter he still had some lettuces, which would have quenched his thirst, but he was naturally reluctant to eat his stock.

Next came an enormous individual, sitting astride a minute donkey. With one hand, the fat man belaboured the poor beast with a stick, while with the other he held a huge black umbrella over his head. He stopped, and without dismounting, haggled over the price of a lettuce, then departed, beating a renewed tattoo on the ribs of the unfortunate moke. A few minutes later, a metallic-grey Mercedes stopped, and this time the driver bought the whole boiling, so we were able to push off without further delay.

The slope was steep and covered with loose stones, so that by the time we reached the village we were completely out of breath. It seemed cleaner than similar places in Syria, but what struck me most was that three generations of women lived together under the same roof: a grandmother dressed in black from head to foot, who could only move with the greatest difficulty, a mother who only went out veiled, to work in the fields or draw water, and the daughters, pretty and gay, wearing mini-skirts, engrossed in the latest film magazines. My mind boggled at the generation gap.

The stable was large, airy and well lit, with a beautifully dry floor, but with one defect. Built for donkeys, neither Mickey nor Donald could possibly get through the doorway. Seeing my disappointment, the lettuce-seller quickly reassured me: 'It's nothing. I'll fix it right away.'

I couldn't imagine what he had in mind, for the opening would have to be enlarged by at least two feet, not from above, unless he knocked down a wall, but from underneath. To make the threshold, an enormous stone like the ones used to build Krak of the Knights had been laid down, weighing at least 300 or 400 kilos.

The man attacked it with a pick, or rather, he tried to loosen it round the edges, then went off to collect reinforcements among his neighbours. Several of them by using a lever raised the stone just enough to slip ropes under it, then, some pulling on the ropes, others working away at the lever, sweating, panting, shouting encouragements, stopping from time to time to mop their faces with a fold of their keffiyehs, they finally managed to move it, though it took them three hours.

I was amazed. I had often heard of Arab hospitality but this was ridiculous! All that effort so that our horses could be sheltered for a single night. Of course they were the descendants of the race who had built the temples at Baalbek and Palmyra, and even the Pyramids.

I tried to convince my friends (what else could I call them?) that it would all be wasted labour, but they wouldn't listen. I measured the doorway: the lintel came just above my forehead, and as Mickey stands exactly the same height at the shoulder as I do, if he lowered his head he might just manage. I made Donald go first, because he's a little smaller, and he walked in without a hitch.

I tied a folded blanket over Mickey's back to make a buffer in case the edge of the keystone rubbed him, and gave him a good push. He moved cautiously forward, measured the obstacle, and looked at Donald who was already munching his oats. I think that must have decided him, for he jumped down on to the lower level, landing with all four feet together. My heart missed a beat, as those kinds of acrobatics could easily end in a fracture, but he landed safely and went on to attack his dinner.

The heroes of the exploit, by which I mean the men who had raised the stone, were invited to the house where the girls had made mint tea. How happy we all were among these simple people for whom generosity is so much more than a word.

Beirut: I didn't care for the chief city of the Lebanon at all, full of luxury hotels, casinos and nightclubs. Of course the women were elegant, sophisticated and often very beautiful, and the men well-dressed and very much *grands seigneurs*, but compared to the misery and poverty of the countryside, I found the sight of so much luxury embarrassing.

The Equestrian Federation of the Lebanon had made excellent arrangements for our comfort. We were installed in one of the palaces frequented by the jet-set, while Mickey and Donald were cosseted like princes in the stables belonging to the local racecourse.

We spent four days in that bustling metropolis, for purely sentimental reasons. We wanted to stick to Godfrey de Bouillon's route as far as Jerusalem, that is, go down the coast and cross into Israel by Ras el-Nakoura and then continue via Sidon, Tyre, St John d'Acre, Haifa, Caesarea and Ramla. From Beirut to Jerusalem was barely 300 kilometres, but since 1948 the frontier at Ras el-Nakoura had only been open to a few officials, United Nations observers or delegates from the International Red Cross. If we couldn't go that way, we would have to make a loop through Damascus and Jordan, adding about 150 kilometres to the route, so it was worth trying to get an official permit.

The French Consul-General in Beirut did his best, for as we couldn't venture alone into the southern provinces where skirmishes between Israelis and the fedayeen were endemic, the only solution would be to attach us to a United Nations or Red Cross convoy, and there was just a chance that he might be able to fix it. But he met with a categoric refusal—each party declining to create a precedent for a private enterprise.

The Lebanese army might, in the last resort, have escorted us as far as the barbed wire barriers at Ras el-Nakoura, but even so, they'd need some assurance from the Israelis that they would let us pass, and to get this assurance our Embassy in Beirut would have to ask the Embassy at Tel Aviv to put in the necessary application via the Quai d'Orsay; in other words, this whole rigmarole might take up a great deal of time and we might still be turned down.

So the question was settled for us: we wouldn't take the Crusaders' route but—oh, St Paul—the road to Damascus.

CHAPTER FORTY-TWO

A Very Persistent Aeroplane

Between Beirut and Damascus the mountains and plains are green, for there is plenty of water: the orchards are leafy and luxuriant and the vines superb. The arak they distil in those parts is similar to Yugoslavian slivovitz or Turkish raki, and they serve 'mezes' with it, dainty titbits of this and that. They claim their arak is the best in the whole of the East.

No difficulties at the border: we meant to stay at the Damascus military riding-club but two things made us stop rather sooner in a small village called Dimas, which is practically the same as Damascus (Damas) in French. Firstly, we were all tired, and secondly I had found a minor road marked on the map that wandered through the mountains and ran south-east to join the road to Jordan at Kiswe. This meant we could bypass Damascus, not only avoiding traffic delays, but saving an appreciable number of kilometres.

We set out on our short cut and found the road surface excellent. Unfortunately peasants kept waving to us to return and go back—they pointed to the heights and pretending to hold machine-guns went 'Bang ... bang ... bang ...'

I thought they were being pessimistic, for although I knew there had been sporadic fighting on the Golan Heights, this was some fifty kilometres away, and as we were on horseback, we would be able to see what lay in front of us. If we should hear any gun-fire, we could always beat a hasty retreat. All of which I tried to convey to the locals, who shook their heads but said no more. The very fact that they weren't more discouraging seemed to me a good sign: I considered they would have stopped us by force if there had been any real danger.

Then we had an unpleasant surprise: the path changed to a narrow asphalt track, so we had to move over onto the verge. Later we took a direct line across the hills, forty degrees southeast, in order to reach the small town of Mouaddamiye. Unfortunately the going was very rough and the horses cut themselves on the sharp flints, so when we came to a path made by tank tracks going in our direction, Corinne suggested we should take it.

We were making good time and it wasn't too hot: Corinne was whistling while I played my harmonica: Pluto was sprinkling I don't know how many rocks, Mickey was beating time with his ears while Donald swished his tail approvingly, when suddenly we heard a low rumbling.

'Listen,' said Corinne, 'thunder. We're going to have a storm.'

I looked up, but there wasn't a cloud in sight, and yet Corinne was right in a way. The growling continued, we hadn't imagined it. Could a thunderstorm come from such a blue sky? After all, we knew nothing of the local meteorological peculiarities, so we shrugged our shoulders and carried on. All the same, I was a little worried when the thunder—if it was thunder—broke out on the other side of the ridge, to the south, and I began to wonder if the tracks criss-crossing the hills might be going towards the front. Perhaps I had made an error in navigation which would bring us much too near to the zone where the gunners and airmen of both sides were hard at work?

We slowed down, the thunderclaps seemed much nearer, and we realised that they were indeed shells. We looked round and saw more and more signs which made us regret not taking the advice the peasants had offered a few hours previously. At the base of a rocky cliff, we could even pick out some khaki-coloured tents surrounded by sandbags, merging into the landscape, while lorries, armoured cars and camouflaged weapon-carriers were drawn up in an immense park. All round were trenches, blockhouses and concrete pillars, which I imagine were anti-tank obstacles.

Nothing moved in the crushing heat.

'There must be a skirmish going on the other side of the

mountain,' I said to Corinne. 'There's no point in digging in here. I'm afraid we must have been travelling too far south from the start—let's strike back north-east.'

The path had petered out, and over broken ground scattered with dried bushes and pebbles, we hurried as best we could. I realised that our best plan was to put as much distance as possible between that plateau and ourselves, at which point Corinne called out: 'Look out! Mickey is getting all tied up in electric wires.'

A network of wires had been laid down over an enormous distance, fixed three or four inches above ground-level. The horses had pulled yards and yards of them away, and began to dance until they could shake themselves free. What were they for? What headquarters were they connected to? Were they intended to detect the arrival of enemy vehicles? How would the Syrians react when they realised that someone was trampling over their flower-beds? All these and many more questions flashed into my mind, none of which I could possibly answer.

Unless the solution came from the sky . . . A few moments later, a small green and khaki-coloured aeroplane began to circle round us, coming nearer and nearer until it finally flew away.

We carried on in the same direction, perfectly calm once we had turned our backs on the fighting zone, but half an hour later, the same little buzz-bomb returned to repeat its antics—more or less as before, except that this time it dived straight at us. The sound of the engine was deafening: the horses bucked and plunged, terrified. We had barely recovered from our alarm when the plane returned to the attack and skimmed just above our heads. I yelled: 'He's barking mad! He'll scalp us both if he goes on like that!'

The plane repeated its manoeuvre several times, but what on earth did it want? If it was a game, it wasn't in the least funny, because every time it passed, the horses went mad and we had the greatest difficulty in calming them.

I realised eventually that the attacks were always on a north–south axis and Corinne suggested that perhaps he was trying to steer us back to the road.

'It's quite possible, so let's do as he says and travel due south.'

As soon as we struck off on this new bearing, the plane settled down to purr overhead at a reasonable height, but he never left us until we joined the main road to Damascus, in the midst of an appalling stream of heavy traffic.

As we came to the city, the road ran beside a railway and we were walking on the right-hand side, leading Mickey and Donald, when a train travelling in the opposite direction passed, making such an appalling din that once again the horses were scared out of their wits. I found myself on the opposite side of the road, still hanging on to the reins, while Corinne, dragged by Donald, was in the very middle of the cars and lorries. Once again we had a narrow squeak.

It took us more than two hours to force our way through the noise and traffic jams to the racecourse, where nobody was expecting us. On the road to Damascus nothing was spared us, not even the traditional stone-throwing by the hordes of urchins who treated us like the woman taken in adultery. You must believe me when I say that the most frightening moment of that day was not the prospect of being machine-gunned or bombed by the Syrians or Israelis, or the possibility of finding ourselves in the middle of a minefield, nor even the particular attentions of an insistent aeroplane, but the fact of being stoned by children who were obviously deprived of any other honest entertainment.

Another experience we couldn't avoid were the interviews with the press. Once we had recovered our spirits, the Cachechos, a family of first-class riders who had offered to put us up, carried us off to the TV studios where the journalists who interviewed us seemed mortally solemn: the sense of humour in those parts had obviously not survived the vicissitudes of their politics, and my only consolation was that the pressmen themselves were even more nervous than we ourselves. One detail upset them especially: our tee-shirts bore not only the imprint of *Le Journal de Mickey* but they announced our objectives: 'Paris–Jerusalem on horse-back'. There was no question of allowing the hated name of the Israeli capital to appear on the small screens of the local TV, and I saw the producer explaining to the cameramen how to solve this problem: he drew his hand across his throat as if to say we should be beheaded on the spot. Indeed, only our heads appeared on the screen and perhaps a vestige of the tee-shirts, but well above the offending inscription.

I couldn't help smiling when I remembered that the Lebanese

papers had told the whole story a few days before, without even omitting that we had the same objective as Godfrey de Bouillon, i.e. Jerusalem. As far as the Syrians were concerned, our journey ended in Damascus.

The day was spent completing the inevitable formalities, beginning, as in most of the capitals we had passed through, with a visit to the French Embassy, which always served as our *poste restante*. We were looked after by the Cultural Attaché, perhaps because our activities came under the cultural heading, or perhaps because of our historic link with Godfrey de Bouillon, or merely because we were special envoys from Mickey Mouse. Whatever the reason, the charming diplomat handed over a pile of letters plus several telegrams, including one from our mother who was very worried because she had had no news from us since we left Antioch. Of course we could have written or telephoned her more often, but everyone knows how casual modern children have become.

The Cultural Attaché informed us that the Ambassador would be delighted if we could lunch with him two days later as he was anxious to hear all about our adventures. In the meantime, could the attaché do anything for us? Did we need anything? Yes, we would be very grateful if he could get us permission to cross into Jordan or Israel in view of the fact that we had no visas for ourselves or permits for our animals.

'Trust me,' he promised. 'We will get in touch with our offices in Amman and Tel Aviv at once.'

Next call was on the Syrian Minister of Tourism who had seen us on the telly. He gave us more than the traditional cups of coffee: pretty boxes in precious wood set with mother-of-pearl, and invited us to call on him if we had the smallest difficulty.

Third visit, the bank, where we expected to find our remittance from *Le Journal de Mickey*. We asked if we could have it paid in dollars and francs, but the clerk declared he could only give us Syrian money, which we couldn't use in Jordan, still less in Israel. However much I argued that we were backed by the Minister of Tourism himself, it took two hours of palaver in office after office before we could exchange our French francs for a cheque made out—in French francs, and negotiable on the other side of the border.

When I voiced a few criticisms of Syrian bureaucracy, one of the Cachecho brothers told me I shouldn't complain.

'Normally, it takes forty-eight hours to get what you have just been given in two. You don't seem to realise you've been granted an enormous favour. Do you know what one of the directors of the bank told me?'

'Probably that we were spies.'

'Dead right. He said: "Why must we do anything to help these girls? Can you trust them? This riding trip is exactly the kind of trick the Israelis would use. I'm not happy at the thought of these girls parading about our country, saying they lost their way in our military zones. The Golan Heights aren't ideal territory for sightseeing." If you hadn't been recommended to him by a Minister, you would never have got what you wanted.'

'You'd be well advised to make tracks at once—that's my friendly advice,' said the elder of the Cachecho brothers, looking particularly serious. So what was happening?

'"They" evacuated all the hospitals last night. It's the first vital measure the authorities take when they are expecting something. Things may hot up any minute now, and you really shouldn't be here if the situation gets serious.'

'Your itinerary will take you through the most difficult and dangerous zone,' added his father. 'If you insist on going through with your plan—and I hope you won't—I advise you most strongly not to move off the road. Listen carefully: you'll be in the middle of a military zone, so even at best, and supposing the sector remains perfectly calm, you are going to be stopped by patrols, and as everyone round here is extremely wary of spies, you'll be questioned goodness knows how often, you may even be locked up for a time while they ask questions about you. Seeing a man would have to be blind not to know you're planning to go to Jerusalem, you aren't out of the wood yet. Before you cross the Jordanian frontier you may have to wait several weeks. Think about that.'

While they waited for us to make up our minds, the two brothers took us to see the oldest city in the world where Abraham, the father of all believers, lived. After the modern city, which was even noisier than Beirut (and that's putting it mildly), we came to the main souk, a casbah where we had to shoulder our way through the most tempting display of all kinds of goodies. It needed tremendous self-control not to give way to the invitations of the merchants who laid out their copper or marquetry goods, brocades, pastries and multi-coloured crystallised fruit for our inspection.

And then, one after the other, two dazzling experiences. First, the Omayyad mosque, majestic and grandiose, with its countless colonnades and rounded portals. Then the Azem palace, a jewel worthy of the Thousand and One Nights, built by a great Syrian lord in the eighteenth century. I have seldom seen a more enchanting or harmonious place, where everything breathed peace and contentment.

Peace . . . On the way back, the younger Cachecho brother who was driving, slammed on the brakes and exclaimed: '*Merde!*' (The middle-class Christian families usually send their children to the local French colleges.) 'The reservoirs have been filled: that's another bad sign. It means they expect it's going to be noisy tonight. You'd be much better advised to get out before the war starts up again. My advice to you is to take the train for Der'a before it's too late.'

Next morning, at dawn, the two brothers repeated their councils of prudence, though the night hadn't produced any excitements. They were probably quite right to be nervous—the cease-fire line was barely sixty kilometres from Damascus—and the capital was only a few minutes' flight from the Israeli aerodromes, but for the time being, the danger didn't seem imminent and my natural optimism and faith in my star urged me not to give in.

'We really can't give up now when we're so close to our objective,' I told my hosts.

'Do you realise hostilities may break out any moment?'

'It'll be one more experience!'

The elder brother gazed at us open-mouthed, then burst out: 'The things you say! An experience! Of course, but it'll be your last. I'd pay good money to see you riding through a battlefield among the tanks, planes and guns of both sides. Shall I show you the pictures of Damascus taken after the October war in 1973? A plane that was aiming at the Headquarters dropped its bombs on a civilian block of flats next door. Believe me, the inmates had the kind of experience you're talking about—the last they ever had . . .'

And then he produced an argument which really touched my heart: 'Your horses won't be able to eat. You needn't think you'll find anyone to feed them. If anyone does do anything for you, it'll be to fling you into gaol. Do you understand? Fine. Instead of making idiotic remarks, come and have breakfast.'

Ever since our arrival in Damascus, the dining-room had been transformed into a forum where the hawks and doves of the family argued over the situation.

The radio was on, and the announcer told us that for the past few days 'incidents' had been increasing on the Golan Heights (we were in a good position to know). That same night, two Israeli fighters had been shot down, their pilots had bailed out and come down in Lebanese territory. The Lebanese had interned them and refused to hand them over to the Syrians.

The younger brother was indignant. 'Those pilots belong to us, since we shot them down.'

'According to international convention,' explained his father, 'the Lebanese must keep them in prison until the end of hostilities.'

'But Lebanon isn't neutral,' countered the mother. 'It's an Arab state and officially it's at war with Israel.'

'In Lebanon,' said one of the sons regretfully, 'no one will force the pilots to talk. We'll never get any information from the Lebanese. Here, we would have known how to treat them, and in any case, we'd have fixed things so that those two airmen would never have attacked us again.'

Didn't I say there were doves and hawks in the family? Some considered that the ruinous war had lasted long enough and that everyone should resign themselves to the existence of the state of Israel—at least 'as long as it is supported by the United States'. Others were dyed-in-the-wool diehards, but they recognised the fact that Syria couldn't get very far unless it was backed by the USSR and they deplored the fact that their country was the only one to support the Palestinian cause: Egypt seemed to be pulling out, Lebanon had always played a passive role, and Jordan, after the disasters of 1967, preferred to wait on the sidelines.

Just then the telephone rang. It was the French Embassy: our

Ambassador regretted, but he would have to cancel his rendez-vous with us, for the King of Jordan had arrived unexpectedly in Damascus and he would have to go to a reception for the diplomatic corps.

It so happened that King Hussein lunched in a restaurant a stone's-throw away from the flats where we were staying, and I was able to check on the tremendous security measures the Syrians had to take: motor-cops blocking all access to the street, policemen posted around the restaurant, while others watched the balconies and windows of the adjoining houses.

'King Hussein is definitely the visitor who gives the security their worst headaches,' explained my hosts. 'Damascus is full of Palestinians who hate him and have sworn to knock him off.'

Whereupon the president of the Riding Club arrived and put an end to the discussion.

'I think the political situation is extremely delicate,' he told us. 'You must also realise that one of your horses is in a critical condition, so if you are absolutely determined to carry on, you ought to try and get into Jordan as quickly as possible. The military situation is comparatively calm over there, so take advantage of the fact. I propose putting a lorry at your disposal tomorrow morning to take you and your horses to Der'a.'

In the heart of the Jebel ed Druz, practically on the Jordanian border, Der'a is ninety kilometres south of Damascus. I accepted with a very ill grace, for while I realised that it was quite impossible for us to cover those ninety kilometres through mountains and valleys (I wasn't likely to forget the buzzing aeroplane), we would have to stick to the asphalt for three days, and it wasn't possible. The president had urged Donald's state of health, but I felt sure Donald was perfectly capable of covering his daily thirty kilometres. What upset me was that the entire team would be motorised for the first time, and I explained my scruples to the president.

'So what?' he reassured me. 'Your performance won't be any less remarkable because you have ridden ninety kilometres less—ninety out of 6,000 don't count, and besides I would remind you that you have no choice. If you don't use the lorry, you can take it that your ride from Paris to Jerusalem will come to an end here in Damascus.'

The president is a man to be listened to, a bona fide horseman who knows what he's talking about. Among other things he had helped us nurse Donald like nobody's business: the poultices he had made for us (recipe: a local stone powdered and mixed with vinegar and salts of lead) had very definitely helped the little horse's tendons. One hind leg was well on the way to recovery, though the other was still swollen.

The president wasn't very optimistic all the same. 'Your horse is better, of course, but I don't believe he could stand up for another twenty kilometres.'

I replied that experts had been saying the same thing since Bry-sur-Marne and Donald had very clearly given the lie to their prognosis.

'All the same, I'll give him an anti-strain injection,' continued the president. 'It will help him over the next week, but don't force him and be very careful.'

He needed all his patience and skill to carry out the injection, for with Donald's pathological fear of the syringe it took ten minutes to get the needle into the right spot.

The lorry in which we were to make the journey Damascus–Der'a didn't inspire me with much confidence. Mickey and Donald were supposed to travel on a platform surrounded by a railing not much more than fifty centimetres high, with no roof, not even an awning to protect them from the sun. I was afraid Mickey might jump over the flimsy barricade the moment he saw a mare, and in addition there was no ramp, though this problem was solved by backing the lorry up against a pile of sand.

I considered we were running a tremendous number of risks. What a contrast to the padded horse-boxes in which my mounts always travel when I go to shows: even if the horse were wedged in with an entire custom-built contraption, I never thought it adequate and transformed them into American footballers with plastic gaiters, neck-guards, tail-guards. If I could have added a complete helmet I would certainly have done so, and the floor of the van was always covered with a thick layer of straw.

What we were being offered was very different, but this wasn't the moment to be difficult. If Arab race-horses could travel in that way, why not our own? We contented ourselves by placing a blanket over their backs—at least they wouldn't catch cold, for the sun was hidden behind clouds and it wasn't at all warm.

When the lorry took off, our anxieties were redoubled, for I realised that on this highway crowded with army vehicles and barred every now and again by checkpoints, our driver relied far more on his horn than his brakes.

All the same we reached Der'a in one piece, and less than two hours later we arrived at the Jordanian frontier post.

CHAPTER FORTY-THREE

On the Banks of the Jordan

The bedouin who acted as watchdogs for King Hussein didn't look at all pleasant, though whether they were soldiers, policemen or Customs officers I couldn't tell. Our arrival on horseback with a dog who immediately lifted his leg against their barrier didn't bring the trace of a smile to their saffron-yellow faces. I considered they looked even less prepossessing than the cameldrivers at Ereğli.

The commander of the post questioned us, poker-faced. 'Where are you going?' he asked in English.

'To Amman!'

'How long do you expect to stay there?'

'Five days.'

Confronted by this jack-in-office I was so nervous that I said the first thing that came into my head.

'And after Amman?'

'After Amman . . . hm . . .'

In Lebanon and Syria we had always said we were going to Jordan and left the rest in the air, now here we were, so to speak, with our backs to the wall, and as the inquisitor repeated his question, I said, 'Afterwards, we'll see . . .'

He frowned.

'What's that mean: we'll see? You ought to know now.'

'We'll try and get back to Paris.'

'What about the horses?'

'We'll take the horses with us.'

He examined us from head to foot, he looked at Mickey and

Donald from their ears to their tails while I was on tenter-hooks.

'Pass,' he ordered.

I was so amazed at getting the green light after my ridiculous answer that I couldn't move.

'Come along, pass!' he repeated, anxious to be rid of such extraordinary customers.

A short way further on, a new barricade and a much bigger Customs post where the man in charge was definitely more amiable.

'Good morning, ladies. Welcome to Jordan. Tie up the horses here, please, and then unload your baggage and spread it out on this table.'

The table was already covered with suitcases and bundles belonging to the motorists ahead of us and they had to be ex-amined by a metal detector, but as Mickey gave signs of an embarrassing excitement, and his kicks threatened to cause serious damage, by general consent we were given priority. No suspicious buzzing.

'If you would be kind enough to put your baggage back on the horses,' said the delightful gentleman, 'you can come with me to see the commander of the post.'

I asked if there was anything wrong . . . a slight understate-ment for we had absolutely nothing authorising us to enter Jordan.

'Anything wrong?' echoed my officer. 'No, no, on the contrary, everything's perfectly all right.'

And in fact the commanding officer received us most kindly.

'Mesdemoiselles,' he announced, 'I have been given instruc-tions from our Chief of Police about you, and would like to welcome you to Jordan. May I see your passports?'

We handed them over, and he covered them with stamps and signatures.

'You're going to Jerusalem, aren't you?' he continued, without a trace of hostility. 'Let me advise you to make for Irbid as soon as you get through Ramtha, and then go down the Jordan. It's the best road.'

'But it's the road along the Israeli frontier. Won't we run into trouble?'

'Just now everything's quiet. Bon voyage, and enjoy your stay in our country.'

Ramtha was reddening under the dying rays of the sun, and in this village which seemed utterly somnolent (it was very hot) the police helped us find lodgings. There was no stable attached to the house they took us to, but a walled garden which would do very well: the horses wouldn't be able to run away, even if they slipped their halters. It was only their second night in the open since we had left Notre-Dame, the first being the night they spent in the Vosges. What a long time ago it seemed . . . unfortunately we couldn't find any hay or barley, and they had to be satisfied with the grass which some children ran off to cut for them.

The women of the household, dressed in severe black jellabas pressed round us. They were not very pretty, and even the youngest had bad skins, but they were kindness itself. I felt a little as I had done during our stay in the Turkish paradise at Neçatiye, and they played with us as if we were dolls, bathing us, washing our socks, and were absolutely delighted, laughing till the tears ran down their cheeks, when they had dressed us in embroidered robes with a scarf wound turban-fashion round our heads. With Corinne there was no problem: the first square suited her to perfection, but they had far more trouble with me, and tried a whole series until they fixed on a mauve job which seemed to be right, judging by their satisfied smiles.

On the map the road from Ramtha to Irbid turned off at right angles, which was why we tried to take a short cut and struck off diagonally across the fields in order to reach the Jordan, but once again we ran into hordes of children who seemed very averse to seeing us anywhere except on the beaten track.

'Not this way!' they yelled, 'Irbid other way.'

We didn't want to know—I was determined to steer due east, and pushed the horses forward, but we couldn't shake off two youths who followed us on their tractor and chased us over streams and up the steepest and rockiest slopes.

To get rid of them, Corinne plunged into the middle of the young corn, already standing high, but my peasant blood turned quite cold: I have always considered it a crime to trample the crops, and barely allow myself to ride along the edge of a field. I called Corinne to order.

'It doesn't matter to them,' she replied. 'They're driving the tractor straight through themselves . . .'

She was quite right. It wasn't the first time I had noticed how in these countries where the land is considerably less than generous, no one makes the slightest effort to protect the crops, and they even allow the animals to graze freely on the springing corn.

However, I have my principles and I embarked on a long detour because I at least respect the labour of those who work the soil, until a succession of trenches forced me to dismount, whereupon the tractor caught up with me. One of the boys jumped down while it was still moving and bombarded me with questions which I couldn't possibly answer, whereupon he grabbed me by the shoulder, made me stand still, and showed me a green and yellow object just in front of me, which looked a little like half a rugby ball.

'Bang! Bang!' he said, 'Israel . . .'

I didn't have to be a qualified engineer to understand that I had nearly stepped on an unexploded Israeli shell.

'There are dozens of them everywhere,' said the lad.

He showed me how to get out of the network of trenches by following a well-defined dirt-track.

'Whatever you do, don't leave the path, and watch where you put your feet. If not, bang!' he explained in gestures, and while Corinne rejoined me, he trotted back to his tractor calling a gay 'Good-bye!'

A light breeze stirred the corn, and a springtime smell tickled our nostrils pleasantly. Far off we could hear the tinkling bells of a flock of sheep and though I couldn't see the shepherds, I knew they were no different from those who had always fed their animals here, even in the days of Jacob, Solomon or Jesus. Such peace and tranquillity . . . but after all, the message of peace and goodwill had originated here.

Suddenly a shot made us jump, followed by another detonation, and then a whole salvo. Soon the bombardment was uninterrupted, punctuated by explosions of shells or mortar fire.

Corinne and I looked at each other. Everyone had assured us that all was quiet on this front. Were we going to be the witnesses—or rather, auditors—of one of those brief but violent skirmishes which broke out every now and then between the Israelis and their neighbours? Unless we had stupidly travelled too far north and were getting too close to the Golan Heights, which wouldn't have been at all impossible. The sun was so high in that latitude that I could easily have made a mistake, and in any case, my compass was more or less out of order.

Not being certain, I preferred to stick to the road the boy in the tractor had pointed out. It ran down into a hollow and climbed up a small hill while the explosions seemed to be coming from the other side.

Corinne, who was slightly ahead of me, called back as she was nearly at the top: 'I can see some red flags waving. What does it mean?'

Knowing perfectly well that if there was one question I couldn't possibly answer that was it, she continued to climb. The idiot! What sort of wasp's nest would her curiosity get her into? I was the elder, and I should have taken much more care, or rather I believed . . . but I could only follow.

My anxiety was changed to amazement when I suddenly heard her laugh, and she turned to me crying: 'Come quickly, it's well worth seeing.'

The spectacle that confronted me when I turned the corner of an enormous rock was quite startling. The two red flags were being waved by a soldier making signals. The detonations? Soldiers firing at clay targets.

A sentinel, not at all surprised at seeing two girls on horseback appear from nowhere, signed to us to wait until the shots, bangs and explosions stopped. The soldiers re-formed round their lorries and put their weapons away while an officer came over and spoke to us in very good English. Our explanation delighted him to such an extent that he handed over his sub-machine-gun.

'Come and put in some target practice.'

I handled it so awkwardly that he took it back before I could have an accident.

'Ladies,' he continued, 'it isn't every day that such lovely flowers spring up in our desert. Will you do us the honour of taking a cup of tea in our canvas canteen, most unworthy to house such graceful creatures? My comrades and I will be delighted to entertain the charming ambassadresses from our friend France . . .'

Ah! I knew it already—I had read Omar Khayyám—that French gallantry cannot compete with Oriental lyricism, and between the two there is as great a gulf as there is between a boiled sweet and Turkish delight flavoured with rose-water.

After Irbid, the scenery changed and the terrain became more and more broken. We were no longer climbing hills, but mountains, and the crevices had become deep gorges. A leaden sun made us giddy and we were perspiring freely. For the last ten kilometres there hadn't been the smallest kind of shelter where we could rest in the shade.

As we approached Beit Yafa where we planned to stop—and if we hadn't covered our scheduled number of kilometres it couldn't matter less—a car stopped alongside.

'Here you are at last!'

The driver was none other than the First Secretary from our Embassy in Amman with the Ambassador's three children. He had driven over to Ramtha as soon as he had heard from the Embassy in Damascus that we were in the area. For several days our representative in Jordan had been falling over backwards to get us all the necessary authorisations, and he had been the one to get us the endorsement from the Jordanian security police. He had been looking for us all morning to organise our crossing into Israel, and get some information he needed. He took copious notes and asked if we could reach the frontier in six days.

'Very likely,' I replied.

'Good. When you get to the Allenby Bridge over the Jordan you'll find all the necessary papers waiting. I think our colleagues in Tel Aviv will have done everything to make it possible for you to enter Israel without any trouble. By the way,' he added, 'I thought you might not have any Jordanian money with you. Here are some dinars.'

I certainly didn't expect that that kind of transaction would take place in the middle of the desert, and when after that people tell me the Diplomatic Corps are hidebound . . .

The *mukhtar* of Beit Yafa welcomed us as if we were old friends, though I did have some slight reservations about his hospitality after I saw the daughters of the house drawing for us what was afterwards served as 'drinking water'.

One little girl collected it from a huge cistern in the middle of the courtyard, pushing aside the weeds which covered the surface together with several unidentified insects, and using a rusty tin to scoop up the muddy contents. Each time she filled her tin, she emptied it into a jar covered with a filter, a rag cut from some ancient garment.

Only a few friends were invited to dine with us, but the doors were opened to a larger crowd at coffee time, which was prepared by the *mukhtar*'s father: while we were eating, the old man had spent his time pounding the beans in a mortar using an enormous pestle, very rhythmically, as if he were beating out a tune, and the harmonious sound rang out an invitation for all the inhabitants of the village.

The road dropped down into a valley where the greenery became sparser, and we were stopped at regular intervals by control posts where the authorities weren't always satisfied with checking our passports, but sometimes asked us to wait while they telephoned Amman to find out what they should do with these less-than-ordinary-tourists. The soldiers who stopped us were always polite, and always offered us the inevitable coffee, but wasted a tremendous amount of our time.

We rode through one village just as the children were coming out of school. They carried their satchels on their heads with the same careless grace as the women draped in black carry an amphora full of water, or a bundle of firewood or bag of corn. I motioned to one of them to stop while I took her photograph. Like so many women of the region her face was covered in green tattoo marks, and she allowed me to take her picture and then took me by the arm explaining that she wanted to take me home with her to be tattooed. I shook my head in refusal for I didn't think the green tattoo line drawn under the lower lip very attractive. At worst, I wouldn't have been too much against the fine line drawn under the eye, and as a good publicist I had already thought of the commercial: 'Be beautiful in bed with our indelible make-up'.

I don't know whether it was the Arab blood, or the spring which was already far advanced in those parts, or our tee-shirts which through being soaked in perspiration showed off our bodily charms too prominently, but a band of teenagers began to tease us more and more. Corinne who had dismounted so as not to tire Donald, was suddenly fed up with the advances of a too-enterprising young man and turned and flew at him. Wouldn't you think that a smart slap combined with a left hook to the stomach would be enough to discourage her admirer? Not in the least, for he beat a retreat and then returned, furious but not in the least discouraged, on his bicycle. It was high time for me to join in. Mounted on Mickey, I pretended to charge him, whereupon he flung aside his bike and began to walk backwards with his arms in the air yelling: 'No, no, no . . .' And yet Mickey had only taken one step in his direction. We never saw the young idiot again.

On the road to Shuma, checkpoints and controls occurred every 500 metres, which seriously upset our time-table, but the man who commanded the final squadron seemed to me really stupid. It was obvious from the way he was examining our passports (upside down) that he didn't understand a word, and the proof was that he asked our nationality.

'You must go to headquarters,' he ordered.

'Where's that?'

'Fifteen kilometres further back.'

I saw red. Did he realise that those fifteen kilometres, plus the same again to get back to his post, implied six hours' travelling? It was out of the question.

'Very well,' he conceded, 'stay there. I must go and see my chief and find an interpreter.'

'When will you be back?'

'About five o'clock.'

'But it's only eleven now.'

Becoming slightly more amenable, he agreed to allow us to move across to a group of buildings where we could at least wait in the shade.

At three o'clock he came back and let us pass. Four hours lost.

When it wasn't the soldiers it was the civilians. After we left

Waqqas where we had stopped to buy some drinking-water—it's a rare commodity in those parts—we were going towards a canal about three or four kilometres away on the route to the Jordan when a group of men stopped us.

'Don't go that way! Over there it's Israel!'

They insisted that we should turn round, and even when I told them we had permission to go that way they wouldn't believe me:

'It's impossible. We tell you that that's Israel.'

Strong in our convictions, we continued on our way, whereupon a dozen of them climbed into a tractor and charged after us. A little further on, a band of children tried to bar our way, but they didn't dare approach the horses. On the other hand, they grabbed Pluto and tried to wring his neck, whereupon Corinne plunged into the mêlée and rescued our dog which I snatched in mid-air and installed on the saddle in front of me while we escaped at the gallop, ducking the stones they hurled after us as long as we were within range.

At a safe distance we stopped to see what they were up to, and saw them arguing animatedly with an older man, until the argument dissolved into a general scuffle. Discord in the ranks of the enemy. After a few minutes, calm was restored and they seemed to be making a plan. What could they be plotting?

We left them to their sinister conspiracies and continued on our way, rounding a small hill and coming on a path that led straight to the Jordan. The river, in other words, the frontier, could only be a few hundred metres away. We couldn't see the water, but we could make out the river walls that contained the stream.

Once again, guns rumbled, unless it was an aerial bombardment, for the Golan Heights were only about forty kilometres away as the crow flies. I lost my nerve, realised that the sector could perhaps be mined, and that our determination to advance so close to their enemies would end up by rousing the Jordanians.

'It can't be helped,' I said to Corinne. 'Let's go back to the last bridge and get back on the road.'

As we crossed the bridge, the group of lunatics we had scattered reappeared in front of us. We just had time to drive the horses straight up a steep cliff beside the road where our tormentors weren't able to follow.

At the top of the rise we found fields of corn, and further on, brown tents with sheep and goats grazing beside them: a bedouin camp. What would their reactions be?

Silhouettes rose silently in front of us. The women wore gold-embroidered veils and necklaces of gold coins. The children were barefoot and in rags.

A chorus of bleating broke out for probably the flocks were upset by our smell and the proximity of the horses. I preferred not to linger among the nomads and called to Corinne:

'Gallop.'

Poor Donald—he who had been cosseted and spared the slightest efforts since Adana was now leaping, or trying to leap, among the rocks like a mountain-goat.

Neither Corinne nor I got very far, for a group of Arabs, machine-guns in hand, called to us: 'Hey, stop!'

Corinne was ahead of me on the skyline, making a perfect target, and an Arab in some kind of uniform laid his hand on my collar (for Donald hadn't followed Mickey).

'Who are you? Show me your passport! Ah! you are French? That's good. France is our friend . . . General de Gaulle was a great man.'

The tension relaxed, and the men put away their guns.

'Follow me,' said the soldier. 'I'll show you the right road.'

At Karayma, once again we had to ask the police to find us food and lodging, which they did in the kindest possible manner.

Having fixed us up in an empty house, they took us to the *mukhtar*'s brother, where a banquet was immediately organised in our honour. The *plat de résistance* was a huge dish filled with rice and pieces of meat crowned by a triangular animal head, with a long muzzle, the teeth very much in evidence. While the guests dipped both hands into the meat and rice and rolled it into balls which they masticated ecstatically, I stared at the head, gazing deep into its eyes. I could have sworn it was one of Pluto's colleagues if I had not known that to Muslims, dogs are as impure as pigs. The realism of the display turned my stomach and I could only nibble the food, making a heroic effort not to upset our hosts.

A compensation awaited us: the mattresses on which we were to spend the night were covered in green brocade: the sheets were in a paler shade of green and emerald-green pyjamas invited us to gentle rest. I would never have dreamed of finding such luxury in such an out-of-the-way corner.

CHAPTER FORTY-FOUR

A Farm in the Desert

The *mukhtar* and the chief of police took us to the banks of the canal parallel to the Jordan, thanks to which the region has become the greenest in the country. The road ran through orange groves and at eight in the morning the sun was still quite bearable. Once out of the orange groves we heard the wind whispering through the banana palms while men were busy hoeing the fields; women came and went with jars of water on their heads, children clinging to their robes, while little girls five or six years old watched the goats. I wanted to sing and laugh.

We travelled for over two hours down that enchanted path, and at least one of us didn't find the sun at all too hot—Pluto. He had discovered the perfect arrangement and didn't trot along the tow-path but jumped into the canal and swam after us. As he couldn't go quite as fast as we did, every few hundred metres he would climb out, race after us, stay with us for a little, and then plunge into the water again.

Corinne and I also wet our heads from time to time, but unfortunately we couldn't take the horses with us down to the canal as the concrete banks were much too slippery. They had to be satisfied with shower-baths provided by hatfuls of water.

As the sun grew higher, the glare became so intense that we had to leave the canal and go back to the road, where the heat soon became overpowering, and the police check-points more and more frequent. It was true that by now Israel was within gunshot range.

In mid-afternoon we heard an explosion, the first of the day.

For once it wasn't gunfire, but a huge motorbike, a Honda 750, which shot past us and disappeared in a cloud of dust.

Half an hour later, the same monster reappeared, drove straight at us, came to a skidding halt and the rider shouted a 'hi-ya' with the purest Yankee accent. With his blue jeans and matching shirt, fringe of beard, wavy black hair and shiny revolver, he made us wonder who on earth this motorised rider could be hailing us as if we were on an excursion somewhere in Wisconsin?

'Well, girls . . . welcome to Jordan. I watched you for a while from my home [he waved towards the top of a neighbouring hill] and I got the impression you were very tired. [Quite right: we had stopped in the shade of a hut to catch our breath and have a drink.] Tell me, where are you off to? There's nothing in the desert in that direction. You ought to stop over at my place, up there. I'll take you on my bike, it'll be quicker, and you'll be less tired. My name is Rafik.'

All this was poured out at top speed in a setting where time seemed to have stood still.

I explained to our handsome bearded friend that we were trying to reach a place that . . .

'Forgive me, I can't pronounce the name. A policeman wrote it down for me in Arabic.'

He read the word. 'O.K., it's only twenty kilometres from here, but you'll find nothing except a monument to the dead of the last war. You'd much better come with me.'

'Our horses are thirsty. Isn't that a lake I can see down there?'

'Whatever you do, don't take the horses there: it's a D.D.T. outlet for killing mosquitoes.'

I was sorely tempted to accept the invitation from the Honda-rider, partly because our horses definitely needed water, and we might not find any for some time, and also because . . . because our motorcyclist struck me as being particularly fascinating. A vestige of prudence, however, made me say that before spending the night with him we should register with the nearest police station.

'Of course! Besides, I know all the policemen hereabouts. They are my friends, but we'll leave the horses in my camp because the nearest station is twenty kilometres further back. I'll take you in the Land-Rover.'

We took the road to the encampment on top of the hill. A few tents had been pitched here and there, among which we saw several men, apparently in no hurry at all. Rafik called to one of them and sent him off to find some barley while we tied Mickey and Donald to pickets stuck in the ground. The horses could perfectly well sleep in the open: it wasn't cold and nobody would disturb them.

Our host showed us his own domain, the centre-piece being his personal lodging, a big roomy tent, a real salon of the sands, with the floor covered in thick carpets strewn with striped cushions. Alongside the tent was an ultra-luxurious American caravan with a kitchen and all mod cons.

'I use it in bad weather,' he told us, 'though not very often, while I'm waiting for the house I'm having built to be finished . . .'

The house in question had hardly been started. The workmen were certainly there but I registered the fact that they spent far more time studying the landscape than using their spades. It was started three years ago, announced Rafik. But when it would be finished, Allah alone knew.

Under the tent, which was cooled by a refreshing breeze, a servant brought coffee and sweetmeats. Rafik left us for a moment and reappeared, having changed his faded jeans for a sumptuous jellaba in pale grey, with a white muslin keffiyeh. Sitting cross-legged on a velvet cushion, with his straight back and sparkling eyes, he told us how, having spent ten years working in an American agricultural college, he had decided to initiate the bedouin into the most advanced modern techniques. He had had the idea of going in for cucumbers and had been delighted with the results: the cucurbitaceae flourished to such an extent, as long as they were irrigated and 'fattened' properly, that he was earning an extremely good living. I could well believe him, for he lived like a prince, and the men who came to see him showed their respect by kissing his hand.

'In fact,' I said, 'you're the local lord.'

'If you like . . . but I treat everyone who works for me extremely well. I've a good name among my workmen as well as the villagers hereabouts, the wandering bedouin, the military and the local police. They say that little gifts foster friendship: what do you suppose I give anyone I have dealings with? Cucumbers. They are extremely popular in a country where everyone is permanently thirsty.'

All this with a mischievous smile. When I said I was surprised at not seeing any feminine touches, I really meant I was curious to know if he was married. I ended by asking him straight out and he smiled even more broadly, his eyes crinkling up with amusement.

'You know that as a Muslim I have the right to four legitimate wives, plus as many concubines as I can afford. Well, as you can see, I don't have a harem, but I haven't taken any vows of chastity either. Let's say I am married from time to time.'

In other words, he left the question open. 'But I don't lead a solitary life here,' he went on. 'I often give parties with music, dancing and film-shows. When I came back from America I couldn't imagine living without my hi-fi, so I installed a generator and I have a splendid collection of American albums my bedouin adore, and I have several films which I show on Friday nights. You know that Friday is our day of rest. Would you like to see a film?'

If anyone had told me an hour before that by nightfall I should be seeing a film-show in the middle of the desert, I should have answered by tapping my forehead with one finger.

Outside, during all this time, the farm people (Rafik always called it 'my farm') were spending a perfectly normal evening: some grilling kebabs over a brushwood fire, others entoning melancholy chants while they accompanied themselves on tambourines, others merely gossiping, as they squatted under the stars.

'You know the rule that can never be broken among us,' said Rafik. 'He who offers hospitality to anyone must treat him royally but the guest is also bound to remain for three days: it's only then that he is free to go or stay.'

'But in three days' time we must be in Jerusalem . . . and it's going to take three good days' travel to make it.'

'In three days' time you'll still be here, otherwise you'll offend me seriously. You don't want to offend me, do you?'

He said that with a look it was impossible to resist, and which I had absolutely no desire to resist anyway.

I got up very quietly before the dawn, as I wanted to walk in the relative freshness of the night. I had barely taken a step when Rafik, warned by some sixth sense, was on his feet, gun in hand.

'I'll come with you,' he said.

'Splendid. It's more romantic when you aren't alone.'

Outside the sky was a fairyland scattered with myriad diamonds surrounding the crescent moon. Then suddenly a ball of white light, trailing a long red streak rose, hung in the air for a moment, lighting up the valleys and hills before going out. I wondered if it was a comet.

'No, a flare: the Israelis are watching the frontier. The Golan Heights aren't far away, and fighting is still going on. But don't look that way, turn round and admire Jordan. I'll show you the desert at its most beautiful hour.'

A short steep rise led to the top of a hill, and Rafik pulled me up with one hand, holding his revolver in the other. The silence of the night was broken by a series of sinister yappings.

'It's nothing,' Rafik reassured me. 'Only jackals. Don't be afraid.'

We stopped beside a prehistoric tomb and at four o'clock watched the sun rise. Valley and sky were confounded in a mixture of colours ranging from blue to mauve to pink to ochre. An ineffable moment when I felt myself sinking into the mystery of nature.

'Why do you want to leave this morning?' marvelled Rafik. 'You're not expected at the frontier for another two days, and we're only thirty-five kilometres away. It'll only take a few hours, and if you arrive too soon, you'll have to wait. In any case, it's nine o'clock already, and if you want to avoid travelling through the heat of the day, you must start by four at the latest. Stay another day.'

We gave way to his arguments, and he drew up our programme.

'Rise at three, leave at four, arrive at twelve. That way you'll only be travelling for two hours in the heat of the day, and in the meantime I'll set up a stable for your horses at the frontier: the police and Customs officials are my good friends: I give them mountains of cucumbers. Then I'll bring you back here to lunch with my family. O.K? Fine, now enjoy life. Would you like a cold drink, or would you prefer mint tea?'

Before us we had the prospect of another day and another night, or rather, part of a night, of *dolce far niente*.

Rafik stuffed our saddle-bags with cucumbers to quench the horses' thirst and ours on the way, and added a supply of water.

'You must drink a lot to keep up your strength, otherwise you may have giddy spells.'

The ground was flat enough, but split by wide, deep crevasses which made the going very slow. Going down wasn't so bad for we could sink into the soft sand, but climbing up was exhausting: the sand gave way under the horses' feet, making them slip back to the bottom again.

By eight it was already more than 30° in the shade, and we stopped in the shelter of a cliff. Some bedouin were already there, resting their camels and drinking tea, which of course they offered to us. A little girl held out some pretty pebbles, which I took, and I offered her a cucumber in exchange. The other children all rushed up, holding out their hands, and each of them was given a cucumber. I gave some to Mickey and Donald, who crunched them up, dropping pieces wet with saliva: I was amazed to see the little Arabs grabbing these too and gobbling them up. Confronted with such poverty we emptied our saddle-bags, and I began to understand why Rafik had such a reputation. What struck me most was that ragged as they were, these wanderers of the desert had a dignity and nobility of bearing that was quite astonishing.

By nine o'clock the sun was so fierce that in spite of our sunglasses the glare hurt our eyes. The Dead Sea, where the Jordan ends, is almost 1,200 feet below sea-level (it is the lowest spot in the world): and we were already 1,000 feet below. There wasn't a breath of air in the oppressive atmosphere. The one who suffered most was Pluto: however much water we gave him, he still panted. He turned up his nose at cucumbers, and didn't care for them at all.

At the crossroads at Shunat, where a slip-road runs to the famous Allenby Bridge, ten kilometres further west, Rafik's Land-Rover was waiting. Our superb and generous sultan had brought along two pretty girls in jeans, and I could feel my teeth clenching. God alone knows what I look like when I'm jealous, so to explain my expression I began to grumble: 'Such heat . . . it's beyond anything . . . what an impossible climate.'

Rafik, who had understood perfectly, burst out laughing: 'Let me introduce my nieces.'

Whew! Immediately my personal thermometer dropped 20°!

The police officer had already prepared a stable for the horses, who would stay securely locked up with two sentinels to watch over them, but no one had found them anything to eat.

'Can't they wait until tomorrow morning?' asked Rafik, anxious to return home where his people were expecting him. 'We'll bring them some barley tomorrow.'

'Of course, they won't die, but they have worked hard today and I'd feel terrible if I left them with empty stomachs while I went off to enjoy a good meal. Couldn't we find them something else to eat—apples, carrots or even some sugar?'

Rafik smiled with a flash of teeth.

'You think you're in a French village. Look around you. This is the desert. Listen, supposing we gave them some bread and rice? That we will be able to find, and we'll give them plenty to drink. Water is most essential . . .'

'. . . with some cucumbers . . .'

'Yes, of course.'

Half an hour later we were settled under the great tent where Rafik's entire family was assembled. One of his sisters-in-law who spoke very good English told me she came originally from Jerusalem.

'I lived in a magnificent house opposite the Russian church but the Jews drove us out in 1948. When I went back, three years ago, to visit one of my cousins, I found that the Israelis had pulled our house down and put up a huge block of flats. They destroy everything. But we'll get our own back, we'll drive them away eventually. We can't wait for the help of God, we must fight for our own rights. That's what I always tell my children: "Fight! Fight! Never give up until we have reconquered Jerusalem."'

When we got back to Mickey and Donald we found they didn't appreciate Arab bread for they had barely touched it. I knew they would have behaved quite differently if we had offered them a good crusty French baguette, but probably the heat had affected their appetites, though they seemed quite pleased to see us when we gave them some barley.

'Get a move on,' said Rafik. 'You've got two hours of trotting before the Allenby Bridge, and soon the heat won't be bearable,' but we had to wait for an hour at least while the horses finished eating and digesting.

And then we embarked on the final Jordanian relay. At the Customs post, the formalities were settled in a flash, and here too the security police had been given their instructions, passed on by the French Embassy. In addition, Rafik had already dropped in with his trays of cucumbers to oil the wheels even more. He had decided to come with us to the other side of the bridge on his Honda, though the heat was crushing. I was feeling dreadful myself, with my stomach churning and my legs buckling under me. However much water I poured over my head, I still felt no better, and wouldn't have taken much persuading to confess my longing to turn back to the 'farm', and indeed, to break off our entire trip, within a day's ride of Jerusalem! Just like those Crusaders who considered the siege of the City of David would take too long, and deserted the army to re-embark at Jaffa.

Rafik had urged us not to leave the asphalt road in case we should find ourselves in a minefield, but when he had gone a little way ahead, we stepped aside on to the rocky verge, not out of contrariness, but because the glare from the rocks was less violent than from the asphalt. We had no problems until the horses entangled their feet in some wires stretched just above the ground, and we were stopped by a military patrol.

'Passports. Where are you going?'

I replied wittily that we had no choice between Israel at the end of the road, and eternity, by striking off into the minefield.

'You have no right to go to Israel,' said the officer, who obviously wasn't susceptible to jokes. 'Your passports make no mention of the fact.'

Of course the ogre was right, but we couldn't make him understand that a welcome party would be waiting for us on the enemy bank and with our French passports, we didn't need visas. Fortunately, as we hadn't shown up, Rafik came back to look for us, and after a quick phone call, and a tray of cucumbers, all our difficulties were smoothed away.

At last we came to a small hut, surrounded by barbed wire and sandbags. A few elderly tanks. Men in uniform, machine-guns at the ready, waved to us to dismount. It was the last Jordanian outpost and before us lay the Allenby Bridge. A bridge? It was more like a tightrope, but at the other end lay Israel, less than a hundred yards away.

Below ran the Jordan, no river, barely a stream, and I couldn't understand how the Crusaders of Louis VII's army had managed to get drowned in it. The chroniclers of the second Crusade reported that the conquerors from France, arriving from Turkey and Syria, had had to construct rafts to cross the 'flood' and that a great many knights who had tried to swim across had been carried away by the current.

The Jordan, in fact, was so shrunk that we could talk to the Israeli post on the opposite bank and see the TV cameras filming us, with a small crowd of people come, we presumed, to welcome us to their country.

It all happened very quickly: yet another stamp on our passports, yet another barrier lifted to let us pass. We remounted because it made a better picture for the cameras, and as Mickey and Donald hesitated to step on to the slippery iron footpath, Rafik seized their bridles and pulled them as far as the Israeli barrier, then turned round abruptly and departed, after wishing us well in two languages, English and Arabic: 'God bless you! *Allah m'âkom!*'

Farewell, most generous prince.

CHAPTER FORTY-FIVE

The End of the Road

The Israeli barrier lifted and we had come to the end of our long journey. A policeman glanced at our passports, but it turned into a very long glance, for Israeli TV wanted to record the scene from every angle. After all, wasn't it part of the history of the original Crusades?

'*Besseder*' ['O.K.'], he said finally, and we were handed over to the small crowd that had come to greet us, addressing us in a babble of Hebrew, French and English.

'Shalom! Welcome! *Broukh ha' bâa! Bravo, bravo . . .*'

I felt giddy and turned to see Rafik's silhouette at the other end of the bridge as he walked briskly away. Hands were outstretched, and we didn't know what to do with all the bouquets, letters and telegrams.

There was a representative from the Israeli Ministry of Tourism who treated us to a discourse full of compliments, the President of the Israeli Equestrian Society who did the same, and Gad Greiver, the director of an important travel agency, who was mad about horses, and told us we would be his guests for as long as we were in the country. He had already laid on a complete programme of visits and excursions. There was a cohort of journalists, too, including correspondents of the French press and television, from whom we couldn't possibly escape: they had been waiting since seven, and it would soon be one o'clock!

How had they known we would arrive that morning? Through our Parisian friends who had been informed by our Ambassador in Amman via the Quai d'Orsay. They included *Le Journal de*

Mickey, Guilde Européenne du Raid, Cercle Equestre de France, who
had watched our departure and followed our progress, almost day
by day, organising relays whenever possible with the help of riders
in all the countries we had crossed. Next day, or even that very
evening, all France would be able to see us on the small screen
setting foot in the Holy Land.

It was time to pass on to more serious business. The horses
having been fastened to pickets and watered, we were taken into
the Customs building. Our bags were thoroughly searched, for
perhaps a terrorist had slipped a bomb into our saddle-bags.
Everyone is so conscious of bomb attacks in Israel that they can
never be too careful. Then it was our turn to be searched.
Girl soldiers in blouses and khaki mini-skirts asked us to undress.

'Don't forget to take off the medals you wear round your
necks,' they advised us. 'Don't keep anything metallic on you,
you're going through a metal detector.'

The buzz of the contraption didn't change: we had passed our
entrance exam.

Then came the problem of Mickey, Donald and Pluto. The
officer was obviously worried.

'What happened in the other countries?' he asked. 'Have you
had any difficulties when you crossed a frontier?'

'Never.'

As if I could say anything else, even if I had had to lie. Fortunately it was true, and I suggested he looked at our passports.
'When we entered a country, Customs usually noted that we had
two horses and a dog in transit, which meant we could leave without any difficulty and without paying any tax.'

'So I see. But here it's different. In principle it's forbidden to
bring any animals from the Arab countries into Israel, and our
rules for protecting our livestock are very strict. There are often
epidemics in Jordan and you know that in the heat, contagion can
be transmitted very easily.'

'But our horses are in prime condition. With such shiny coats
and such flesh on their bones, you don't need a vet to see that they
aren't suffering from anything.'

The officer became more and more undecided.

'How did you get into Jordan?'

I got the impression that he didn't want to seem more pernickety than his neighbours.

'As easily as anything,' I told him. 'They gave us a visa and a cup of coffee.'

'I see. Will you wait a moment? I'll make some inquiries.'

A few moments later he returned to give us the verdict.

'We must make certain that your horses and dog aren't carrying any infections, so you must leave them here in quarantine until we've had the results of the veterinary tests. The Minister of Tourism will place two other horses at your disposal to take you to Jerusalem.'

'But that doesn't make sense! The whole point of the journey was to ride into Jerusalem on the same horses we had at the start.'

'Oh, I see . . . And after Jerusalem, what are your plans?'

'Jericho–Jerusalem is our last stage on horseback. After that we'll allow the horses to rest and then we'll repatriate them.'

'It isn't usual, but we'll try and fix it.'

Finally a man from the Ministry of Tourism undertook to plead our cause with his colleagues from the Ministry of Agriculture. In the meantime the telphone rang in the room where we were waiting.

'This is something you'll find interesting,' said the chief Customs officer as he put the receiver down. 'I've been asked to tell you that your mother has just arrived in Israel. You'll see her this evening in Jericho . . .'

'Maman on the Jordan! What an excitement for her!' I could just see her with tears in her eyes, and her nose quite pink from emotion.

The tourist representative returned, a triumphant smile on his lips.

'It's all been arranged. You'll be escorted to Jericho and Jerusalem, because you can't travel alone through the occupied territories, and your escort will see that your animals don't come into contact with any others. Jericho is only eight kilometres away: you can sleep at the hotel and your horses can spend the night in one of the hotel courtyards. The escort will fetch you tomorrow morning at five so you can reach Jerusalem at noon. Then the horses will be taken to quarantine in Haifa.'

'An excellently organised programme, thank you, gentlemen.'

Before leaving for Jericho we went through the messages of congratulations waiting for us. The Prefect of the Nièvre was delighted to inform us that we had been awarded the Department's medal of honour: the Minister of Youth and Sports had also awarded us his silver medal. There was a telegram from Loulou, Mickey and Donald's former owner, congratulating the riders—and the ridden. It was a great day for him: his horses had stayed the course to the very end, even if Donald had had a few bad moments. In fact, they both arrived in remarkably good condition: no one would have guessed they had just covered 6,000 kilometres, and not always under the easiest of conditions. They had grown, and were looking better and more lively than when they left. Loulou had made a good choice, and his equipment had also proved itself over and over again. I realised we owed him a tremendous amount, as well as Louis Giordanino from Saint-Estève-Janson. I could imagine him saying to his wife in his melodious voice: 'Hey, Maria, the little ones have made it!' Among the pile there were even letters from American friends sent on from Ankara.

Our stuff had been piled into a car, and we set off after filling our canvas hats with water from the Jordan, like the pilgrims who used to come to the very spot where John the Baptist had baptised Jesus of Nazareth. In our case this was all the more important because the thermometer was registering 40° in the shade, and there wasn't even any shade. The sun's heat was crushing and our tongues hung out. Talk about mad dogs and Englishmen . . . no one else would have thought of taking to the road at a time when the whole of the Near East was enjoying its siesta.

Jericho was an admirable oasis: for miles around there was nothing but orchards and palm-trees. The city was already thirty centuries old when Joshua conquered it at the head of the Jews returning from Egypt, and it was probably their first victory in the Holy Land. I couldn't help smiling at the thought of my beloved Crusaders attempting to repeat the trumpet trick outside the walls of Jerusalem. Invested by the soldiers of the Cross, the Holy City defied every assault by Godfrey de Bouillon, Raymond de Toulouse, Robert of Normandy and their peers. A visionary monk, named Pierre Desiderius, announced that Adhémar,

Bishop of Le Puy, one of the organisers of the Crusade, who had recently died, had appeared to him in a dream. Adhémar had asserted that if the Crusaders marched in procession round the ramparts, Jerusalem would fall after nine days, but there must be no drums or trumpets. Priests and prelates, princes and knights, soldiers and pilgrims paraded barefoot round the walls, under the jeers of the Infidels, and when these tactics proved abortive, the Crusaders had had to resort to more martial practices.

At the hotel in Jericho, which was almost a luxury palace, everyone greeted us with '*Salam aleikom*' . . . but if our rooms were ready, the improvised stable wasn't: the courtyard where the horses were supposed to stay was merely a dump for broken furniture, worn-out refrigerators and detritus of all kinds, including several rolls of rusty barbed wire, but once the mess had been cleared away, it wasn't at all bad.

Even more journalists were waiting for us, and for the thirty-sixth time we had to give an account of the most frightening, the best, the worst and the most uncomfortable moments of our trip.

At last came the person we had been waiting for with the greatest impatience: Maman, and as expected, mopping her eyes.

'My little girls! What a long time since I've seen you—how I've worried! You gave me such appalling frights. Why leave us so long without a word? I haven't had a sound from you since Antioch. I was imagining so many things . . . You could have been imprisoned in Turkey, carried off by a Palestinian commando . . .'

'But we did write . . .'

'Not often enough . . . But it's all over now. I'm so glad to see you in one piece, looking absolutely splendid. You'll have so much to tell us . . .'

We had to cut short our transports for the journalists were insatiable.

I tossed and turned all night while memories jostled each other in my mind. I couldn't believe that the next day would see the end of our troubles, and also the end of a chapter which hadn't been without its happy moments. Tomorrow our endeavour would be crowned with success, however wild it had seemed, and never had I appreciated the fact more than at that moment.

I could hear the horses whinnying and stamping and wondered if Mickey might not be about to indulge in one of his runaway acts? I got up to check that he was safely tied up.

At four o'clock I got out of bed, for the sky was already beginning to pale above the Jordanian mountains. When I went down to the courtyard to get the horses ready, I could have sworn they were surprised to see me so early:

'You must realise, my darlings, that in a few hours it'll all be over.'

While Maman entered Jerusalem in a comfortable police car, we climbed into the saddle, with the strictest instructions to stick to the main road which went up and up. We were at 1,000 feet below sea-level, while Jerusalem is 2,000 feet above and the climb through the Judean desert, perhaps the stiffest we had met, was very tough. Straight ahead of us was the Mount of Temptation, where after forty days of fasting, Jesus successfully resisted the blandishments of the devil, and to our left lay the dull green mirror of the Dead Sea. Behind us were ruined villages, abandoned ever since the Six Day War.

By seven o'clock the heat was terrific. Mickey was covered in foam and both horses were suffering a good deal. They hadn't had time to lose their winter coats, and were still covered in thick layers of hair, so we dismounted to give them a bit of a breather. The more I stared around me the less I understood why anyone should want to fight for those lunar deserts.

After twenty kilometres the heat became more bearable and we could see three towers on the far horizon. Jerusalem in sight! Hosannah! Alleluya! I had quite a lump in my throat.

The last hours were interminable. The mists in the Jordan valley had lifted, the colours were brighter, the sky a dazzling blue, the suburbs of Jerusalem bright mosaics of pink, yellow, ochre, fawn. A light breeze brought a touch of freshness.

The outlines of the Holy City grew clearer. Above the walls built by Saladin, a prodigious number of towers, minarets, belfries and domes blossomed in the transparent air. We could see the Mount of Olives, the valley of Jehosaphat, with Mount Sion opposite, where the Crusaders, after endless bloody assaults, pierced the first breach in the city walls. To the left were the heights of Bethlehem, a scene of such peace where so much blood had flowed, so many dramas had been enacted, including the greatest of all, that I was absolutely shattered. I fell in love on the spot with Jerusalem the golden, the city of bronze and light.

We didn't enter through the Gate of Lions like Godfrey de Bouillon: our escort wanted us to ride round the walls to admire the fortifications, and as we crossed a section of the new city, passers-by recognised us from the newspapers and TV and cried '*Bravo!*' and '*Vive la France!*' Many of them who spoke French came and inquired if we were tired, if we wouldn't like a cold drink.

We rode past the Tower of David, then the Jaffa Gate, where we left the horses. We would have liked to have ridden as far as the square outside the Holy Sepulchre, but it wasn't possible: the streets leading to it through the bazaar are broken by flights of slippery steps.

A few minutes on foot and we stood before the Tomb of Christ, the real end of the road as far as we were concerned. Today was 18 April 1974; it had taken us seven months to make the journey. Godfrey de Bouillon, was buried on this very spot, in the crypt of the church that St Helena, the mother of the Emperor Constantine, had had built in the fourth century.

I was horrified to discover that the holiest spot in all Christendom had been invaded by hordes of people who jostled and shouted as if in a fairground.

'Queue up here . . . Don't push. Five at a time only . . . Watch the roof . . . the ceiling is very low . . .'

In front of the marble slab which covered the Tomb, a priest sat waiting with a huge blue dish beside him full of coins and bank-notes of all currencies and denominations: the tourists' offerings.

'You are Catholics?' he asked. 'Then you can light a candle and say a prayer . . .'

But how could one pray in the midst of all that commotion? My disappointment was so great that I couldn't summon up the least enthusiasm.

'Come along, say a prayer,' repeated the cassocked guardian, or in other words: 'Get a move on, there are so many others waiting.'

Corinne glanced at me inquiringly. What could I do? Ashamed of my hypocrisy I genuflected and prayed that He who wore the crown of thorns would forgive me.

'This way out,' announced the priest. 'The next five, please.'

We emerged, sad, bewildered and depressed. I wanted to be alone and slipped away down the neighbouring alleys, among the small shops and cafés full of narghile smokers. Luck led me to the Via Dolorosa, then on to the esplanade with the mosques of Omar and El Aqsa. Here I stood looking up at the sky, cloudless and serene until finding peace at last, I was able to make my way back to the Holy Sepulchre and Corinne and our friends.

It had been agreed that our horses would be taken to quarantine in Haifa, and that Maman, Corinne and I would do a little sight-seeing, Maman for a few days only, Corinne and I for as long as it would take to organise the return of the entire team.

As far as we were concerned, Gad Greiver took care of everything. We had hardly joined up with our horses again after visiting the Holy Sepulchre than he scooped us up in his car and installed Mickey and Donald in a trailer, we bound for a hotel in Tel Aviv, the horses *en route* for quarantine.

Two blow-outs one after the other upset this plan, as it was impossible to get them repaired: it was Friday afternoon and the garages would only reopen on Sunday morning.

'In a way,' said Gad, 'we've been lucky. We're quite close to a place that belongs to one of my friends who breeds horses. Let's take him yours while we wait to take them to quarantine. Our friend will drive us to Tel Aviv.'

A few days later, Gad told us we wouldn't have to send the horses to Haifa: they could stay in his stable where a vet would make all the necessary examinations. In the meantime, the best thing we could do was to see something of the country.

From Galilee to the Red Sea, from the Mediterranean to the lake of Tiberias and Sinai; we went everywhere. In buses, with tourists, in private cars with friends, and even hitch-hiking: not that this latter is the best of ideas, for it's the method most practised by soldiers of both sexes and they have priority. We also had a few handicaps, for it isn't easy to give lifts to two girls loaded with baggage and a dog of sizeable proportions. Further-more, we happened to be in Israel at the time of the terrible tragedy at Ma-alot: three Palestinian terrorists had taken a group of school-children hostage near the Lebanese frontier, and an appalling massacre had followed. France, like other countries, had protested, but in terms that might be considered moderate. Whenever they discovered we were French, our benevolent motorists couldn't prevent themselves voicing their dissatisfaction with our government. 'Our children are massacred,' they complained, 'and your President sends us a telegram to express his sympathy. Sympathy, indeed . . .'

Two weeks, three weeks, slipped by. We waited impatiently for news from Paris, as the information we had in the interim hadn't been very reassuring. The efforts made by our friends as far as the Ministry of Agriculture was concerned had produced no effect. 'We are up against a blank wall,' *Le Journal de Mickey* had written. Our other friends warned us that our hopes of obtaining satisfaction were very slim.

When we came back from one excursion to the shores of the Red Sea, still dazzled by the beauties of the underwater banks of coral, we discovered that we hadn't yet seen the worst.

'I have some bad news for you,' announced Gad. 'One of your horses, the little one, has had a positive reaction to the dourine test. If the diagnosis is confirmed, he'll have to be put down.'

'But it's impossible! Five days ago they were both perfectly healthy!'

'There are no external signs, but I say again, the test for one of them is positive. You should have seen the commotion in my stables when the vet discovered it! He took your horses off at once to quarantine, not at Haifa, but at Ramla which is about twenty kilometres from here. What a business! I have insisted on a minimum of three more positive tests before they decide to shoot the horse.'

'I don't understand. The disease is transmitted through mating and our horses have been gelded. In any case, it's an extremely contagious disease, so if our horses are infected, yours must be as well!'

I was so upset that I became quite unreasonable and impossible, and was even furious with Gad (and goodness knows he had already done enough for us) for not understanding why we were so anxious to take Donald and Mickey home with us. He had pointed out that their transport would be very costly, and if we sold them in Israel we would be able to make a handsome profit. He was quite right, of course, but right had nothing to do with it, it was a purely sentimental affair. We had promised our horses that we would take them home with us to live out their lives in peace, and we would never forgive ourselves if we had to abandon them.

Gad remained calm. 'Why don't you go and see the vet? He can give you all the details himself.'

My rage gave way to despair, and I told myself that Donald's general condition during the past few weeks hadn't perhaps been due to the state of his tendons and badly fixed shoes, or the heat and poor food, but that there had been something else, and if the vet hadn't noticed any disturbing clinical signs, I certainly had myself: I had put it down to fatigue, but it might just as easily have been the result of an internal abscess.

And then something that had happened in the Lebanon came back to me: we had stopped to buy some bananas by the roadside, and while we were haggling, the horses had gone off to eat the grass in a nearby field. A donkey had come up and began paying court to Mickey, who had given him a swift kick and sent him about his business. The little beast had then started on Donald who, only concerned with his stomach, hadn't bothered to react. The donkey grew bolder, had mounted him and behaved as if he wanted to make Donald a mother, while Donald continued to munch calmly, until the other's attentions became too much for him and he bucked him off. If that donkey had been carrying the germ of dourine, that might explain how Donald had been affected.

When we left Gad's home, we went for a breather to the corniche overlooking the beach at Tel Aviv. Corinne lent on the parapet, in floods of tears, and I watched a boat on the horizon, wondering if a day would come when we would all five find ourselves on a ship bound for France. After a few minutes I hailed a taxi to take us to the bus station, and less than an hour later were in the stables at Ramla.

'The doctor isn't here,' the watchman told us, 'and my orders are not to open to anyone.'

We discussed the situation, and he finally relaxed.

'Don't tell anyone I let you see your horses. They're fine specimens, you know. D'you want to take them back to France?'

'Yes, but it seems one of them is sick.'

'Sick? They're both perfectly healthy. Look, they're over there.'

'Over there' was a fenced enclosure where our darlings were tied up to numbered pickets. Just like convicts! They showed their displeasure at having been abandoned by ignoring us. When the watchman took them a bundle of dried clover, they barely tasted it. We clapped them affectionately on the shoulder, but got no reaction.

I finally managed to make an appointment with the vet to find out what was happening about the tests, and all he could say was that the labs were all on strike for an indefinite period, and we would have to be patient.

For the next week we went to see the horses every day, and managed to get them transferred to an enormous meadow where they were able to enjoy a relative freedom. They didn't seem at all sick, but the vet still had his doubts: he had just discovered a case of confirmed dourine in a horse coming from Syria, through which our horses had been.

The strike continued and I sent blood samples from the horses by air to a laboratory in Lyons as we had at least two reasons for speeding up matters: first, the cost of maintenance for the horses was being met by Gad, and we couldn't presume too far: and our own funds were growing dangerously low. The French Company of Navigation gave us a final nil return: horses don't stand up well to the sea trip, they told us: at least two-thirds have to be put down on arrival, and air freight would be much more suitable. Unfortunately, Air France had no cargo planes on that route, and El-Al asked 20,000 francs to take the horses to Orly.

Among all these vicissitudes there was one good piece of news at last: the Ministry of Agriculture would allow the horses to be repatriated on condition that they passed the normal health tests. Apparently this was an exceptional concession, but after all, hadn't our two provençals proved themselves totally exceptional too?

Another piece of news that might have been good in different circumstances came from Mlle Ferrière, our Vice-Consul in Tel Aviv. She had been working wonders to help us and announced she had found two berths on a cargo-boat belonging to the

Israeli society Zim, and we could take our horses with us, provided of course that the veterinary tests were negative. The cost was very reasonable, but there was only one snag: the boat, the *Iris*, was leaving in forty-eight hours from Ashdod, fifty kilometres south of Tel Aviv.

I flew to the Ministry of Tourism to explain our situation, and the man who saw me was wonderful.

'O.K., I'll put in a request that the strikers make an exception in your case, and if they won't co-operate, I'll get in touch with people better placed than I am. When the orders come from sufficiently high up, any strike can be broken. I quite appreciate that you want to take your horses home with you.'

Next morning—there was less than a day to go before H-hour—we rushed off to see the vet.

'The strike was suspended especially for you,' he told us as soon as we reached his office.

We waited for the results with our hearts in our mouths while he took his time to make his effect, the mean thing! Finally, he said, 'The verification tests have shown up negative to dourine, so you can take your horses back to France, they are unquestionably healthy. I can sign the certificates forthwith . . .'

There were quite a lot of things still to be done. First, the certificates had to be translated and certified by the French Consul: then we had to find 4,500 francs for our passage. We got together anything we had that looked like money, and found bits and pieces of German marks, Austrian schillings, unused traveller's cheques, dollars we had had since I don't know when, various odds and ends discoloured by our sweat (we had kept them in our boots) and duckings in chalky water.

We embarked on the necessary calculations, and taking the most advantageous rates, eventually reached a total of 4,300 francs. We had the nerve to lay this monetary potpourri before the cashier in the Zim office, relying on a miracle or our personal charms to make up the difference.

The cashier surveyed the pile with admirable equanimity and then proceeded to solve the problem with the aid of his calculating machine.

'O.K.,' he said. 'It's just right. You can pick up your tickets from the desk opposite.'

It took less than fifteen minutes for us to pack. It wasn't our personal effects that were so bulky, but the presents we had been given on all sides, among others, some books we prized very highly, *My People* and *My Country*, which their author, at that time the Minister for Foreign Affairs, Abba Eban, had signed for us, and also various works written by Israeli specialists on the Crusades, including Meron Benveniste.

Gad was waiting for us with his trailer already hitched to his car, for while we had been running all over the shop, he had been buying the fodder the horses would need for the five days' crossing.

First stop: Ramla to load up Mickey and Donald, then full speed ahead for Ashdod. We prayed there would be no more blow-outs, but when he realised I was nervous, our driver said, 'Don't be so impatient. These cargo boats never leave on time. We've got a comfortable margin.'

At the port, the formalities went through in the time it took to take a couple of flash-pictures: the policeman who stamped our papers didn't even glance at them, so flattered was he at being snapped with us, with Pluto, with the horses. The director of Zim presented each of us with a bunch of roses, which decorated our cabin during the crossing.

Once on board, our first concern was to find the best possible spot for Mickey and Donald. On the bridge there was plenty of air, but no shade, and the sun was pretty fierce at that time of year: besides, the pitching and rolling would be much more marked than anywhere else, and the horses might be seasick. In the hold, the movement of the ship would be less, but the noise of the engines would drive them mad. The most suitable place was in the stern, and we spread some tarpaulins on the steel deck which we covered with a thick layer of sawdust and sand. This would prevent the horses from slipping, and if they liked, they could even lie down in reasonable comfort. They also had adequate provisions of hay and corn.

We went on deck to watch the sailors cast off.

'Shalom! Shalom!' our friends called from the quay.

'Shalom!' we replied, and as night fell the engines purred, and the lights of Ashdod dwindled on the horizon.

We were the only passengers on board, and the captain, the

four officers and twenty-six sailors and engineers, who all spoke English or French, couldn't do enough for us. They fixed up a small sea-water swimming-pool on the bridge and once, when I was chatting to the captain and told him I was an amateur painter, he sent me pots of paint and brushes, as well as various old marine charts instead of canvases, so I could daub to my heart's content. The officers gave us lessons in navigation, and when I thought of the mistakes I had made, trying to steer by the sun, and with a broken compass at that, it certainly wasn't a waste of time.

Our horses, too, lived the life of Reilly, though Mickey still tried to take up as much room as possible. As an additional treat they were given water-melons liberated from the cargo, which they adored, as well as endless crusts of real French bread.

The only miserable member of the team was Pluto. He kept looking for a patch of ground so that he could behave normally, and sulked until we came in sight of Corsica, when suddenly he started to sniff the air. His nose quivered, his tail wagged, and pricking up his ears, he began to bark happily. Perhaps he was catching the smell of his native land?

Sunday, 28 May 1974 at 11.00 p.m. the *Iris* tied up in the port of Marseilles. It was Mother's Day and I know that for Maman the return of her daughters to hearth and home was the finest present she could get. For her the nights of anxiety, the visions of Turkish brigands or Syrian bandits were over. My father could be happy and even proud of us, though he would never admit that our whole adventure hadn't been crazy from start to finish.

In all honesty I had to agree that he had been perfectly right. Where would we have been on so many occasions if luck hadn't been with us? And it had taken a very large slice of luck indeed to carry us through the Balkans and Anatolia in sub-zero weather, and trot through the Arab countries at war, with an ailing horse, at that.

The *Iris* ran out her gangway, but even before it touched the jetty, Pluto had fled down the ramp and leapt onto French soil. Henry de Barrin was already on board and helping to put socks on Mickey and Donald so they could get back on dry land without slipping: Loulou was there too, radiant and enthusiastic, even more exuberant than ever, for wasn't this success story his as well? He hurled his cowboy hat in the air!

'Hey! Holy Mother! You've come a long way, haven't you?' Good old Loulou!

Three of the team took the road to Nevers, because Mickey and Donald had gone off to quarantine, but in a month, provided they passed all the tests, they would rejoin us to live, as I had promised them, like lords for the rest of their lives.

In the meantime I had the joy of being reunited with my magnificent Concorda. There he was, haughty and arrogant, in his favourite spot, the top left-hand corner of the meadow, with the white star in the centre of his forehead giving him a slightly malicious expression. When he saw me, he ran up, chest thrust out, neck curved, carrying his head with the grace of a gipsy dancer. He kicked up his heels and went into a delirium of caprioles to celebrate my return, refusing, naturally, to allow anyone to catch him.

Months have passed. Corinne has taken a liking for independence and dreams of nothing but travel. She talks of going round the world on her scooter, at the very least.

Mickey, still in good form, and Donald, whose legs have fully recovered, are happily installed in a green meadow, but never so happy as when we put a saddle on their backs.

Pluto was the only one who showed a touch of old age, or perhaps it was reaction after extreme fatigue. If the other members of the team had covered 6,000 kilometres, he had clocked up twice as much or more, thanks to his habit of zigzagging about, rushing forward only to rush back to our side. Then suddenly he recovered completely and I'm quite sure if we were to do it all over again, he would wag his tail and cock his ears, as if to inquire: 'When do we start?'

And what about me? I have opened my atlas again. The world lies before me: Lapland, the reindeer's paradise: a long trek over the snow: might be interesting. Or what about the Canadian North-West, home of the Mounties . . . or further south, black Africa: I could retrace Stanley's itinerary, or ride up the Nile from the sea to Lake Victoria, oddly enough, another 6,000 miles. But what about that other enormous green space, on the other side of the Atlantic, Amazonas, that jungle of vegetation which is neither hell nor heaven, to quote the expression used by the *Guilde Européenne du Raid*, which offered to help if we went ahead. A real return to nature in the jungle, why not? On horseback, of course.

Yes, definitely—I have made up my mind, and my next trip will be to ride up the Amazon.

Index

accidents, 64–7, 222–3
Adana, 223, 224, 228–30, 296
Adhémar de Monteil, 206, 310–11
Adnan, of Jeble, 258–60, 271
Aleksinac, 156–8
Alexandretta, 233, 237
Alexis, Emperor, of Constantinople, 166, 197
Allenby bridge, 7, 292, 303, 305, 306
Alsace, 36, 39, 42
Amanus plateau, 237
Anatolian bandits, 29, 199–200, 237
Antioch, 237, 239–41, 243
Anzbach, Maria, stud, 85–8
Arğithani, 212
army manoeuvres, 68–70, 256, 277–9, 281, 290–2, 295
Arqua, 272
Ashdod, 318, 319
Assam, of Konya, 214–16
Austria, 74–102; bureaucracy, 4, 19, 73, 75, 101–2; hospitality, 85–8, 91–4; vets, 73, 74
Azem palace, 282

baggage, 18–19, 59–61, 209, 219, 252
Ballalanli, 189
Baniyas, 259, 261
Bar-le-Duc, 36
Barrin, Henry de, 12–16, 320
Bataszék, 112–13
Baudouin, brother of Godfrey de Bouillon, 224
Béchau La Fonta, M., 19–20
Beirut, 274–5, 276, 281
Beit Yafa, 292–3
Bela Palanka, 165
Belgrade, 3, 148–51
Beli Manastir, 115–16
Belovo, 174
Belpinar, 209
Benveniste, Meron, 319
Bertoldsheim, 64
Black Forest, 44–8, 96
Blois, Comte de, 3, 205
Bohémond de Tarente, 205–6
Bolvadin, 211
Bosporus ferry, 198

Bouillon, Godfrey de, see Godfrey de Bouillon
Bovota, 127–9
Braljina, 152, 154
Branco, of Bovota, 128
Branko, of Lapovo, 147–8, 158
Brie region, 30, 33
Budapest, 107, 108
Bulgaria, 166–80, 181, 183; bureaucracy, 4, 167, 179; hospitality, 168–9, 175–6; New Year's Eve in, 168–9
bureaucracy, see under individual countries
Burgenland, 101–2
Büyük Çekmece, 189

Cachecho family, of Damascus, 279, 281–4
Caesarea, 275
Camalan, 222–3, 224
camels, 220–1
Capoue, 74
Ceyhan, 234, 235
Chalons, 36
Champagne, 35
Chateau-Thierry, 34
La Chaumière, 31–2
children, pestering, 203–4, 212–13, 230–1, 258, 261–2, 263–5, 267, 279, 289–90, 295–6
Cirey-sur-Vézouse, 38
Clarisse, of Belgrade, 150–1, 152, 154
clothing, 11, 18, 22, 54–5, 57–8, 61, 77, 108, 151, 198, 233
Concorda, 4, 15, 20, 321
Condé, princes de, 33–4
Constantinople, see Istanbul
Coquet, M., 8–10, 42–3, 320
Coquet, Mme, 42–3, 71–2, 155, 311–12, 320
Crusaders, 1–3, 17, 21, 47, 56, 131, 158, 166, 188, 197, 198–9, 205–6, 214, 230, 239, 241, 269–70, 274–5, 305, 306, 310–11, 312–13

Damascus, 275, 276, 279–86
Dam-Sharko, 254
Danube, 55, 63, 68, 81, 82, 97, 107
Dara, of Martinci, 134–5

Debrc, 136–8, 144
deer, 95–9
Degirmenkoy, 211–12
Der'a, 282, 284, 286
Desiderius, Pierre, 310–11
Devorac, 129–30
Dimas, 276
Dinon, 38
dogs, wild, 189–90, 192–5, 200, 230–1
Domrémy, 36
Donald (l'Enclume), 15–16, 24, 25, 37, 39, 44, 52, 63–4, 75, 177, 193, 234–6, 246–8, 321
Donan, 38
Donaueschingen, 49, 55
Donjevin, 37
Dormans, 34
dourine infection, 315–17
Drava river, 127
Dubrovka, 122–3

Eban, Abba, 319
Edirne, 180, 183, 188
Emirdağ, 210
Epernay, 34, 35
Ereğli, 220, 221, 224, 286
Eskisehir, 3, 205, 206–7

Fathi, of Neçatiye, 185–6, 187
Ferrière, Mlle, 317–18
finances, 6–11, 59, 90, 280, 318
Flanders, Comte de, 205
France, 23–43; bureaucracy, 315, 317, 318; hospitality, 24–6, 32, 34–5, 41
Franco-Yugoslav Riding Association, 160–1
Freiburg-im-Breisgau, 43
Fritz, chauffeur, of Ulm, 57–8

Gakmak, 221
Georges, the Goblin, 172, 173, 175, 176, 177, 178, 179–80
Germany, West, 43–73; bureaucracy, 4, 70–1; hospitality, 50–3, 54–5, 56–8; vets, 42, 57, 58
Giordanino, Louis (Loulou), 13–16, 19, 20, 22, 58, 76, 100, 310, 320–1
Goblin, *see* Georges, the Goblin
Godfrey (Godefroi) de Bouillon, 1, 3, 11, 43, 131, 136, 166, 188, 197, 198–9, 205–6, 214, 224, 239, 241, 274–5, 280, 310, 313
Golan Heights, 78, 276, 281, 283, 291, 295, 302
Gols, 101
Gopbogasi, 238
Gorski-Izvor, 178

'Green Mare', Citroën 2–cv, 178–80, 190, 194, 200, 204, 208, 209, 229
Greiver, Gad, 307, 314–19
Gschwendhof, 85–90
Guilde Européenne du Raid, 4, 308, 322
Gunduzbey, 204
Györ, 106, 107, 108

Haifa, 275, 309, 314
Hamidiya, 261–7, 269
Hegyelshalom, 105
Herbiye, 241–2
hospitality, *see under individual countries*
'Hubert, St', 97–9
Hungary, 102–14; bureaucracy, 4, 102–3; vets, 103–5, 111–13
Hurriyet, 197, 201, 206, 207
Hussein, King, of Jordan, 284, 286

Ibrahim, of Konya, 215–16, 217
Iconium, 214
Ilgin, 212
Ingolstadt, 68
Irbid, 288, 289, 292
Iris, 318, 319–20
Iskenderun, 233
Israel, 307–19; bureaucracy, 5, 292, 307, 308–9; hospitality, 314, 317; vets, 314, 315, 316–17, 318
Istanbul, 3, 173, 188, 196–8
Ivan, 'Chin-Chin', 171–2, 173–4, 175, 176, 177
Ivan the Driver, 172, 175
Ivo, of Bovota, 128–9
Izmit, 199, 200, 201–2

Jabucje, 138–42
Jean-Lou, of Nancy, 36–7, 38
Jeble, 257, 258–9
Jericho, 309, 310–12
Jerusalem, 312–14
Jockey Club of Istanbul, 197
Jordan, 287–306; bureaucracy, 5, 287–8, 294, 305; hospitality, 289, 291–2, 293, 296–7, 300–4; women, 289, 293
Jordanka, 174–5
Le Journal de Mickey, 6–11, 20, 59, 90, 142, 279, 280, 307–8, 315

Kadinham, 212–13
Kapitan Androvo, 177
Karaisali, 224, 227
Karayma, 296–7
Karchzarten, 43
Kelebec, 227
Kilij Arslan, 205–6
Kiro, of Bulgaria, 172, 173
Kisildere, 231–4

Kislac, 242–3
Kiswe, 276
Konya, 3, 212, 214–19, 225
Kostenec, 173
Krak of the Knights, 269–70, 273
Kruševac, 142–3

El Ladhiqiya (Latakia), 252, 254–6
Lapovo, 146–9, 15
Lebanon, 267–76; bureaucracy, 4, 268–71; hospitality, 272–4
Ligny-en-Barrois, 36
Linz, 78
Louis VII, King of France, 199, 306
Loulou, *see* Giordanino, Louis

Ma-alot, 315
Mahmudiye, 208–9
man-mountain, of Hamidiya, 265–6
Marne, 22
Marras, 224
Marseilles, 320–1
Martinci, 133–5
Masonmagyarovar, 104, 106
Medina, 111–12
Mehmet, of Edirne, 183–4
Melk, 78
Mersin, 228
Mickelsdorf, 101
Mickey (Ondo), 15–16, 24, 27, 29, 45–7, 81, 84, 86, 101, 132, 161, 212, 237, 240, 246–8, 257, 320, 321
Miloš, 86–8
Mohács, 113–14
Mollafeneri, 200
Montheillet, M., 197
Morava river, 146, 152, 154, 156
motorway hazards, 159–64, 196, 279
Mouaddamiye, 277
music, 53, 88, 193, 218
Musihe, of Adana, 229

Nancy, 36
Neçatiye, 185–8, 289
New York, 3
Niš, 3, 158–9
Notre-Dame, Paris, 20–2

Obernai, 39, 41
Olivier, 178–80, 183, 190, 200, 204, 209
Ommayyad mosque, 282
Orontes river, 240
Osijek, 118–27, 188

Pataud, *see* Pluto
Patrick, 179–80, 183, 190, 195, 200, 204, 209–10, 222, 227, 228–9, 232–3, 237, 251–2

Pazardzhik, 175–6
Pépé, of Osijek, 118–23, 127
Peter the Hermit, 165, 166, 188, 197
Pirot, 165
Plovdiv, 176, 177
Pluto (Pataud), 27–9, 30, 38, 76, 81, 93, 122, 124–6, 134–5, 192–5, 320, 321
Pol Roger, Madame, 35
Popoviça, 177, 178
Porsuk, 221–2
Poteau stud, 24–7
Pozanti, 221
preparations, 3–23

quarantine, 309, 314, 315, 321

Rafik, of Jordan, 299–306
Ramla, 275, 315, 319
Ramtha, 288, 289, 292
Ras el-Nakoura, 275
Ratisbon, 68
Raymond de Toulouse, 3, 205–6, 214, 269–70, 310
return journey, 319–20
Richard, Cœur de Lion, 261
riding, long-distance: feed, 25, 75, 86, 105–6, 107, 167, 190, 208, 235, 251, 289, 304; illness, 82, 117–22, 127, 167, 189, 233–50, 261, 285, 315–17; runaway, horses, 247–50; selection of horses, 7, 12–17; shoeing, 18, 60–1, 82–4, 198, 225; swimming, 235, 237, 240, 257–8
Ried, 56, 78
Robert of Normandy, 310
Roques, Henri, 2
Rosières stud, 36
Runciman, Sir Steven, 3

Sade, Marquis de, 33–4
St John d'Acre, 275
Saint-Martin-d'Albois, 34
Samandira, 199–200
Sarimazi, 233
Schärding, 73, 74–5, 97
Schmidt family, of Vogelgrun, 42–3, 78
Sexey, 36
shoeing, 18, 60–1, 82–4, 198, 225
Shuma, 294
Shunat, 303
Šid, 130–2
Sidon, 275
Silivri, 190–1
Sinan, of Konya, 216–17
Société Hippique Nationale, 43
Sofia, 167–71, 178, 180

Spanish Riding School, 85, 88–9
Stalać, 152
Stoikovo, 178
Stoytchev, General, 4, 166, 167, 168–9, 170–1, 177, 197
Syria, 245–67, 276–86; bureaucracy, 5, 245, 267, 280–1; hospitality, 254–5, 258–66, 280
Székesféhervár, 109
Szekszárd, 112

Tartus, 263, 264, 269
Taurus mountains, 47, 219, 227
Tel Aviv, 314, 316
Tel Qulaat, 261
Titisee, 53–5
Tossunoglu, 212
Toulouse, Raymond of, *see* Raymond de Toulouse
Turkey, 181–244; bureaucracy, 4–5, 181; hospitality, 185–8, 190–1, 201–2, 206–7, 215–18, 227–9, 243–4; vets, 234–5, 239–40; women, 186–8, 191, 215–16
Turunglu, 235–6
Tyre, 275

Ulm, 56–7
Usnier, of Konya, 216

Vakarel, 173
Vermandois, Comte de, 205
vets, *see under individual countries*
Vienna, 10–11, 19, 89–90
Vitry-le-François, 36
Vogelgrun, 42
Vosges mountains, 36, 37, 39, 95, 289

Waqqas, 295
Welde, Mr, 100–1, 168
Wels, 78
Winkler, Paul, 6–8, 11, 36. 164
wolves, 205

Yayladagi, 243–4
Yonikoy Nazimbey, 231
Yugoslavia, 115–65, 173; bureaucracy, 4, 140–3, 145–6, 156–7, 164; Christmas in, 152–5; hospitality, 116, 121–4, 128–30, 137–9, 144–9; vets, 115–16, 133–5

Zim, 318, 319